CONSTANT
COMEDY

CONSTANT COMEDY

A Memoir

How I Started
Comedy Central
and Lost My Sense of Humor

ART BELL

Published by:
ULYSSES PRESS
P.O. Box 3440
Berkeley, CA 94703
www.ulyssespress.com

ISBN: 978-1-64604-089-6
Library of Congress Control Number: 2020936436

Printed in the United States by Versa Press

Editor: Jane Rosenman
Proofreaders: Renee Rutledge, Elizabeth Lotito

This book is a memoir. In telling these stories, I relied primarily on my recollections rather than documentary evidence. Since the bulk of this takes place thirty years ago, my less-than-perfect memory may have led to inaccuracies or misrepresentations. There are a few places where I made changes for the sake of good storytelling, but mostly I wrote things the way I remember them. Some names have been changed, and most of the dialogue has been re-created and possibly embellished from the bits and pieces I remember. Most of the humorous remarks attributed to others is mine, and what they really said was probably a lot funnier than what I wrote.

For Carrie

Everything is funny, as long as it's happening to somebody else.

—Will Rogers

Tragedy is when I cut my finger. Comedy is when you fall into an open sewer and die.

—Mel Brooks

How Do You Get
to the Russian Tea Room?*

On a summer day in 1995, I walked into the Russian Tea Room, one of Manhattan's most famous restaurants, located on Fifty-Seventh Street near Carnegie Hall. I'd walked over from my office at Comedy Central, where I was the executive vice president of Marketing. Comedy Central had been around for six years. It was starting to get a big audience, starting to make a name for itself in the comedy world, and on the verge of making money. There were hundreds of people working at the channel. But I still felt that it was ultimately my responsibility to make Comedy Central successful, since I was the one who started it.

The Russian Tea Room had been a favorite of artists, actors, and people who worked in show business since the 1920s. Tourists who could afford it came to watch the rich and famous, hoping that a Hollywood star would drop by. I was there to meet a hero of mine, a stand-up comedian I'd first seen on television thirty years earlier when I was ten years old.

---

* A guy pulls up to a New York City cop and says, "How do you get to Carnegie Hall?" The cop says, "Practice, practice, practice."

• • •

There were lots of funny people in my family, and from an early age I wanted to be funny, too. I thought of it as a required skill, as important as reading or hitting a baseball. I found that by making kids laugh at school, I could be part of the crowd, get invited to parties, and get noticed by girls. It also helped me avoid getting beat up on the playground and bullied in gym. Being funny was a path to survival and reproduction.

Comedy was an obsession for me in grade school. I listened to the comedy albums of Bill Cosby and tried to mimic his story-telling. I studied Marx Brothers scripts and marveled at their verbal acrobatics and comic timing. I read *The Essential Lenny Bruce* and felt Bruce's pain through his comedy. I read Woody Allen's *Without Feathers* and discovered the art of writing comedic short stories. I studied Jonathan Swift's "A Modest Proposal" and started writing my own satire. I subscribed to *Mad* magazine and *National Lampoon* and collected back issues. I started an underground satirical newspaper. When I got my driver's license, a friend and I drove home from school every day and ate lunch in front of the television, so we could watch *Get Smart*.

Television comedy provided a window on the larger comedy landscape. From the time I was eight years old I loved watching the stand-up comedians on *The Ed Sullivan Show*. One of my favorites was Richard Pryor. He was twenty-four years old when he first appeared on *The Ed Sullivan Show*, looking uncomfortable in his black suit, white shirt, and skinny black tie. His suit clung too tightly to his slight frame as he described growing up black in Peoria. Richard talked about being bullied on the playground. First, he impersonated the bully: "After school...I'ma bite off your foot." Then he did his reaction—mortal fear. Richard's eyes went wide and darted right and left. His shoulders hunched in anticipation of being hit and he forced his mouth into a half smile that was both supplicating and frightened. My brothers and I had our own playground challenges, mostly about lunch money, and we could relate.

And there was Jackie Vernon. His routine was to describe his life in a continuous slide show. He held a clicker that imitated the sound of a slide changing. There were no actual pictures, only his descriptions of them. "I went on safari in Africa," he'd say. "It didn't go too well. I'd like to show you some slides." Click. "Here we are starting off on our safari." Click. "Here we are just before we hit the quicksand." Click. "Here's a waist-up shot." Click. "Here's some hats and ropes and things."

But my favorite was Alan King. He'd show up on the stage dressed in his suit and tie and holding a cigar. His face would be screwed up a little, his mouth in a sour frown, as if he found merely *talking* about his life to be a burden. His whole approach to the audience would be, "Can you believe what I have to put up with?" His eyebrows would rise, his lips would purse. He would wave around his cigar, stabbing for emphasis, gesturing grandly. His material was basic Borscht Belt stuff: wives, partners, in-laws, the everyday indignities of life.

"I remember the day I got married. Such a wonderful ceremony! My bride, beautiful in her wedding gown, stood next to me crying tears of joy. In Jewish weddings it's traditional for the groom to end the ceremony by stomping on a wine glass—this is

11

supposed to drive off the evil spirits. I broke the glass, but when I looked up...*my mother-in-law was still there.*"

•   •   •

The Russian Tea Room's maître d' greeted me, informed me that I was the first in my party to arrive, and escorted me to a table set for three. I opened my menu and did a quick search for something that could be eaten with a knife and fork without making a mess. Something dry, without any sauce that might land on my favorite and most expensive red paisley tie. I was a sloppy eater, and more than once when I'd dropped a forkful on my lap at dinner, my wife had asked, "Do you eat like that at business lunches? It can't be good for business."

When I looked up from my menu, there was Nancy Geller, the producer of a series we were running on Comedy Central called *Inside the Comedy Mind.* She greeted me with a smile and a kiss. Nancy, tall with long blond hair and a big smile, stood next to the host of *Inside the Comedy Mind.* He held an unlit cigar in his mouth, but it didn't stop him from smiling. I stood up as we shook hands. "I'm Alan King," he said. "It's a pleasure to meet you."

Alan sat on the banquette; Nancy and I sat on the chairs facing him. I settled myself and looked across the table. There he was, bathed in the low amber light of the restaurant, framed against the plush red velour of the banquette, and smiling regally at me, his presence warming the room.

People at the tables nearby turned to look, whispering and pointing. "Of course it's him," they said. "Look at his hair, his eyes." He said nothing for a moment while he scanned the room. He nodded to a middle-aged woman sitting nearby. She put her fork down and walked over.

"Oh, Mr. King, I'm so thrilled to see you here. I've been a fan since I was a little girl. My father thought you were the funniest man alive. That's what he'd say. He'd say, 'Tessie,'—that's me, I'm Tessie—'Tessie, Alan King is the funniest man alive.' He'd laugh so hard tears would come to his eyes."

"Thank you, sweetheart," Alan said, smiling up at her. "I'm so glad you came over today." He pulled a fountain pen and an index card from his pocket and wrote, "To Tessie, All the Best, Alan King." Tessie took the card, thanked him, and scurried back to her table to share her adventure with her husband.

"Nancy said you wanted to meet me," Alan said. "And she told me you're a big-shot network executive at Comedy Central, so I said to her, 'Sure, why not, maybe he won't cancel my show.'"

"I love *Inside the Comedy Mind*, Mr. King—"

"Call me Alan!"

"I love your show, Alan, and I hope it stays on forever."

Nancy put her hand on my arm. "Art, you're so nice! I told Alan you're the only one at the network who knows what they're doing." This was Nancy buttering me up, thinking that I could somehow get his show renewed.

"Nothing's been decided as far as I know. But I'm not in Programming anymore, I'm the marketing guy, so..."

"Come on, Art," Nancy said, "everyone knows you run things over there."

I turned to Alan and said, "Nancy likes to make me feel important."

"She does the same thing to me," he said, "always with the compliments and the big laughs at my jokes."

Nancy beamed. She put one of her hands on his and the other on mine. "I'm so glad I could finally introduce you two, because I love you both."

We ordered lunch and chatted about Comedy Central and some of the comedians Alan had interviewed on his show. He told us how he "discovered" Barbra Streisand when she was a teenager singing in some dive club in Greenwich Village ("She was just a skinny kid, but man, when she opened her mouth to sing, everyone in the place practically fell over!").

When I asked him what he thought of an older Borscht Belt comic who was attempting a comeback, Alan said, "Him? I haven't said two words to that creep in forty years. Not since we had a fistfight."

"You hit him?"

"One night after a show we were doing, I walked into the alley for a smoke. There he was beating up his girlfriend. I walked over and told him to knock it off, but he says, 'Mind your own fucking business' and goes to hit her again. I grabbed his arm and spun him around. That's when I punched him in the nose." Alan smiled at the memory. "He cried like a baby. I helped the girl to her feet and told her, 'Sweetheart, you're too good for this bum, find somebody else.' He never forgave me."

We talked all through lunch about the comedians and performers Alan knew and loved. At one point he said to me, "You really know your comedy, don't you? You're a real student of comedy. It's good to know somebody at that channel has some respect for the past."

Alan King was right. I did know my comedy.

Nancy said, "Alan, did you know Art started the channel? Art, tell Alan about how you started Comedy Central."

Before I could answer, somebody came up to the table and put his hand on Alan's shoulder. He was an older gentleman, dark skinned, very handsome, and somewhat familiar. "Jesus, Harry, what are you doing here?" Alan said. "Meet my friends Nancy and Art. Guys, this is Harry." It was Harry Belafonte, the world-famous singer and actor.

"Sit down, Harry," Alan said. "Art was just about to tell us how he started Comedy Central."

CHAPTER 1

Pitching Comedy

I never thought I would have a career in the television business; or, more precisely, I was convinced it was nearly impossible, in the same category as becoming an astronaut or a rock star. Despite my interest in comedy throughout my childhood, my parents believed strongly that I shouldn't try to make a career in entertainment because: 1) Why throw my life away on something as frivolous as entertainment when I clearly had the brains and the drive to become a doctor (note: to become a doctor was the pinnacle of achievement for first-generation American Jews because it afforded both wealth and the admiration of the community in a way that no other career could; while this had become a caricature by the time I went to college, it was still pretty much dogma); and 2) There was no guarantee of success. What guaranteed success? Accounting, law, medicine. "Get your CPA so you can have something to fall back on," my mother said, and my father agreed. He'd hired me to work in his accounting office while I was in high school, so I knew enough about accounting to not want to fall back, forward, or sideways on it.

College offered an alternative that I hadn't even heard of let alone considered—economics. When I enrolled in Introductory Microeconomics in the first semester of my freshman year, I had no intention of taking another economics class after that. Three weeks into that class, I studied hard for the first exam, so I was surprised when my professor handed it back with an F on it. Having failed my first test ever, I realized that this economics stuff was harder than I'd thought, and if I was going to learn it, I'd have to change my approach. By the end of the first semester, I'd decided to major in economics. When I told my father, he said that economists were useless and reiterated that accounting was a better bet.

At the end of my sophomore year, I'd taken a bunch of economics courses and was hungry for more. I had been eager to learn about something called econometrics (a more quantitative approach to economics that involved statistics and was the basis of economic forecasting models), but as it turned out, it wouldn't be offered my junior year because the professor who taught it would be on sabbatical. Further, if I wanted to take econometrics at Swarthmore, I had to be enrolled in the "honors" track, which consisted of seminars instead of classes. That pissed me off. The classroom system had served me well since kindergarten and I wasn't looking for a change, so I signed up for some other courses and grudgingly gave up on econometrics.

A few days later I got a note from the economics department saying, "Congratulations on being accepted into the Honors Economics Program." Thinking there must be some mistake, I marched off to see the head of the department. There'd been no mistake. Apparently, I was being drafted into the honors program.

After hearing this, I stewed in my dorm for a few hours. I *didn't* want honors; I *did* want econometrics. I decided it was time to address both problems head on and find a solution. I went to the library and found the econometrics textbook *Principles of Econometrics*, written by Dr. Jan Kmenta, who, according to the information in the introduction, was Professor of Economics at The University of Michigan in Ann Arbor. Noting this I returned to my dorm, collected as much change as I could find in my room (including my roommate's drawers, thank you very much) and parked myself in the pay phone booth down the hall.

I dialed, deposited an impossible amount of change, then waited.

"University of Michigan, Admissions, Miss Dellman speaking. How can I help?"

"Hi, I'm a sophomore at Swarthmore College. Can I ask you something? Do you have a professor there named Jan Kmenta?"

"Um, yes, Professor Kmenta is in the economics department."

"Does he teach undergraduates?"

"Yes."

"Great. I'd like to transfer to your school next semester. Can you tell me how to do that?" There was a very long pause. "Who is this?" Miss Dellman asked.

After a few minutes of conversation during which I told Miss Dellman about myself and my grades and that I was deadly serious, she said, "Well, yes, I suppose you can transfer here. You'll need to fill out the paperwork, though."

I had taken my education into my own hands. Nobody was going to kick me into honors against my will. I'd found a way out. Everyone—my professors, my friends, my parents—thought

I was crazy doing what I did, but I didn't feel crazy. I did what I had to do—change everything. It was like changing the television channel. Instead of watching a show until the end, I cut into something else to see if it was better. And I felt the jolt of being alive, in control by being slightly out of control.

I spent the next year at University of Michigan and did, in fact, study with Jan Kmenta. He was a terrific professor and a charismatic man who had made a daring escape as a seventeen-year-old from his home country of Czechoslovakia during the Second World War, a story he'd told during one of our classes. His accent was almost unnoticeable except for the mispronunciation of a few key terms, including reciprocal which came out "reh-ci-PROC-al." Nobody dared correct him.

During one meeting with him in his office, he asked me what I intended to do after I graduated.

"I think my parents wanted me to become a doctor," I said.

Kmenta nodded thoughtfully, then said, "Doctors don't always have such interesting lives. I'm an economist. I get to travel all over and talk to very smart people about important problems—and solutions. Maybe you should become an economist." It was the first time I even considered it. But I admired Kmenta and took his advice to heart.

My year at University of Michigan was exactly what I needed in order to feel that I was in charge of my education and my life. But by the spring I was ready to return to Swarthmore. I graduated in 1978 with a degree in economics and was hired right out of school by a consulting firm in Washington, D.C., where I worked for three years on various projects for the Environmental Protection Agency and Department of Energy. My education had paid off, and as Kmenta had promised, I got to work with very smart people devising solutions to tough problems, and I found the work fascinating and gratifying. Then one day, I was sitting at my desk reading a copy of *Coal Weekly* when I realized this was not my life's work. I still wondered what it would be like to work in the movie or television business. I decided to quit consulting and go back to business school, hoping that an MBA from Wharton was just the credential I needed to land an exciting job in entertainment.

On my first day at the Wharton School, there was a barbecue on the quad for new students. I sat on the low brick wall watching the smoke rise from the grills and observing rather than participating. A young woman walked up to me. "Mind if I sit down?" She held out her hand and said, "I'm Emily."

She was young and attractive, and I assumed she was a fellow student. "Hi, Emily. I'm Art. Where you from?" I asked.

"Nowhere," she said. "I mean, I live here. I work for Wharton in administration. I oversee Student Affairs."

"We're not free to have affairs on our own? This place is stricter than I thought."

Emily smiled. "Very funny. No, it's about student life, clubs, extracurricular activities, stuff like that."

"Is there an Entertainment Business club?"

"Um, I don't think so. You could start one."

"Thanks, but not my style."

"A lot of the students here who are interested in performing arts end up doing the Wharton Follies." Emily went on to explain the Wharton Follies was an annual musical comedy review written and performed by students. "It's very popular. You should check it out if you're interested." She scribbled a name on a piece of paper.

I auditioned for the Wharton Follies and joined the cast. Several of the students were quite accomplished, including the director (who'd previously acted in and directed several off-Broadway plays), the choreographer (oh no, I was going to have to dance!), and the musical director (and sing!). And there were a bunch of veterans of the Harvard Hasty Pudding Show, the granddaddy of all student-performed satirical shows, and these guys were seriously funny.

The Follies wasn't my first theater experience. In college I wrote and performed comedy skits, and I'd been Motel the tailor in the school production of *Fiddler on the Roof*. I got to sing "Miracle of Miracles," which I pulled off with the help of a very patient voice coach and a lot of wide-eyed enthusiasm in my delivery. I enjoyed being onstage, and I had loads of fun doing the Follies my first year.

The second year I was chosen to be head writer, based on the fact that I got a lot of laughs the previous year. Plus, I volunteered. The first thing I did was to put up a notice on the activities board inviting anyone interested in writing for the Follies to a meeting. Twenty people showed up at the meeting. I spoke for a few minutes about the process. Everyone there was welcome to submit skits and songs making fun of the school, professors, or job hunting, and then I would put them together into a cohesive show that I would write myself.

A woman raised her hand. "Can you give us some tips on writing comedy?" she asked.

I froze. What did I know about comedy? "Sure," I said, and proceeded to talk about what I thought made a good comedy skit, funny song, and target for satire. I gave examples from *I Love Lucy*, the Marx Brothers, and *Get Smart*, describing funny scenes that were well constructed and had a beginning, middle, and end.

When I finished, the woman said, "Gee, you've thought a lot about this, haven't you?" And I realized I had.

One of the pieces I wrote was called "Video Resume." The idea was that when video became more generally available, job seekers would no longer use printed resumes but instead make videos highlighting their career histories and accomplishments. I enlisted the help of the Wharton visual aids guy, who had experience in film and video. I directed everything, and we all laughed as we were performing for the camera, but when he came back with the edited version, it wasn't funny. "It's edited wrong," I told him, and we went back to the editing room, where I re-edited for several hours until it all finally worked.

As I sat editing the vignettes in "Video Resume," I thought, Wouldn't it be fun to be able to watch the funniest scenes from movies and television? Just the classic funny scenes rather than the whole show or movie? Maybe it could be a show...or a television channel...devoted to great comedy. The more I thought about it over the next few weeks, the more I liked the idea. During the previous three years, more than a half-dozen new cable channels were started, including all sports (ESPN), all news (CNN), and all music (MTV). Why not an all-comedy channel?

That spring, armed with my MBA in finance, I was one of only a handful of people who graduated without a job offer. I was holding out for something in entertainment, but not many entertainment companies were recruiting at Wharton. I finally got hired at the beginning of the summer—as a financial analyst at CBS Television Stations. It paid me roughly half of what I'd been making as a consultant in Washington, D.C., before starting graduate school.

But, at the age of twenty-seven, I was in show business. Sort of.

I moved from Philadelphia to New York and took an apartment on Twenty-Ninth and Park, an area of Manhattan known for two things: furniture stores and prostitutes. It was comforting to know that a coffee table and some rentable companionship were right outside my door. CBS was located at Fifty-Second Street and Sixth Avenue, a short subway ride away.

Working at CBS Television Stations, I quickly learned, was like working at any other large corporate company. I was almost completely removed from the production of television and spent most of my time churning out spreadsheets that reported on assorted financial measures of how profitable my division was. The short answer: *extremely* profitable. But the executives liked to see that in black and white and read the detailed reports in order to better manage the business, or so I was told. I felt good about my contribution to the overall effort until I learned that a lot of my financial analysis and reporting was hardly used. After working there for about a year, I suggested to my boss that one of the reports I'd been preparing was not useful to anyone. I knew this because I had asked a lot of the people who received it. When I asked if maybe I should spend time on something else, my boss was horrified. I slunk back to my office, wondering how I was going to make my first foray into television more personally and professionally rewarding. So far, working at this giant corporation was not what I'd pictured.

In December 1983, a few months past my first anniversary at the job, I got a call from a former CBS colleague who'd recently been hired by HBO. "This place is great," he said, "and they need someone who knows how to do economic modeling. Interested?" Two weeks and several interviews later I was hired as a marketing analyst by HBO.

Working at HBO was a completely different experience. CBS was a huge corporation fighting for a slightly bigger share of the network television pie. (At that time, there were only three networks: CBS, ABC, and NBC. Cable television was not yet considered a serious competitive threat.) Working there was like working at the post office, although the pace seemed slower.

On the other hand, HBO was a small, relatively new company crammed into a couple of floors in the Time & Life Building across from Radio City Music Hall. It was started in 1976 with the idea of providing first-run movies to cable subscribers for a monthly subscription fee. In 1978 they began to deliver the service via satellite so they could go national. As long as a local cable system had a satellite dish, they could offer HBO to their cable subscribers. HBO was an almost-immediate success.

My new job was to develop a methodology to forecast how many people would subscribe to HBO over the next ten years. Even though I had a degree in economics and had worked on forecasting models of all sorts after I graduated from college, I knew this wouldn't be easy. I taped Casey Stengel's famous quote to the wall next to my desk: "Never make predictions, especially about the future." But that was my job in its entirety: to make predictions about the future.

At the time I was hired, HBO had been monstrously successful, with millions of new customers signing up every month. As soon as I got there I could feel the adrenaline. HBO was like a football player who'd just run eighty yards for the winning touchdown, strutting, dancing, high fiving, and celebrating. When I arrived, the mission of the company was clear: "We are going to change television." I believed it, and I was as excited by this as everyone else.

After a couple of years forecasting subscriber growth, I was transferred to the New Business Development department. My boss, Linda Frankenbach, and her team were developing and test launching a new cable television channel. Research had shown that one of the reasons people didn't subscribe to HBO was that the movies had too much sex, violence, and bad language, and many viewers didn't want objectionable content coming into their homes. Armed with this information, HBO designed a new cable channel called Festival.

Festival was a lot like HBO: there would be recent Hollywood movies shown without commercials, and viewers would pay a monthly subscription fee. But Festival would only show movies suitable for the entire family or movies that had the offensive content edited out. Festival was intended to be a "clean" HBO.

During the Festival test phase, the team traveled around the country talking to hundreds of television viewers about their TV viewing habits (favorite shows, how much they watched each week, what they liked to watch, and so on). Through this research, we were trying to learn how to program, market, and sell Festival. I not only heard a lot about how people watched television, I found that by listening closely during these interviews I got a firsthand look at how these people thought, felt, and lived their lives. And I discovered that their lives were hard.

"My husband died in an accident at work four years ago, so I work and take care of the kids. Television is my escape."

"I have a son who's in a wheelchair and he's got a lot of problems. I love him, but he's a handful. He's fifteen now, and he loves watching cartoons."

"My wife, God bless her soul, she passed away last summer right after I got laid off from the factory, so I haven't got much in my life but the television. Sports and news mostly, and I'm embarrassed to admit I watch Days of Our Lives. *Yessir, almost every day."*

Another thing that came up talking to these viewers about television was how much they liked comedy. We asked people in focus groups whether they would watch a movie channel that had less sex, violence, and bad language, and most agreed that it sounded like a worthwhile idea.

Ever since the idea had first occurred to me while writing and performing the Wharton Follies, I kept thinking about how great an all-comedy television channel would be. New cable channels were launching all the time and I expected someone would announce an all-comedy channel any minute, but nobody did. I'd run the idea by a couple of my friends, including the possibility of using comedy clips from movies and television. They all agreed it was a cool idea, but nobody knew how to get it started. I watched as more and more cable channels with single-subject formats were launched in the 1980s. The Discovery Channel showed documentaries. The Entertainment and Sports

Programming Network (soon to be known as ESPN) was riveting audiences by broadcasting second-tier sporting events, like college volleyball and lacrosse. And MTV—music television, all music all the time—was changing the cultural landscape.

The time seemed right for another reason: live stand-up comedy was suddenly everywhere. The club scene was raging in cities across the country; clubs were packed with patrons willing to pay the cover charge *and* a two-drink minimum to watch headliners as well as up-and-coming comedians. Comedy clubs, previously a big-city phenomenon, began opening in cities and towns across America. Even small-town bars had comedy nights. Clubs featured open-mike nights, where anyone could get up and try out their act in front of a live audience (at their peril). A feature article in *Rolling Stone* magazine on the comedy club explosion noted that in 1988 there were 300 comedy clubs in the country compared to a handful in the early 1970s. In the same article, the comedian Richard Belzer put it this way: "Comedy's kind of taken the place of rock & roll. Kids in the fifties wanted to strap on a guitar and be Elvis; now they want to be Jay Leno or Eddie Murphy or Steve Martin or Robin Williams."

Television took advantage of the live comedy boom, in no small part because it was relatively inexpensive to produce. In 1982 A&E launched *A&E's An Evening at the Improv*, originally taped live at the Improv comedy club in Los Angeles, and the show stayed on the air, capturing the acts of hundreds and hundreds of comedians, many of whom went on to become stars. There seemed to be an endless supply of new comedians clamoring to get their careers supercharged by television. While a few minutes on NBC's *The Tonight Show Starring Johnny Carson* was still coveted as *the* career-building television appearance for new comics, HBO was now offering breaking talent an opportunity to showcase their material in its Annual Young Comedians Special. HBO was helping to make comedy careers. And HBO was also having great success programming one-hour stand-up comedy specials with top comedians like Robin Williams, Sam Kinison, and Whoopi Goldberg, whose acts were presented uncensored and without commercial interruption. Comedy was suddenly everywhere.

Why *not* a comedy channel?

I decided to meet with Bridget Potter, HBO's head of Original Programming, to run the idea by her. I phoned her assistant and said I was a director of New Business Development working on Festival and other new channel ideas (that part wasn't really true) and I had a programming idea. She put me on hold for a minute, then said that Bridget would see me the next day in her office at ten o'clock.

The following day I arrived promptly and her assistant waved me in. Bridget, standing in front of her desk with her arms crossed, invited me to take a seat and start my pitch. She listened to me for about thirty seconds, long enough to understand that I was suggesting that HBO launch an all-comedy channel, before cutting me off.

"Arthur, Arthur, it can't be done," she said as I sat on a couch in her office. Bridget knew me as Art; nobody called me Arthur except my mother. "There's so much comedy on television all over the dial, why would anyone need a twenty-four-hour-a-day comedy channel?" She pranced around the office operatically, grandly waving her arms as if she were about to be hoisted aloft by an invisible wire before bursting into song. "HBO became famous by putting great comedians on television, uncensored! And when we put a comedian on HBO, we made their career. Whoopi." She left off Goldberg, because who else would it be? "Billy." Crystal. "Robin." Williams.

Bridget Potter had risen to the top of the HBO programming team because she was opinionated and, I assumed, some kind of genius. Blond, British, bombastic, and wearing oversized glasses, Bridget lectured me enthusiastically. Her voice was loud and grating, and every now and then her long-buried London accent seeped through. "There's too much comedy out there already, Arthur," she continued. She didn't so much win me over to her point of view as bludgeon me with repetition. "What comedians would be on the channel? Nobody good. Robin? No. Billy? No. Whoopi? Absolutely not. Their management would *just die* before they'd let them appear on a comedy channel. And there's no way you could *consider* making a comedy channel without A-list talent."

And then, all of a sudden, Bridget became quiet and walked toward the couch. Softly, calmly, almost soothingly, she said, "Arthur, you're not a programmer. You know nothing about comedy and very little about television. There are probably two dozen channels out there already. Do you really think that people want more?"

With that, she returned to her desk. She picked up her pink message slips and began to flip through them. Without looking up, she said, "Thanks for coming by, Arthur."

"Thank you, Bridget," I said and hurried out. I thanked her assistant, walked to the elevator and thought about where things stood. It was 1987. I had been at HBO for three years, and I was thirty-two years old. It had been five years since I left business school and almost six years since this comedy channel idea began bouncing around in my brain.

Bridget had left no doubt in my mind that she hated the idea, and if I couldn't convince Bridget Potter, any hope of getting HBO to start my comedy channel had just died in her office. But even as I returned to my desk rattled and chastened, I knew she was wrong.

CHAPTER 2

Meeting the Chairman

My meeting with Bridget was discouraging, but she raised some objections that were worth considering. First, there was plenty of comedy on television already; a full-time comedy channel would be redundant. Second, the new channel would be unable to attract famous comedians, and without them the channel would fail. And finally, who the hell was I, walking into her office with some cockamamie idea? As Bridget put it somewhat more diplomatically, I didn't know anything about the comedy business, and therefore no senior television executive would take my idea seriously because it was coming from me.

Bridget may have been right, but I remained convinced that the world needed a comedy channel. I'd taken a chance and been shot down, but I would try again. I had gotten Bridget to listen, so maybe someone else would listen, too. Or, if HBO wasn't interested, I would try other entertainment companies. Bridget hated the idea of a comedy channel, but maybe someone else would see what I could see. I silently nursed my wounds, told no one about my meeting with Bridget, and promised myself I'd try again soon.

In the meantime, I had plenty of work to do on the Festival channel to keep me distracted. We were marketing Festival as the family-friendly alternative to HBO, but the test marketing was not going well. Our research revealed what any random teenage boy could have told us: "A movie channel with no sex, violence, or bad language? Nobody's gonna watch that."

The final nail in Festival's coffin came as a complete surprise. The Disney Channel, which had been a television channel for children, started programming movies and advertising the channel as "entertainment appropriate for the whole family." Festival was facing a serious and well-funded competitor.

We'd worked for more than a year on Festival, tweaking the programming model, trying different advertising approaches, and lowering the price to almost nothing. In the end, nothing really worked, and we couldn't pretend any longer that we would find the magic that would make Festival successful.

Linda, my boss, called me into her office. She was only a few years older than me, but I considered her a seasoned executive. "What do you think?" she asked as I sat down across from her.

"Honestly?" I said. "I think we're done."

Linda shook her head, slowly, and she bit her lip. "Maybe we should give it one more push."

I shrugged. "Why? Festival's just not working. We can't figure out how to sell it. Even the people who do like the channel don't like it very much." I sat there, waiting for her to say something. "And one more thing. I got the feeling HBO brass is not really behind this anymore."

Linda laughed. "What, you mean Festival, the family entertainment channel, isn't cool enough for Michael Fuchs?" Michael

Fuchs was the chairman of HBO. He'd established his career by giving HBO specials to top comedians: George Carlin, Whoopi Goldberg, Robert Klein, Billy Crystal. The specials were successful not only because they gave brilliant comedians a one-hour television showcase but also because the shows were completely uncensored. Festival, reflecting the family values found in America's heartland, was probably not Michael's favorite project.

Linda leaned back in her chair and laughed. "You got that right." I started laughing, too.

When we stopped laughing, neither of us said anything for an awkward moment. "What do we do now?" I asked.

"We write a memo saying it's time to shut this baby down." Linda's eyes watered up.

She had put a lot of herself into making Festival successful. We all had.

Linda and I wrote the memo that afternoon. The next day, we announced that Festival was shutting down.

•   •   •

Festival had been my only project, so while I was still employed as a director of New Business Development, I had nothing to do. I assumed I'd need to start looking for a job, either inside the company or elsewhere, but Linda said we were all still employed and we would be assigned to "special projects."

Sure enough, Linda stuck her head in my office the next day. "You got your first special project. You're on a committee to figure out whether HBO should get into the basic-cable business."

There were six senior executives on the committee and they had already met twice. I suspected that I was added as an afterthought so that I'd have something to do. I learned that we were tasked with examining whether HBO should launch a new advertiser-supported channel that would be carried on basic cable and have commercials. HBO was a pay service that charged a monthly subscription fee and became successful by *not* showing any commercials. We spent six weeks collecting data, looking at business models, and preparing a recommendation. I alone on the committee felt strongly that HBO should expand into basic cable. The handful of existing basic-cable channels, A&E, Discovery, ESPN, MTV, and others, were staking out niche audiences with programming not found on the broadcast networks. They were growing audiences and revenues. It looked like a successful television business model. And HBO knew how to create quality television. Why shouldn't HBO jump into the basic-cable business?

When we were ready, we scheduled a meeting with Michael Fuchs to discuss our findings and recommendation. The group was already seated in a small conference room when Michael walked in. He was wearing a pale-blue tailored shirt that hugged his arms and torso like a second skin, so tight you could practically see the veins in his arms. He looked around the room and then right at me. "Art," he said as he pulled out the empty chair next to me, "I assume you did most of the work on this, so I'll sit next to you." Everyone laughed, partly because it was Michael who said it and partly because they knew it was true.

The committee told Michael that given the proliferation of cable channels and HBO's lack of expertise in advertising sales, HBO should not develop an advertising-supported basic-cable channel. Michael turned to me. "You agree with this?"

I swallowed hard. "No. I definitely think we should be in the basic-cable channel business."

"That's what I thought," Michael said. He stood up and addressed the group. "Thanks, everyone, for your good work. Let me digest the report and get back to you if I have anything else to say."

We stood up to leave. The other committee members were probably not thrilled that I'd told Michael how I really felt, but nobody said anything to me. Despite my display of chutzpah at the end of the meeting, we never heard a word from Michael, suggesting he had accepted the committee's recommendation. I felt it was now official: HBO would not acquire or start a basic-cable channel.

My meeting with Bridget was the first blow to my comedy channel idea. This was the second.

•　　•　　•

Larry Carlson, HBO's executive vice president of New Business Development and my boss's boss, loped past my office just as I looked up. He turned his head and our eyes met for an instant.

Then he continued loping past my doorway and toward the elevators.

Larry had been responsible for several new business projects in addition to Festival, but Festival took up most of his time. I assumed he was working on some of the other projects, although I had no idea what they were. Maybe he wasn't working on anything, either.

Loping came naturally to Larry, partly because of his lean, six-foot, four-inch Nordic frame, but also because he had the laid-back attitude of a seventeen-year-old Malibu surfer. Larry took life in stride, and everything was always great with him. He had a beautiful wife and two beautiful children, and he was successful and well off. With his blond hair, easy manner, and mischievous smile, Larry looked like an overgrown Dennis the Menace.

Five seconds later, having evidently thrown his lope into reverse, Larry reappeared at my doorway. "Hey Art," he said, deadpan.

"Hey Larry," I replied, also deadpan.

"Working on something?" he asked. Larry knew I didn't have any work to do since my cable committee project had ended and I was waiting for my next assignment. But there I was, obviously working on something. I had papers spread out on my desk and I was scribbling furiously on a yellow legal pad. No sense denying it, but I was reluctant to tell Larry what I was doing. I didn't want to tell anyone at HBO that I had begun to circulate my resume, along with my idea for a basic-cable comedy channel, in order to get a new job. But Larry was curious and I wasn't going to lie to him.

"Remember I told you about my idea for a twenty-four-hour cable comedy channel?"

"Yep. Sounded like a good idea."

"Well, nobody else around here likes it."

"Really? You try Bridget Potter?"

I winced at the memory of that meeting. "She was lukewarm," I said.

Larry laughed. "I've never seen Bridget lukewarm about anything."

"Okay, she hated it," I said. "Anyway, I thought I'd write up the idea, staple it to my resume, and try some other TV companies." I said this to Larry knowing that any idea I came up with as an employee of HBO was, legally, the property of HBO. Even though I'd first thought of it before coming to HBO, I wasn't looking to have that fight. I knew I could get in trouble for taking it elsewhere.

"What, you're sending it to *Viacom*?" he asked. Viacom owned MTV and Nickelodeon, two channels that were taking off. They seemed more willing than HBO to take chances, so I thought they might be receptive. Even if no one at Viacom liked the idea of a comedy channel, maybe it would get me a job, or at least an interview.

Larry sat down in the chair across from my desk, his large frame overwhelming the small chair. "Can I see that?" I handed him my work and he scanned it, making out what he could of my nearly illegible handwriting. Then he looked at a printout of financial projections I'd put together showing how a successful comedy channel would make millions of dollars in just a couple of years. "Okay, I get it. But before you send this, let's go see

Michael and tell him what you're thinking about." He got out of his seat and walked to the door. I assumed he was leaving, but he turned and said, "C'mon, let's go see Michael."

"Now? He's the chairman—don't we need an appointment?"

"Nope. Michael's my boss, but we're friends, too. I know he's in his office because I was just there." I didn't move, so Larry said, "Come on, Art. We'll drop in for a quick chat." I grabbed my pen and the pad I'd been writing on and followed Larry out of my office.

•   •   •

Larry Carlson and I walked down the hall together. Larry's longer stride and his apparent enthusiasm for our mission required me to jog every few steps to keep up. Other people in the halls hustled out of the way for their own safety. Larry reached the elevator first and it opened as soon as he hit the button, as if it had been waiting for us. I leapt into the elevator as the door started to close. As I stood gathering my thoughts, Larry moved next to me, put his arm around my shoulders, looked down at me from his great height, and smiled. "Don't worry, Art. This'll be fun."

The elevator opened, and I followed Larry through the double glass doors that led to the executive office suites. Beyond the doors was a receptionist sitting behind a large desk in a waiting room with several couches and floor-to-ceiling windows. Larry walked past the receptionist with nothing more than a wave. He turned left, walked down a short corridor, and entered the large area outside Michael's office, where Michael's assistant, Merav Brooks, sat at her desk typing. Prim and slender, her dark hair pulled into a bun, Merav was a handsome woman in her forties who looked like she could be your favorite high school English teacher. Larry walked behind Merav's desk and stood next to her before she could even look up.

"Larry," she said, "would you like to see Michael?"

"*Art Bell* and I would like to see Michael," he said, correcting her.

Merav turned her head toward Michael's open door and, raising her voice slightly, said, "Michael, Larry Carlson and Art Bell are here to see you." Without waiting for a response, Larry started to walk into Michael's office. When I didn't follow, Merav said, "You can go in, Art," so I followed Larry in.

Michael was sitting behind a glass desk, which was so large and deep it looked like one of those kidney-shaped swimming pools with a couple of pens and a telephone floating in it. "Lars," Michael said, using Larry's nickname. "Weren't you just in here half an hour ago?"

"Art and I want to talk to you about something he's been working on. Can you spare a few minutes?" Michael gestured to the couch, and Larry and I sat down. We waited as Michael walked around the couch to face us. He remained standing and folded his arms across his chest.

"Arrrrrt," he said, lengthening my name by adding several r's. "What have you been working on that's so important that it couldn't wait for you to schedule a proper meeting?"

I paused before answering, not out of fear or apprehension, but because I wanted what I was about to say to have maximum impact. "I've been working on a plan for a twenty-four-hour comedy channel. For cable TV. I think HBO should launch an advertiser-supported cable comedy channel."

"Really. You talk to Bridget about this?"

"She hated it," I said. "She thinks there's too much comedy on television already, but I think a comedy channel would work." I let that linger for a second to see if Michael was buying any of this. "Nobody does comedy like HBO, Michael, you know that. We've got the best comedians doing stand-up specials. Billy, Robin, Whoopi. You gave them their own specials, and HBO helped make them famous. Nobody has better relationships with comedians than HBO. The only other possible competitor is A&E, with their stand-up comedy series, but why let them take over our turf?"

Michael nodded. "Anything else?"

"Yes," I said. "I spent a long time on the road talking to people about Festival and asking if they thought it was something they'd watch. Some did, some didn't, but I kept hearing the same thing in every town: everyone loved comedy and they wanted more. There's a hunger for it. I just know it. How do I know? Because growing up I loved comedy; it was part of what kept me going all my life. I saw how much people loved to laugh, how much a part of everyone's life comedy was, especially me and my friends in high school and college and...and now. Comedy's like music—it's one of the things that makes life worth living. You love comedy, too, I know you do, and you know how passionate people are about their favorite comedians, and comedy movies, and comedy scenes."

I paused, wondering if I'd overdone it, if the passion spilling out of me was the call to arms I meant it to be, or if I just sounded a little crazy. Nobody stopped me, so I kept going.

"We can start small, use our comedy library, and program the channel with old comedy movies and comedy clips. We could keep our programming costs low."

"Comedy clips? What comedy clips?"

"You know how MTV gets music videos for free? The record companies get tons of promotion for their bands because MTV airs the music videos. We can do the same thing with comedy— take funny scenes from movies, stand-up shows, television shows, and play the clips as promotion for the movies and television shows. Nobody in the entertainment business turns down free promotion, right?"

"Interesting. Free programming. I like that."

"And HBO has all the other back-office stuff we'd need, like legal and finance. The only thing we don't know is advertising sales, but how hard is it to hire some sales guys?"

My enthusiasm propelled me and I was talking fast. I hadn't prepared for this ad hoc presentation, but I'd thought about it for so long that the words had poured out of me. Then I looked at Michael and said, as calmly as I could, "If we don't do it, somebody else will."

I stopped there and sat back on the couch a little, signaling that I'd finished. Michael was quiet. Finally, he turned to Larry. "Lars, what do you think?"

"Michael, you're the boss and you know best about comedy programming, but it sounds good to me."

"Okay, Art," Michael said, "where do we start?"

Larry and Michael were both looking at me. When I repositioned myself so that I could address them both, I accidentally dropped the pad of paper that had been perched on my lap. When I leaned down to pick it up, I noticed my hand was shaking. Nobody had ever asked me where I would start. All my thinking up to this moment had been focused on envisioning the channel fully formed, not how to get it there. As excited as I was by Michael's question, I suddenly felt like somebody had called my bluff, and I was, for a moment, unable to form a coherent thought, let alone a plan with a beginning, middle, and end. Larry looked at me and gave me an encouraging nod, and I found my voice again.

I suggested that we needed audience research, that we should refine the financial projections, and that we should produce a twenty-minute demo tape to show what the comedy-clip format would look like. Michael thought about all this for a few seconds and said, "Fine. And I want you to work with Stu Smiley on this." Stu was the head of Comedy Programming at HBO. "You have two months to get this together and then we'll see what's what."

"Okay…" Two months didn't sound like a lot of time, but I didn't voice my concern. Instead, I asked, "What about a budget for this stuff?"

Michael waved that away. "Not an issue. Figure out what you need; Larry will work it out with you. Call Stu. And you know what, get Fran Shea to help on the demo tape." Fran was vice president of On-Air Promotion. "Thanks, Art," he said, dismissing us.

Michael turned and sat down at his desk, then shouted out the door as we were leaving, "Merav, where's my lunch meeting?"

CHAPTER 3

In the Weeds

Following my brief but consequential meeting with Michael and Larry, I began thinking that I was totally in over my head. But I had gotten marching orders from the chairman and I had no intention of letting him down.

HBO was a small company with fewer than seven hundred employees in 1987. Almost everyone was young, energetic, ambitious, and smart. The long hours and shared quarters often turned working relationships into friendships and romance. The company had recently moved from the Time & Life Building in Rockefeller Center to a newly renovated building all our own, at the corner of Forty-Second Street and Sixth Avenue. The offices were new, clean, and comfortable. Almost nobody worked in cubicles back then, and most staffers had their own offices with big brown desks and credenzas. We'd been allowed a say in the office décor. When an interior designer showed me some fabric swatches and carpeting, I had no idea what the heck I was looking at or why, but I pointed to one of the three or four choices and grunted. That seemed to please the designer, and she moved on to her next victim.

One improvement, for HBO at least, was that the new building came complete with a high-end company cafeteria. I recall hearing that the cafeteria was intended to replace a Time Inc. corporate ritual that had both fascinated and appalled me. Time Inc-ers (as even HBO employees were known while we were in the Time & Life Building) were encouraged to take each other to lunch at the finest Midtown restaurants as often as possible. This ritual allowed even a low-level employee to ask an executive to dine with them, but it took a certain level of gumption to really bust through several org chart layers for your lunch dates. In the end, we took advantage of the policy mostly to save money and supplement our nutrition, and to grease the wheels of cross-departmental cooperation.

Everyone was expected to dine out relentlessly in order to build their reputation and find common cause with others in the company. In fact, after my first month at HBO, my new boss confronted me with my anemic expense report, holding it between her thumb and forefinger at arm's length as if the toxic smell of it would overwhelm her. "Art," she said, "you'd better start asking people out to lunch and taking them to the best places. Or there will be consequences!" After that, I had three or four company lunches a week.

Eventually the company realized that buying everyone lunch was getting expensive, so the plan for the new HBO building included a company cafeteria. HBO would be budget conscious and provide a place for employees to mingle and dine without sending company profits to neighborhood five-star restaurants.

When I entered the new cafeteria for the first time, I took a tray and started down the line, passing by the fruit and cereal and stopping at the grill. The grill man had his back to me but must have sensed my presence. He turned and gave me a huge smile. I recognized him, but from where?

"How you doing, man, good to see you," he said.

"Jake?"

"Yeah, I'm here now. How 'bout that!"

I first met Jake when I worked at CBS Television Stations. He could handle a dozen people at a time—take their orders, start things rolling, and keep the line moving for hours without messing up. Some people were good at their jobs. Jake was a master. Leave it to HBO to poach the best grill man in the business.

"Whaddya having, man?"

"Two fried eggs, over easy, bacon."

"You got it."

The cafeteria had Jake, and the food was generally fabulous, another perk of HBO's success. But I soon realized that the cafeteria was, like any high-school cafeteria in the country, where it all got sorted out: who was cool, who was hip, who was connected, who was on the way up, and who was on the outs. You could look at the company org chart and see the organizational structure and who reported to whom. But it was the cafeteria that revealed what was really happening.

Shortly after my meeting with Michael, my assistant, Rosa Lombardo, told me that Dick Beahrs had scheduled lunch with me. Dick was the executive vice president in charge of Cinemax

Sales. He'd actually been my boss's boss when I was hired at HBO five years earlier.

Dick had been at the company since the beginning, and before that he'd been at *Sports Illustrated*, owned by Time Inc., HBO's parent company. He had dark hair and a pale complexion, a forelock that hung down toward his left eye, and slightly protruding front teeth that made him look like a distant Bobby Kennedy cousin. He came to the company almost directly from UC Berkeley, where he'd been student-body president during some of the anti-Vietnam War protest years, and he had the ability to bring an undergraduate revolutionary passion to everything he did. While I admired Dick's energy, he took on every business challenge as if it were a campus confrontation with the National Guard. Dick spoke proudly of his hippie days at Berkeley, but he'd fully transformed himself into the corporate guy, with short black hair and the navy-blue suit, white button-down shirt, and red tie of the sales executive commuting from Connecticut.

After four years at HBO, lunch with Dick was no big deal, but I wondered why he had asked me to lunch since we weren't really working together anymore. The answer came before we took the first bite.

"I heard you and Carlson had a meeting with Fuchs about starting a new channel." I nodded. "Can you tell me about it?"

"I guess so," I said. "It's a twenty-four-hour cable channel devoted to comedy."

"Just comedy?"

"All comedy. Constantly. Comedy clips from movies, TV, and stand-up performances."

Dick pondered that for a minute. "I thought licensing clips is really expensive. How's that gonna work, financially?"

I told Dick he was right; licensing a two-minute clip from a movie to use in a television show you're producing can cost a small fortune, because everybody associated with the clip, including the actors, the writers, the musicians who wrote the music in the clip, etc., all have to be paid. Union rules. That's why it wasn't done all that much. There were a handful of movies that relied on clips (the movie *That's Entertainment* was hugely successful) and a few television shows, too, but the high cost made clip shows the exception.

So how could we do a channel full of comedy clips from movies and television? I'd found out that there was a way to get these clips for free: by using them for promotional purposes (as in a commercial or a preview of an upcoming show or movie).

I summed up: "So we can use clips from movies and television and, if we put the name of the movie on the clip while we're showing it, it's considered promotion. Since we're promoting the videotape, which the studios are trying to sell or rent through video stores like Blockbuster, we can use the clip for free."

Dick looked skeptical. "And you can program a whole channel like this?"

"Think about how MTV started," I said.

"What do you mean?" he asked.

"Well, MTV got music videos for free from record companies because the channel promoted their bands. Eventually, MTV added other stuff, like live concerts, request shows, interviews. And that's what we can do. Start with comedy clips, and over time add movies, specials, original series, all that stuff." (MTV blazed a trail by adopting music programming as their format. They also cleverly appropriated the anti-establishment, bad-boy persona lifted from the rock & roll world. They became the unofficial home for the music industry. And because MTV was considered by some conservatives and cable operators to be juvenile, profane, and even godless, it had a hard time getting national television distribution until they launched a brilliant advertising campaign. "I want my MTV" was screamed with malevolent glee into the camera by David Bowie, Madonna, Mick Jagger, and other famous rock musicians. MTV's surly teen attitude was the best part about the channel.)

Dick sat back. "It's brilliant."

"Really?"

"This thing could be huge!" I realized Dick was going into one of his paroxysms of enthusiasm, from which there was no turning back. "Wow, I think this could be the biggest thing in cable television! I've got to be part of this." He was practically shouting, and the people at the next table looked over, saw it was Dick, shrugged, and went back to their own lunch conversation.

Dick was one of the best sales executives at HBO and had been there for a long time. That, and the constant management shuffles and reorganizations that gave Dick responsibility for huge swaths of the company, made him something of a senior statesman at HBO. His approval of my idea wasn't critical, but I knew his enthusiasm could make a difference to the way people thought about it around the company. And every time someone else said something favorable about my idea, I had a rush of pride and confidence that lasted for as long as twenty minutes before I returned to my usual worried self. So I was glad Dick was as enthusiastic as he was.

Dick seemed so excited about this comedy channel that I knew he would find a way to be part of it. Sure enough, a short while later Dick was named to the team that would explore the viability of the channel. Having worked with Dick before, I wondered if he was the best guy for this project. But despite my initial skepticism, Dick turned out to be instrumental in plotting a course for us over the next few months.

News of my meeting with Michael was roaring through the building, and things were happening fast. Stu Smiley, the most appropriately named vice president of Comedy in the history of the comedy business, had teamed up with Fran Shea, vice president of On-Air Promotion, to create a presentation tape that would demonstrate the format of this new channel. I met with Fran and Stu in Fran's office to talk about what the tape would look like. I wasn't a complete stranger to creative projects; I'd written and performed in shows in college and graduate school and I'd made some short films. But this was different. This was my first creative meeting at HBO, or anywhere in a professional context for that matter.

Fran waved me into her office without a word. She was standing alone in front of her desk, engrossed in something playing on a TV monitor. I realized she was concentrating, so I kept quiet. Fran was in charge of producing the thirty-second commercials that advertised HBO programs and aired on HBO between movies and other programming. The department also created the "look" of the channel, producing channel IDs ("You're watching HBO"), tune-in spots ("Tonight at seven on HBO, tune in to *The Godfather*"), and image advertising that often consisted of sixty-second montages of the blockbuster movies on HBO. This, like any advertising, was extremely important to the success of the channel, since it made HBO seem like a great value, a channel worth paying ten bucks a month for.

"That's great!" Fran said when the on-air promo she was watching ended with a shot of fireworks and the HBO logo, all accompanied by a hip soundtrack. "That's really terrific! Art, check this out." As Fran rewound the tape, I thought about how many young, attractive, talented people worked here, and how HBO was proud of the fact that they hired only the best and the brightest.

Fran played the spot for me proudly, then looked over for my approval.

"Wow, it *is* great!" I said, although I wasn't really sure why it was great. It looked like a lot of other promos to me. Fran yelled to her assistant, "Can you tell Chris I love this spot and have no changes?" Then, returning her attention to me, she said, "So how's it going? We're doing, what, some kind of tape for your comedy channel idea?"

"Yeah." I looked at my watch. "Isn't Stu supposed to be here for this?"

"You know Stu—he has to make an entrance," she said, laughing. "I'm sure he'll show up eventually. So, tell me about this comedy channel—what's it all about?" I repeated to Fran what I'd told Dick Beahrs. We would start out like MTV, with hosts and comedy clips making up most of the programming, and over time add more traditional comedy programming, like movies.

"But," I said, "the demo tape should probably show what the hosted clip shows look like."

"Okay. We can do that." Fran paused, then said, "I guess we better make sure it's funny. Hard to sell comedy without making people laugh."

That was the first time anybody had put it that way. It was my first lesson in the art of promotion for the new comedy channel. I realized that whenever we pitched the channel, whether to top management, cable companies, or potential advertisers, we had to make people laugh for them to take us seriously. I had no idea how difficult that would turn out to be.

I asked Fran the question I'd been asking myself a lot lately. "You think this'll work? The all-comedy channel, I mean."

"Yeah, it's great. HBO should do a comedy network. No reason it shouldn't work. But I think it's gonna be really hard." She paused, as if reflecting on what she'd just said. Then she said, slowly this time, "Yeah. It's gonna take a lot of work by a lot of people." I knew she was right.

A few seconds later, Stu announced himself with a knock on the door and walked into the office.

"Hey, Fran."

"Hey, Stu. You know Art?"

Stu and I shook hands. I knew very few people in the Programming department and Stu, on the front lines of comedy programming, spent a lot of time with comedians at comedy clubs. While I'd seen him around, we hadn't had any reason to talk before this.

Stu said, "So, you're the guy with the big idea." He laughed, not a good-natured laugh, not the kind of laugh that might break the ice with someone he's just met, but an edgy, wise guy kind of laugh. Stu looked to be about the same age as most everyone else around HBO, somewhere between twenty-eight and thirty-five, and had longish wavy dark hair. He was short, though not as short as me, and wore a loosely fitted, blue suit with brown suede shoes that somehow enhanced his overall tough-guy attitude. I looked at Stu in his tailored, baggy blue suit, radiating an arrogant confidence, and wondered if I was way out of my depth.

• • •

My first baggy blue suit was a band uniform made from the finest nylon acrylic.

When I started high school I played trumpet well enough to be in the marching band. On the first day of practice we were handed our band uniforms. They were blue and white, our school colors, and included white leather spats that buckled over our shoes, blue and white–striped suspenders that crossed in the back, and a fuzzy blue hat that stood up high on our heads and looked like the bride of Frankenstein's hairdo. I hoped the hat might make me look taller, because I was the shortest kid in the freshman class.

Because I was so short, I worried that the uniform might not fit. As soon as they handed it to me, I fished around inside the jacket for the size tag: XXS, the smallest they had. I took the uniform, hat, spats, and suspenders home, ran upstairs to the privacy of my bedroom, and put it on. The pants were so big that I could hold the waist six inches from my body. I looked up and saw myself in the full-length mirror. The jacket swallowed me whole, and the sleeves hung down to my knees. With the suspenders and spats it looked like I was wearing some kind of clown suit. The only thing missing was the big red nose.

I had a week before the first game, enough time to make alterations, but my mother didn't sew, and I was too embarrassed to ask anyone else to do it. I found a box of safety pins and began the process of pulling, folding, and pinning the uniform into a tolerable size. I shortened the pants and sleeves. I pulled in the waist so that it could be belted without bagging. When I'd finished I slowly climbed into the uniform, contorting to avoid the hundreds of safety pins holding the excess material in check, and stood at the mirror. While the pants and sleeves were the right length, the jacket drooped and draped as if thrown onto a tiny clothes hanger. The pants crotch still hung down well below my actual crotch, and the zipper fly looked and felt like it was two feet long. I gazed in horror, knowing there was nothing more I could do.

On game day, uniformed and holding my fuzzy blue hat, I sat silently as my father drove me to the high school. "See if you can get a ride home," was all he said when I climbed out of the car, fighting the acres of acrylic blue fabric. As I walked down the hall to the band room, my pant legs broadcast a swish, swish sound. I braced myself for the inevitable withering looks, unkind remarks, and cruel laughter.

But when I got to the band room, nobody seemed to care how I looked. Even though the uniform didn't fit...somehow I fit in.

•　　•　　•

Stu radiated confidence. Fran knew what she was doing. Me? I was shaking in my shoes, wondering whether I'd crossed over from the relative comfort of my former professional life of numbers, finance, and marketing plans to some kind of alternative reality where things didn't neatly add up, where creativity was king, where thinking outside the box meant throwing out the box completely. That's how Stu made me feel. Then he said, "Well, Mr. Big Idea, whadda we do now?" How did Stu know that I had absolutely no idea what to do now? I'd had an idea and I'd gotten it this far. But Stu didn't make me feel welcome at all. He made me feel like an interloper that had to be shown up or flushed out.

Before I replied, Fran said, "Oh, Stu, lighten up. We need to figure out what this tape's gonna look like, and we don't have a lot of time, or a lot of money for that matter. Sit down." I loved the way Fran took charge.

I sat down with Fran and Stu. Fran couldn't have been nicer, or more accommodating and helpful. She was going to make this work. Stu...well, working with Stu would be more of a challenge.

"Hey," Fran asked. "What are we calling this thing?"

I wanted to call it The Comedy Channel. It was 1988, and there were only a handful of channels on basic cable. I never thought of calling it anything else. "I guess we're The Comedy Channel," I said.

"Okay, good, yeah, I love that. Better have legal check it out, make sure it's available. But for now that's our name. I'll get the design guys to work up some logo treatments." Fran and Stu started bouncing host ideas back and forth, but I was too electrified by the moment to listen. We had just given my channel a name. I'd been standing at the starting line for so long, and now I was hearing the shock of the starter's pistol. The television channel I had imagined was concrete in my mind, complete with comedy clips, comedians, and comedy programs; I also imagined it would be something of a repository of classic comedy. But I realized that as much as I'd thought about it for years, my all-comedy channel was still amorphous, a fog of an idea that needed to solidify, to crystallize into a real channel, with its own look and feel and attitude. Now talented people like Fran and Stu were helping to concretize my notion of a comedy channel and that energized me. It was exciting but at the same time unsettling, the way you feel when you reveal a secret you've been keeping for a long time. And when you reveal a secret, it changes everything.

Fran, Stu, and I set to work on the demo tape. Fran and Stu produced the host segments, and I provided a bunch of funny scenes from movies that would be the first "comedy clips." Six weeks later I was back in Fran's office to take a look at the latest version. She stood in front of the TV, one hand in the pocket of her gray skirt, the other holding the remote. I stood next to her. "Okay, Art, check this out." The TV lit up with color bars, then a title card that said "Comedy Channel Pilot." Suddenly, loud sound effects (BOING! HONK! CRANK!) played over quick cuts of comedy classics (*The Honeymooners*, the Marx Brothers), and then a voice screamed, "COMEDY! COMEDY! COMEDY! TWENTY-FOUR HOURS A DAY!" There was nothing subtle about this introduction. Watching it, I felt I was being bonked over the head with a giant rubber hammer.

Then the very first Comedy Channel logo appeared on screen: a large, three-dimensional *C* with "The Comedy Channel" written inside it.

The logo faded out to reveal a small studio where the host was standing. The host introduced himself as Brian O'Connor. He was kind of a raggedy-looking guy, young but not a kid, shaggy dirty-brown hair, creased face, casually dressed in ill-fitting clothes. Brian was a prop comic but not a well-known one. Prop comics built their acts around objects, like toys, appliances, or dolls. The most famous prop comic was a skinny guy with a mop of crimson hair. His name was Scott Thompson; he performed as Carrot Top and was very successful, but he was relentlessly ridiculed by other comics. For this reason, I was surprised that Stu had chosen Brian. But Fran and Stu said they liked his manic energy for the tape.

"You're watching The Comedy Channel," Brian announced before repeating that it was all comedy, all the time. He moved around the set and announced the comedy clips, clips I'd chosen from *The Naked Gun* movie franchise and from *The Kentucky Fried Movie*. After each clip, Brian came back and did a short comedy bit. By the time the tape ended, I'd laughed out loud several times. Fran asked, "Does it work?"

I said, "Yeah, it looks great and it made me laugh. I just hope the rest of the world thinks it's funny."

Fran agreed it was funny. "I showed it to my staff this morning and they laughed, and they're a tough audience."

The tape was well produced and funny and gave a sense of what the channel could be. But it wasn't exactly the comedy channel I'd envisioned. It was a little too...madcap. And it felt like the host wasn't really interested in the comedy clips. I'd imagined him more like one of those FM progressive-rock DJs who introduce their songs by giving a little information about the band, or the songwriting, or the album it came from, and who seem to truly love the music they play. Brian just said, "Here's a clip from—" and named the movie. He didn't seem to have any relationship or connection to the material. I felt that was missing in the tape, but maybe I was the only one who felt that way. I mentioned it to Fran.

"Yeah," she said, "you may be right. But all the tape has to do is sell the idea. Once we're on the air we can fine-tune things."

"If we get on the air," I added.

"I'm betting we will," Fran said with characteristic optimism. She put down the remote and leaned back on her desk. "Okay, now what?"

"Audience research," I said. "We show it to some focus groups and see whether people think an all-comedy channel's something they'd watch."

The HBO Research department put together a series of focus groups with viewers around the country to find out whether they'd like an all-comedy cable channel. We showed the tape. People laughed. The moderator asked the people in the focus group what they thought. They said they liked the idea but hoped it would be more than just clips (or, as we began calling it, "short-form comedy"). The focus group participants unanimously said they'd definitely check out an all-comedy network.

The HBO Finance department descended on me like a team of FBI agents looking for evidence of money laundering and fraud. "What are the start-up costs?" they asked. "How much advertising can we expect in the first year? What about affiliate revenue? How many people on staff? Is the staff full time or shared with HBO?" I thought these were excellent questions, and I'd actually started thinking about some of this, but now putting together the numbers and the financial plan became a huge project in itself. Luckily, I had plenty of help from the HBO Finance guys, who seemed afraid that the new channel wasn't such a great business idea.

I was serious about getting all this financial information right, but I knew from past experience that you basically make the numbers up. Whatever you expect to spend ends up being wrong, often too low, and often by a lot. Whatever revenue and profit you forecast are also likely to be wrong, often too high, and often by a lot. All new business forecasts tell the same story: the business will lose money for a couple of years, but then profits will soar and everyone involved will be rich! No—really!

Ultimately, after all the prodding and probing from the Finance department, after all the hard questions about costs and staffing and marketing and operations and legal and everything else, we put together a business plan that looked spectacular. Now we had a funny tape, consumer research that showed people loved the idea of an all-comedy network, and a business plan.

We visited some advertising agencies to see if they thought their clients, companies like Coca-Cola and Ford, would buy advertising on the channel. The agencies loved it. We visited the movie studios and asked them if they would supply clips for the channel from their movies and TV shows on a promotional basis. They said they would. One studio executive asked if they could invest in the channel. No investment was needed, thank you very much, but we took the compliment. We asked some cable companies if they would carry the channel. They said they would, depending on how much they had to pay for it. They asked if they could invest in the channel. Once again, we politely declined their offer.

It had been a fast two months since my meeting with Michael Fuchs. Now it was time to present our research findings, the financial plan, and the demo tape to Michael and his executive team. Dick Beahrs, who had been instrumental in introducing The Comedy Channel to cable operators, was now the senior executive in charge of The Comedy Channel effort, so he and I were responsible for the presentation.

We had two weeks to prepare.

CHAPTER 4

The Presentation

Dick Beahrs was a natural salesman. He'd done hundreds if not thousands of presentations selling HBO and Cinemax to cable companies across the country. He knew how to convince cable operators that HBO could make them money, big money, and satisfy customers, and he was partly responsible for the early, rapid adoption of HBO as America's first and most successful pay-television service. Could the two of us deliver a presentation that would bring The Comedy Channel to life?

I usually started work at 8:30 a.m., but on the day of our presentation, I was at my desk at 7:15. I made a point of arriving early on days when I was giving an important presentation. The early morning came with empty halls, closed doors, and dimmed lights, and the quiet helped me stay calm and focus. Typically, I would make some last-minute notes or tinker with the presentation slides. This was less about the presentation and more about convincing myself that I'd done everything I could to prepare. That I was ready.

As soon as I sat down at my desk, I noticed that my voicemail light was on, so I picked up the phone to hear the message. The voicemail lady said, "Message received today at 6:30 a.m." That was followed by Dick's voice. "Art, it's me. I'm in my office going over the presentation. Come by when you get in."

When I got to Dick's office, I found him staring at the pile of presentation decks on his desk. His assistant had made forty copies of the thirty-five-page presentation, and they were stapled and neatly stacked in front of him. Next to the copies was a manila folder holding transparencies that we would use on an overhead projector. The tech people were encouraging everyone to use computer projection, but neither Dick nor I had taken the time to figure out how to use it. Besides, we didn't want to risk something going wrong. Overhead projectors and transparencies were old fashioned, but relatively foolproof.

The presentation was scheduled for 9 a.m. Dick and I put on dark-blue suit jackets and made our way to the fifth-floor conference room to set up. As we rode the elevator, I turned to Dick and said, "This is the most important presentation since my bar mitzvah." Dick smiled, nodded, acknowledged the moment. I added, "I hope this one goes better than that did."

Dick laughed and said, "Yeah, I hope so, too."

"Well, at least this time my notes are in English."

He laughed a little more, and as the elevator doors opened, he turned to me and said, "Let's not fuck this up."

. . .

My bar mitzvah may have been an early, important presentation, but it was not my first. One day when I was in the fourth grade, I was pressed into service at my fourth-grade assembly. They needed a student to stand up on stage and introduce a safety movie they were going to show. Even now I have no idea how this task fell to me, since I didn't consider myself much of a showman, but I agreed to do it. I listened to the principal as he briefed me on what I was supposed to say. He didn't give me notes or a script, and I didn't think to ask. When he was done, the principal asked if I understood, and I nodded. "Do the best you can, Arthur," he said. Then he left. I stood backstage by myself for a few minutes, waiting to go on.

I should have been petrified at the thought of addressing a few hundred kids in an auditorium on short notice, but for some reason I felt no fear, no butterflies, no trepidation at all. When the time came, I marched onto the middle of the stage, stood up straight, and began addressing the audience as if it were the most natural thing in the world for me.

I was standing in front of a microphone positioned near my forehead and was initially startled by the sound of my amplified voice coming through the loudspeakers. I noticed the kids in the front row gazing up at me as I spoke. None of these sights and sounds overwhelmed me or kept me from speaking slowly, clearly, and deliberately. It just seemed to come naturally, and I enjoyed being onstage.

I said everything that the principal had told me to, then added, "I hope you all enjoy the movie. And I hope it's not boring like those other safety movies." Everyone laughed, and I walked off the stage to the sound of applause. The principal, standing in the wings, said, "Good job, Arthur," and I tried not to smile at the compliment. When the film started, I took my seat to watch with everyone else.

Later that day, Mrs. Bartolf intercepted me in the hall. She had long, dark hair, alabaster skin, big brown eyes, and a beautiful smile. She was the prettiest teacher in the school.

"Arthur!" She stopped me, knelt down to look me in the eye, and put one hand on my shoulder. I could smell her perfume. I'd never been this close to her before, and I stood there without moving a muscle, my eyes wide, my stomach fluttering. "I am so proud of you! You were so poised on stage, so grown up! Where did you learn to do that?" And then she said again, "I am so proud of you." My knees got rubbery and I was, ironically, tongue tied. As my brain spun around in my head searching for something to say, Mrs. Bartolf put her arms around me and gave me a hug and a kiss on the cheek.

•　•　•

I thought about my little speech that day and Mrs. Bartolf's kiss as Dick and I walked into the empty conference room. I still had no idea what I had done that impressed Mrs. Bartolf, but I hoped whatever it was, I could conjure some of it for our Comedy Channel presentation.

I found the light switch, and the fluorescent lights flickered on. The room was empty and silent except for the barely audible hum of the lights. We set up the overhead projector. We made sure the video player worked. We checked and rechecked our slides.

Everything was ready.

I was ready.

Ten minutes before the start of the meeting people started streaming in. The room filled up fast. The top executives took the seats up front, and everyone else scrambled for the chairs in the back or stood against the walls.

There were about forty people in the room, including all of the department heads. Michael Fuchs sat right in front of me, and Bridget Potter sat next to him. Larry Carlson stood off to the side. Fran Shea was seated next to Stu Smiley, and when I caught her eye, she mouthed, "Good luck." My old boss, Linda Frankenbach, was among the last to come in, and she squeezed my arm as she walked past.

Dick looked over at me and nodded. I nodded back. Then he stood up and called for quiet, and everyone stopped talking. The forty people in the room turned their attention to Dick and waited for him to start. I remained seated to his right.

"A few minutes ago," Dick said, "Art told me that this is the most important presentation since his bar mitzvah." That got a small laugh. "Well, I think it's an important moment for all of us here, and for HBO."

Dick stood next to the projector and put up the first slide of his portion of the presentation. He talked about how the new channel would be received by cable operators, since they would be instrumental in determining how quickly the channel would achieve distribution to all sixty million cable households in the country. And he made the case for why it wasn't too late to introduce a new channel and how we could charge cable operators a fee for carriage. This was important to the channel's success, and Dick's experience in Affiliate Sales gave him credibility that I lacked. Everyone in the room followed Dick's every word, fascinated by the prospect of a new business. They knew, as I did, that if this presentation went well, we would start a comedy channel. They also knew, as I did, that Michael Fuchs would be the decider. Michael sat up front where everyone could see him. He alone would give the thumbs-up or thumbs-down at the end of our presentation. It was like a gladiatorial spectacle.

Dick moved briskly through the first several slides, but soon he began to drag, and I sensed the room's restlessness. I needed to tell Dick to pick up the pace. From my seat, I caught his eye and began vigorously nodding my head, as if in agreement, but really to encourage him to move it along. He got the message and went directly to his closing slide. "Has the train left the station?" he asked. "Meaning, is it too late for HBO to start another basic-cable channel?" This was my cue. I stood up, moved to the head of the table, and began.

"No," I answered, "the train has *not* left the station. Our timing is perfect. HBO is the leader in comedy on television, and we can either take this lead and create a twenty-four-hour comedy channel or let somebody else steal the opportunity out from under us. But we're going to have to move fast."

I spoke for twenty minutes outlining what the channel would look like, then played The Comedy Channel demo tape (hosted by Brian O'Connor) that Fran and Stu had made. Everyone in the room laughed. When the lights came up, I put up my final slide, the one that summarized the financials. "This slide shows our investment and projected cash flow." I turned to look at the slide and paused to examine it, as if I were seeing it for the first time. "These projections show that The Comedy Channel is a business that can make money." I paused. I could feel the energy in the room. I felt that everyone was with me. "A *lot* of money." I knew it was a great last line, so I said, "Thank you," and took my seat.

When the applause died down, Michael looked around the room. He located Stu Smiley. "Stu, what do you think?" Stu nodded his approval. Then he turned to Bridget Potter, who had shot me down a few months earlier. "Bridget?"

"I think it's *wonderful*, Michael," she said.

Michael called on more people. I think he was really asking whether it was worth risking HBO's reputation, and his own, by starting an all-comedy basic-cable channel. He looked each person in the eye as they answered. Michael was not just asking for their opinions; he was making certain that he had everyone's word that they were willing to do whatever it took to make this successful, that they were *committed.*

Finally, Michael seemed satisfied that he had everyone's support. "Okay, Art," he said, "let's get this thing up and running before the end of the year."

I looked at Dick, and he looked at me. We'd nailed it.

As the meeting broke up, people stopped to shake my hand, to tell me how exciting this was for HBO, and to wish me luck putting it all together. I said "thank you" over and over. When Larry Carlson shook my hand, he said, "That's the biggest smile I've ever seen on you. You usually look like you're about to cry."

"That's just my regular look, Larry. People used to come up to me in school, people I didn't know, and ask me if everything was okay because I looked so miserable."

Larry laughed. "Well, it's nice to see you happy. Hold on to that feeling. You deserve it. This thing, this comedy channel, could be a home run."

"Hope so," I said. "If you hadn't put me in front of Michael, this wouldn't have happened."

"I didn't want to see a good idea die." He patted my shoulder and said, "I'll miss working with you."

"You're not staying involved?"

"No, I've got other things on my plate. I think Michael wants Dick Beahrs to run with this."

"Did he mention anyone else?"

"You. And Stu, probably, since he knows comedy."

"Yeah, Stu does know comedy."

Larry said, "I have one programming suggestion. You should do a news show. A funny news show. Like *Saturday Night Live* does with 'Weekend Update.' Maybe a half hour, weekly, or even daily."

"That's a good idea. I'll talk it up. To whoever ends up programming the channel."

"Isn't that you?

"We'll see," I said. "Right now, I'm just glad that this thing's really going to happen."

"You should be. You've done a great thing for the Home Box." Larry and I shook hands again. It hit me that I wasn't working for Larry anymore, and that I'd miss his warmth, his self-confidence, and his mischievous sense of fun.

Then the conference room was empty except for Dick Beahrs and me. We looked at each other and started laughing. We were like Butch Cassidy and Sundance right after a successful bank robbery.

•   •   •

Michael wasted no time announcing plans for The Comedy Channel to the world. On May 17, 1989, Michael held a morning press conference in Los Angeles and laid out our plans exactly as Dick and I had described them in our presentation. Minutes before Michael was set to speak, I found myself standing next to Billy Crystal, one of the many invited comedy luminaries, as we moved past the impressive bagels-and-lox spread. Billy Crystal turned to me and said, "Who are you?"

"Art Bell. I work at HBO in New York. I'm vice president of Programming for The Comedy Channel."

"Yeah? You work with Stu Smiley?"

"I do. We're supposed to get the new Comedy Channel up and running." I paused. "The one Michael's announcing today."

"I figured that was the one." Billy reached for a basket of bagels and held it out for me. I took a sesame, and Billy said, "Well, good luck with that."

The way he said it, I thought I detected a hint of skepticism.

Michael stepped up to the microphone and began. "HBO has been in the comedy business for a long time. It is our manifest destiny to launch a twenty-four-hour cable comedy channel." I stood with my sesame bagel on a plastic plate and marveled at the swagger Michael put into the announcement. As he continued his remarks, I looked at the roomful of people watching and scribbling on their notepads, and thought, *I am responsible for all this*. The combination of nervous excitement and fear of failure made an odd cocktail. I felt like an astronaut, sitting atop an atlas rocket, knowing there were hundreds of people working to make sure the launch was successful. If the rocket failed, everyone in mission control would be sad, but they'd go home. But it was me in the capsule.

•   •   •

Two days after our press conference, MTV put out a press release saying they, too, were planning an all-comedy network. Their channel would be named HA! The TV Comedy Network, and it would launch April 1, 1990. I assumed this was just a competitive response, that they'd put no more thought into a comedy channel than, Hey, that sounds like a good idea, we should launch one, too. But as I flew home from California and pondered MTV's press release, the full implications of their intent to launch an all-comedy channel hit me.

While their initial press release was short on programming details, it made clear that HA! would show mostly classic television sitcoms; in other words, reruns. They'd already played that game on their Nick at Nite channel. Nick at Nite was started when executives at Nickelodeon, the channel for kids, realized that their audience was in bed after eight. To fill the airtime in the evening, they acquired some inexpensive television reruns from the '60s and '70s and packaged them using hip advertising and promotion to give the vintage shows a fresh look. The repackaged reruns attracted an audience, and Nick at Nite was a success. I realized HA! would use the same strategy. They knew how to do this. They were good at it. And they appeared to be in it to win.

With the two entertainment giants just beginning to draw up their plans, there was no telling how this battle of the comedy networks would be fought, how long it would last, or which side would prevail. But the landscape had changed. We were no longer just launching a comedy channel. We needed to be the first, the funniest, and the best, or we would be no comedy channel at all.

CHAPTER 5

Larry's Birthday Party

A month after the big presentation, my assistant, Rosa, called to me from her desk outside my office. "Jody Crabtree's on the phone for you."

Jody was Larry Carlson's wife. Why would she be calling me? I picked up the phone.

"Art, Jody Crabtree here."

"Jody, hi, everything okay?" I'd met Jody a few times when Larry brought her to company parties. She was a good match for Larry: very tall and strikingly beautiful, with a big smile and dark hair. She laughed loudly and had a trace of a Southern drawl, especially when she'd had a drink or two.

"Yes, everything's great," she said. "Listen, Art, Larry told me you played piano. That's so cool!"

"Well, yeah, I play but I just started taking lessons. I mean, I've played since I was a kid, but now I'm taking jazz."

"Yeah, I love jazz. Listen, I don't know if you know this, but Larry's fortieth birthday's coming up, and I'm having a little surprise party for him next Thursday. I want everyone at our apartment by nine o'clock, so when we come back from dinner, SURPRISE!"

Surprise? That's for sure—I couldn't believe Jody was inviting me to Larry's surprise party.

Then she said, "And I thought it would be nice to have some music there, so if you wouldn't mind playing some jazz piano at the party, I'd really appreciate it."

"I, uh, sure Jody, I'd be happy to play a tune or two..."

"The party's from nine to midnight, but you'd only have to play for about an hour or so, starting around, like, nine thirty or quarter to ten. Something like that."

"Jody, you know I'm not a professional musician. I'm not that good—"

"Oh, you'll be great, Art. See you there. Oh, you know where the apartment is, right?" She gave me the address and hung up.

I looked at the phone and thought about calling her back and telling her that I couldn't make it after all, that I'd just remembered I had a family thing that night, so sorry. Or maybe I should wait until the day of the party and say I had food poisoning.

As I was generating fake excuses, my friend Doug Lee knocked on the open door and walked in.

"What's the matter with you? You look pale."

"Close the door."

I needed advice and Doug would know what to do. I'd met him a couple of years earlier when we started working together, and we'd become friends. He'd been at HBO longer than me and worked in Programming. Everyone at HBO wanted to work in Programming, because it involved movies and comedy and deciding what programs got on the air and how it was all scheduled. And sometimes you got to work with the talent and Hollywood producers on original productions and all that. And, best of all, if you worked in Programming, you were automatically thought of as pretty cool.

Doug fit the bill. He was a Chinese American who dressed for work like he was tending bar at a club in the East Village: black pants, black shapeless jackets, skinny ties, and lace-up boots. He was smart and sophisticated and lived with a bunch of smart, sophisticated friends in a huge apartment on the Upper West Side, where he threw frequent and fabulous parties. He was the Hugh Hefner of my circle, hosting these parties with an ease and elegance that I envied. I asked him once why his parties were always so successful, and he said, "Easy. I make sure there's twice as many girls as guys." Doug knew his way around Manhattan, and he knew everyone at HBO. Hanging out with him was like having a cool older brother to tell you how to handle tough situations. Like dating. Or office politics.

"You're not gonna believe what just happened," I said.

Doug pulled up a chair and settled in for a coaching session. "Personal or professional?"

That stumped me for a second. "Um, both I guess. Larry Carlson's wife just invited me to his surprise party. At their apartment. Next Thursday."

"Cool," he said. "Hold on, why wasn't I invited?"

"What is this, high school? You weren't invited because maybe you don't have any special entertainment talent."

"What's that supposed to mean? I'm endlessly entertaining."

"The reason Jody invited me is she wants me to play jazz piano at the party. You know, as the entertainment."

"Really? She offer to pay you?"

"No, of course not! She invited me, then dropped it on me that I had to put on a show. Can you believe that shit?"

"You *can* play piano, right? And think of who's gonna be there. This could be a great career move. Plus, don't you love playing jazz?"

I loved *trying* to play jazz.

I was introduced to jazz as a teenager by a friend. "You gotta hear this," he said as he cued up the classic Miles Davis song "Kind of Blue." That's when jazz, specifically jazz piano, grabbed me for the first time. Whoa, how does he do that? I wondered. When the album finished, I asked my friend to play it again. As I listened, I thought to myself that I needed to solve this. I couldn't play it; maybe I'd never be able to play it. But jazz had entered my life, and I could tell it was there to stay. I loved it on two levels: the haunting intimacy of the music that made me want to hear it again and again, and the baffling puzzle of it—the unfamiliar chords, the melodies invented on the spot, the rhythms, the interplay of the instruments, the swing of the beat, the sizzle of the cymbal. Figuring this out wouldn't be easy, but I promised myself I would try. Years later when I moved to New York City, I knew it was time to make good on that promise.

I had found a wonderful jazz piano teacher named John Valzano and I'd been practicing every night after work for two years, but I felt I wasn't yet good enough to perform. If I was going to play at Larry's birthday party, I was going to need John's help.

• • •

Two days after Jody invited me to play at Larry's party, I arrived at John's apartment door for my weekly piano lesson. His wife let me in and directed me down the hall to the piano room, where I found John seated at the piano, wiping down the keys with a white cloth. I shrugged off my suit jacket and tossed it over a chair, then wrestled with my tie until it was loose enough to pull over my head and throw on top of my jacket. Then I pulled my music binder out of my briefcase and sat down at the piano with slumped shoulders. John said, "You look tired. Tough day at work?"

"Busy, that's all. Lots going on, trying to get this comedy channel launched."

"Sounds like fun."

"Fun? It's exciting, and I guess sometimes it's fun, but it's not, like, going to the beach fun."

John laughed. "Okay, let's get started. The last tune I gave you was—"

"John, before we start, I gotta talk to you about something. A couple of days ago I was asked to play some jazz at this party at my boss's apartment. I said yes, but I'm feeling I shoulda said no. It's just that I was kind of trapped into it." I expected him to tell me why I would be crazy to try and play at the party. Instead, he reached for my music book and started flipping through it.

John asked, "When's the party?" I told him and he nodded. "You've been doing pretty well with some of these tunes. Let's pick out the ones you know best and work on them a little. I'll get you ready." He continued to look through the tunes. John thought I could do it. I could tell Jody no, I couldn't play at the party, but how could I let John down? How could I let myself down?

So began my crash course in jazz performance. John's steady voice and direction kept me calm as I focused on what he was saying. We worked on the intro for each tune. We talked about alternating up-tempo tunes with ballads. We planned how long I should improvise. As John prepared me for my first gig, I actually started to get a little bit excited.

Toward the end of my lesson, John stood up and said, "Don't move, I'll be right back." A minute later he walked back in with his wife, his teenaged son, and his eleven-year-old daughter. John said, "Now let's try it with an audience."

"I'm not ready!" I protested.

"You're ready. Maria, Chris, and Tessa, I want you guys to act like you're at a cocktail party."

Tessa screamed with delight and said, "I'm a kid. I've never been to a cocktail party. What do I do?"

"Ignore the piano player. Talk to each other. Don't worry about making noise. Walk around, walk behind the piano, laugh out loud."

Chris said, "I can't do this right unless I have a real drink in my hand. Where's the scotch?"

"Very funny, mister," his mother said as she gave him a playful push and Tessa laughed.

"But that's a good idea." John said, "Except for the scotch. Grab some glasses. The most annoying thing can be the clink of glasses when you're playing." Tessa and Maria went to the kitchen and came back with four glasses full of ice water. "Okay, everybody, let's party. Art, you can start whenever you're ready."

At the end of my rehearsal, they all applauded and John's wife said, "You sound so good! Kids, doesn't he sound good?" They nodded. Okay, I thought, I can do this.

$$\cdot \quad \bullet \quad \bullet$$

"Hey, Art, didn't expect to see you here." I turned and faced Mark Benson. He was tall, thin, with fins of dark hair on either side of his balding head. He stood slightly askew as if weighted on one side, and he was pigeon-toed the way some natural athletes are. Mark was a distance runner.

"Mark." I shook his hand but bristled at his greeting. "It's a surprise party. I'm your first surprise," I said. As much as Mark's greeting had irritated me, I understood why he was surprised I was invited. The large living room, with floor-to-ceiling windows and sleek modern furniture, was filled with HBO's top executives and their wives. The head of Affiliate Relations was in the corner chatting with the EVP of Marketing and the senior vice president of Finance. And Michael Fuchs stood munching nuts from a bowl on the piano. This wasn't a business meeting, but Michael was clearly in charge. Power radiated from him like heat from a furnace. People wanted to get close, but not so close they risked being incinerated.

Everyone in the room was a president or executive vice president or senior vice president. This was HBO's ruling class. I was merely a serf, or maybe a knave. And Mark seemed to enjoy my unease.

"Jody invited me because Larry was my boss," I said.

"Yeah, but you guys aren't really friends, are you?"

"Well, we were working together on this new channel—"

"Oh, that comedy thing. Jeez, Art, you really think that has a shot?" Mark asked.

I shrugged. "Michael Fuchs is into it. He wants it to work."

"Uh-huh. Wait 'til things start going sideways. He'll be on to the next thing, and you'll be left holding your dick." Mark was looking over my shoulder now, locating his next mark.

"Well, at least I have that to look forward to."

"Good talking to you, Art," he said, not looking at me, and he moved away.

I was the only person at the party not in a position of authority. And there I was, standing alone with my back to the wall, watching all these guys drinking and laughing as their girl-friends and wives stood close by. I recalled something a comic once said from the stage when he was totally bombing: "I hope that's sweat running down my leg."

I stood in the same spot for what seemed like an eternity, talking to no one, nursing a gin and tonic, and hoping I looked like I belonged, but feeling lost. Then somebody yelled, "They're here...SHHH...Everyone be quiet." The lights went off and the room disappeared into darkness. I stood waiting for my eyes to adjust and looking toward the door. One of the women giggled and everyone shushed her. "Sorry," she said, and everyone shushed her again. Thirty seconds later I heard the snap of a key going into the lock and held my breath. The door opened, and Larry Carlson walked into his apartment, followed by Jody. When Larry flipped on the lights, we jumped up and screamed, "Surprise!"

I watched Larry's face radiate alarm, followed by confusion and finally pleasure, as he figured out what was going on, at which point he said, "Jesus, you've got to be kidding me." He turned to his wife, hugged her, and then opened the door as if he were leaving. Everyone laughed. The party was on.

Larry took off his coat and said a few words of thanks to everyone for coming. When he finished, he began walking around the room greeting guests individually with his big smile, a handshake, and a hug. I moved away from the wall as he closed in on my corner of the room.

"Art, hey buddy, great to see you here, thanks for coming!"

Larry gave me a hug, and I considered, while I disappeared into his embrace, whether it felt genuine. It did. Mark's words had stung, but Larry and I *were* friends. Once again Larry's warmth made me feel better. "Happy birthday, Larry."

Jody said, "I asked Art to play some piano for us this evening."

"Really? Well, that would certainly be a treat."

"Yeah, I'll play a few tunes," I said, trying to appear enthusiastic.

"If you just wanna drink and enjoy yourself here, that's okay, too. Right, Jody?" Larry waited for her response.

"Sure," she said.

Here was my opportunity to beg off. Instead, I said, "It's my birthday present to you, Larry." I wondered if some part of me wanted to play, wanted to show off what I'd learned.

Oh, God, I thought, don't let me make a fool of myself.

A few minutes later Larry had finished welcoming everyone. I felt the rhythm of the room return to where it had been before Larry walked in, with people clustered in groups of two or three, drinking, talking, and laughing. Servers circulated among the crowd with hot and cold hors d'oeuvres. There was no sign of my favorites, pigs in a blanket. Just as well, since I couldn't pass them up and I hated playing piano with greasy fingers. I felt my hands sweating, so I wiped the perspiration on my suit pants. It was time.

I made my way toward the piano as inconspicuously as possible. The few times I brushed by someone, I smiled and quietly said, "Excuse me, I'm sorry." When I got to the piano, I hesitated for a moment as I recalled my piano teacher's advice: "Remember, try to get to the party early so you can sit at the piano, get a feel for the bench, the lighting, and play a little something so you know how the piano feels." I hadn't done that—I'd arrived too late; the place had been almost full when I got here, so I'd blown the opportunity. The piano sat quietly, ignoring me, like a stranger on a bus hoping I wouldn't sit down next to him.

I felt the perspiration on my back as I sat on the rock-hard wooden piano bench. I should have taken off my jacket to be more comfortable, but I didn't want everyone to see the puddle between my shoulder blades or the stains at my armpits. The first tune on my playlist was Erroll Garner's "Misty." I heard the lyric in my head: "Walk my way, and a thousand violins begin to play." It made me wish I had some violin accompaniment. I placed my hands on the piano. A bead of sweat zigzagged from my hairline down the side of my head, past my ear and onto my shirt collar. I closed my eyes tightly for a second. When I opened them up, I began to play.

Nobody noticed.

I'd played a few tunes before some of the people I knew came by to chat with me. "Art, I didn't know you played." It was Mark again. "Sounds good." He moved on. Later, my former boss, Linda Frankenbach, came over and put her hand gently on my shoulder. "You are quite a guy, Art, quite a guy." Linda and I knew each other well. We'd worked closely together for years, and as a result, we had our coded phrases. I knew she wasn't complimenting my piano playing. She was saying I had a lot of balls to perform at a party like this given my obvious limitations.

On the other hand, I'd done it.

After I finished playing, I hung around for the obligatory compliments. Even if they weren't completely genuine, the compliments felt good. I left the party and walked onto the sidewalk toward the curb intending to hail a cab, but of course there were no empty cabs. I watched as the lucky ones, the people who'd found cabs, raced by me. It had been hot when I arrived earlier in the evening, and nervousness had kept me sweating despite the air conditioning. Now, with my jacket over my shoulder, my tie pulled away from my collar, and my top shirt button open, I walked slowly up Second Avenue, enjoying the cool nighttime air. Like Sinatra in Vegas after playing the Sands, I thought. It was twenty blocks to my apartment, about a mile walk. At one in the morning there were still a lot of people on the sidewalk, talking and laughing. The city seemed welcoming and alive with the promise of good things to come.

CHAPTER 6

Early Days

Michael Fuchs wanted The Comedy Channel up and running by November. He didn't ask whether the timetable was viable, and in the excitement of the moment, I didn't think to question it. Weeks later, as the newly formed Comedy Channel team struggled to put an entire channel together, I realized this was going to be much more complicated than anything I'd ever done before. And it would require me to do things I'd never done before, like producing comedy clips and getting them ready to air. Actually, nobody had ever done that before, so there was nobody to ask. I needed help and I wasn't sure where I would find it.

There was nothing else for me to do but jump right in. I hired a couple of production assistants to screen every comedy movie in the HBO library (there were hundreds, with more added every day) and find the scenes that could stand on their own as comedy clips. Each clip had to be edited so that it could be viewed and understood outside the context of the source film, it had to be less than two minutes long as mandated by our deal with the Directors Guild of America (DGA), and it had to be funny. The production assistants and I were teaching ourselves how to do this, and it turned out to be more difficult than I had imagined. First you had to screen the movie looking for funny scenes. Then you had to decide if they could stand alone, with a beginning, middle, and end, without any prior information on the characters or the story. Then you had to cut the clip so it fit into the two-minute time constraint. We weren't allowed to edit within the scene (again, DGA rules), so all we could do was pick where to start and where to stop. With some films, this was easy. For example, there is a scene in *The Odd Couple* that takes place in a diner. Felix and Oscar have just ordered when Felix starts snorting loudly. Oscar asks, deadpan, "What are you doing?" Felix answers that he's clearing his sinuses and proceeds to do so loudly enough for the other patrons to turn around and stare. The scene goes on until the final loud snorts by Felix. It's a perfectly contained funny scene with a good setup that made it work for us. But this turned out to be rarer than I'd hoped, especially given the fact that we couldn't edit within scenes.

Easier to work with were stand-up comedy shows, and HBO had made a bunch. We also found large tranches of stand-up comedy footage owned by the producers and not by the comedians. This footage turned out to be a mother lode of clips, because it was easy to find two-minute bits within any comedian's act.

We also began hunting for funny short films from Hollywood (like the Three Stooges two-reelers that played in theaters in the 1930s), award-winning short films, and funny commercials from around the world. We needed thousands of clips and other short-form comedy in order to keep from repeating too much. Too many repeats would drive away the audience. I was confident we would find enough clips.

The clips, the backbone of the channel's programming, were to be introduced by comedians the same way MTV "VJs" (video jockeys) introduced music videos. Stu Smiley, recently promoted to be head of Comedy Channel Original Programming, was responsible for hiring the comedians, producers, and writers, and for creating the "shows." He was also responsible for getting a studio built where all of this could happen. The studio was designed with several different sets, one for each show, and took up an entire floor in a building on Twenty-Third Street near Madison Avenue. While the primary purpose of the "comedy jocks" was to introduce the clips, Stu was insistent that each show have its own look, feel, and attitude, and that the comedians be given enough room to deliver their own brand of comedy between clips.

Soon after we started work on the channel, I suggested to my boss that we get together with some of the staff to review the clips and see what my clip team was coming up with. My boss, John Newton, was in charge of all of Programming, and Stu and I both reported to him. With his impish grin and constant joshing and joking, John was a good-natured leprechaun of a man. He'd worked for HBO in Film Acquisitions for several years, negotiating the multimillion-dollar movie deals that kept HBO flush with exclusive first-run movies. I assumed Michael Fuchs had plucked John from his job in Film Acquisitions to run Comedy Channel Programming because of his experience with programming deals and his many contacts in Hollywood. I trusted him.

"Good idea," John said, "and make sure Stu comes to the meeting." I wasn't anxious to let Stu in on my early progress, because we'd just started the clip-finding process. I wasn't all that confident that the clips we had were funny enough. My hope was we'd get better at it, and I didn't relish Stu throwing stones from the sidelines. "And," John added, "bring the cliptomaniacs." John had nicknamed the clip producers the cliptomaniacs, and that's what everyone called them.

The first clip review session took place the next day over lunch, and it was just John, Stu, the three cliptomaniacs, and me. We watched for an hour, occasionally laughing or noting a particularly funny clip or a particularly bad one. "That one doesn't work," John would say. "Let's fix it or lose it."

When we finished screening the first batch of clips, John told the cliptomaniacs that they could go back to work, and they left the room. When they had left, Stu said, "Uh-oh."

"What's that supposed to mean?" John asked, but I assumed he knew.

"C'mon, Stu," I said, "it's the first batch. We're just figuring out how to do this." I was defensive because I was also concerned about the clips.

"You better figure it out fast. Lotta losers on that reel," Stu said.

"We will," I said. "By the way, how're things going with the studio?"

"Better than things are going with the clips."

John held his hands up. "Knock it off, the both of you. It's a good start, and it's early days. But it shows one thing: you gotta crush a lot of rock to get to the gold."

"Yeah, I know," I said. "I'm working on it."

We left the room. While John was supportive, Stu was clearly not impressed. But there was nothing I could do but keep at it.

•　　•　　•

At the same time, my personal life was looking up. Several weeks earlier, just before The Comedy Channel was thrown into high gear, a friend set me up on a blind date. I'd never had any luck with blind dates, but I called this woman anyway. Her name was Carrie Livingston, and she suggested I meet her at her apartment.

I knocked on her door and braced myself for the inevitable crushing disappointment. Still, a small part of me hoped for a miracle. The door opened. Miracle. Carrie Livingston was cute, with curly dark hair resting on her shoulders, blue eyes, alabaster skin, and a lovely smile. Behind Carrie was an apartment filled to the brim with books. After saying hello, I asked if she'd read all those books. She looked behind her. "No," she said, "they're just for decoration." I must have looked confused, because she said, "Of course I read them." She was evidently intelligent, well read, and fully equipped with a sharp sense of humor.

Our drinks turned into dinner, and when I suggested we hear some jazz, she said great. By the end of the night I knew I wanted to see her again, but in two days I would leave for a week-long trip to Italy with friends. I didn't want her to think I wasn't interested, so I called her the next morning.

"Hi, Carrie? This is Art."

"Who?"

Evidently the date hadn't been quite as miraculous for Carrie. "Art Bell." No response. "From last night? We had dinner together? Remember?"

"Oh, yeah, of course I remember. It's just that I'm at work and..." She trailed off. "You know...context."

"Right. Anyway, I called to tell you I'm heading out of town for a week."

"Okay...," she said, sounding unsure of why I was telling her this.

"I mean, I just didn't want you to not hear from me for a week and think I didn't have a good time. Last night, I mean."

"Oh...yeah, I had fun, too."

"Good."

"Well, have a good trip."

"Thanks. I'll call you when I'm back."

"Okay."

When I returned from Italy, we started seeing each other a lot. I was glad I'd met her before work on The Comedy Channel completely took over my life. I was glad I'd met her, period.

• • •

In June, about a month after The Comedy Channel announcement, Stu hired Eddie Gorodetsky, a twenty-something comedy writer whose work he admired, to be head writer for the channel. Stu planned to divide the day into several distinctive two- to four-hour shows and hired a comedian/host and a production team for each one. That would allow each show to be written for and tailored to the host/comedian. Eddie, as head writer, would oversee the writing for all shows so that The Comedy Channel had a singular and consistent comedic voice.

Stu invited me to his office to meet Eddie. I opened Stu's door and walked into a wall of thick blue smoke that wafted off a cigarette held between the tar-stained fingers of a beefy, beer-bellied guy wearing a white tee shirt featuring a dark-haired pinup girl in black stockings. He looked up at me and in a low growl said, "I'm Eddie." He stood up, put the cigarette in his mouth, and ran his right hand over his shaved head. We shook hands.

"Art. Nice to meet you."

"Charmed, I'm sure," Eddie said, cigarette dangling from his lip. His voice floored me—it sounded like a pickup truck with a busted muffler. Stu suggested we grab some lunch in the cafeteria. Eddie looked around the office for an ashtray, and finding none, dropped the remainder of his cigarette into his coffee cup.

As we walked toward the elevator, I asked Eddie who was on his tee shirt.

"Bettie Page," he said. "I'm kind of obsessed." Eddie explained that she was an internationally famous pinup girl from the 1950s. "Then one day she disappeared," he said, and his gravelly voice got a little quieter. "Nobody knows what happened to her."

"Jeez," I said.

"Yeah. Lotta women claimed to be Bettie Page since then, but they turned out to be impostors."

"Like the whole Anastasia thing, huh?" I said. Eddie ignored that.

We walked into the cafeteria, got our food, and sat down.

"So, Eddie," I said after taking a bite of tuna sandwich, "Stu tells me you're not only a great comedy writer, but you know a lot about comedy."

"I know plenty," he replied. "I know that this channel needs some comedy with attitude, and I know we won't do comedy with a *K*."

I wondered what he meant. Comedy with a *K*. Komedy? Was that like Eastern European comedy, or Keystone Kops comedy? "Sorry, I don't understand. What kind of comedy aren't we doing?"

Eddie eyed me coldly before answering. "Dopey comedy. Pretend comedy. Stupid sitcom comedy...Ya know, comedy doesn't always have to be funny."

I was beginning to see that comedy was a religion, complete with its own laws and doctrine and maybe even priests and saints. This was Eddie and Stu's religion. If I was going to be a convert, there were clearly a lot of things I needed to learn, or incorporate into my world view, that I'd never even heard about. I loved comedy, but I'd spent my career doing other things: economics, finance, marketing. Would I ever be accepted as an acolyte? I wondered.

$$\cdot \qquad \cdot \qquad \cdot$$

What I knew about comedy I had learned mostly from watching comics on *The Ed Sullivan Show* and listening to funny people at school. Mr. Novarro, my fourth-grade teacher, was my first funny teacher. He'd been our gym teacher the year before, and I liked him because he didn't treat me like a mutant even though I was the shortest kid in the class. He was tall and stocky but solid, with a little pudginess in his face that made him easy to like, as if he were a panda bear made human. He wore his brown hair short and had a generous but narrow mouth, his lips concentrated into a small area of his face. And he made us laugh when he taught class.

"Can I go to the bathroom?" I asked Mr. Novarro one day in a whisper from my seat in the first row, directly in front of his desk, where he sat grading papers. Going to the bathroom in fourth grade seemed like a personal decision that was nobody else's business, except that you still needed permission. When Mr. Novarro didn't seem to hear me, I whispered more urgently, "Excuse me, Mr. Novarro, may I go to the bathroom?" Without looking up, he replied in a booming voice, "Yes, Mr. Bell, you may go to the bathroom." So much for whispering.

The whole class stopped what they were doing and looked up. I froze. Then I said loudly enough for everyone to hear, "Well, you don't have to *announce* it!" The room was silent. For a second, I thought, Did I just go too far? Am I in trouble? But then the kids all started laughing, and Mr. Novarro laughed, too. I'd just played my first audience. Twenty-three kids and a grown-up had just laughed out loud at something I'd said, and I was so proud, I smiled all the way to the bathroom.

•   •   •

The more Eddie and I talked at that lunch, the more I realized that we weren't likely to become best friends, but I admired him.

He was chatty and spoke with a lot of New York swagger. He was proud of the fact that he'd never gotten a driver's license and boasted that he would never move to LA. At one point, apropos of nothing, Eddie said, "My mother died when I was a teenager. I cracked jokes at her funeral." Once again, I had no response, other than to nod as if I completely understood. I guess this was Eddie's way of demonstrating his bona fides as a true writer of comedy, someone who would imbue The Comedy Channel with the right mixture of funny and edgy.

Eddie turned out to be a huge influence on the channel. "It's gotta look handmade. Everything has to seem like it was hand-crafted; it's gotta be a little rough around the edges." Eddie had us modify our logo, the big *C* with the words *Comedy Channel* inside, so that it looked hand drawn.

Something else Eddie talked up was a "watch-us-watch" show, where comedians would make comments about a movie or TV show while it was in progress. We all thought that sounded like a good idea, and Eddie and Stu started talking about how to make it happen. A few days later, a videocassette came in the mail addressed to The Comedy Channel from a local television station near Minneapolis. *Mystery Science Theater 3000* had premiered on KTMA in Minneapolis in November of 1988. It featured a comedian named Joel Hodgson and the two puppets he'd created, Crow and Tom Servo. The three of them, silhouetted in front of a movie screen, made fun of a movie while they watched. Our watch-us-watch show had miraculously arrived in the mail. None of us had seen anything like it, but there it was—unexpected, original, and, most importantly, funny.

Joel Hodgson and his team had decided to contact us on their own, based on our announcement that we were launching an all-comedy channel. Stu and Eddie wasted no time getting in touch with them and making a deal. Hodgson and his production company, Best Brains, would produce a series in which Joel, Crow, and Tom Servo would watch cheesy movies (like bad sci-fi and horror films from the 1950s and '60s) and make fun of them. *Mystery Science Theater 3000* would premiere on The Comedy Channel as soon as we were on the air.

If we could attract this kind of offbeat and brilliantly funny show before we even launched, I knew we were on to something great.

But first, we had to get on the air. Our announced launch date, November 1, 1989, was only six months away. The way things were going, I wasn't sure we would make it.

CHAPTER 7

I Hope this Works

Each day seemed crazier than the last, and I could feel a collective sweat breaking out. I had to find a way to cut through the increasing pandemonium and quell everyone's sense of panic, including my own. I wasn't sure what to do, so I decided to just bring everyone together for a big meeting.

Even though I had some experience running meetings and working across departments, this was bigger than anything I'd ever done, and I was frankly intimidated by some of the older department heads at the meeting. Who was I to tell them what to do? Or even to ask them for their help? I was thirty-four years old, but sitting at the table for the first time, I felt like a twelve-year-old in a suit and tie trying to run a meeting full of grown-ups. But I pushed myself to stay calm and run the meeting professionally. We had a launch deadline to meet, and I needed all the participants to understand their own role and how it dovetailed with everyone else's roles.

Thirty people crowded around a large round table. After starting the meeting with a few tentative remarks about teamwork, I asked each person to update the group on their progress, problems, and coordination issues. We went around the room, and each person spoke for a few minutes. As they spoke, and as others listened attentively and asked questions, I could feel the fog lifting. I couldn't believe how much we accomplished. By the end of the meeting everyone seemed excited and energized. I decided that this group would meet at 8 a.m. every morning for the next four months leading up to launch day.

This was my meeting and I was in charge, but I knew the successful launch of The Comedy Channel ultimately would rest with the Broadcast Operations department, run by Dom Serio.

As executive vice president of Broadcast Operations, Dom oversaw the huge group of people responsible for keeping HBO on the air. The very idea that Dom was at my meeting, and subsequent meetings, was intimidating to me. He was a legend in the world of broadcasting. He'd been with HBO since the late '70s and had spent years building and perfecting HBO's satellite operations center and editing facilities. Now they were considered the best in the business. Dom boasted that his Broadcast Operations facilities were so secure that in the event of a nuclear attack, HBO would be able to continue broadcasting. So while the apocalypse might not be televised, the survivors would still be able to enjoy the best Hollywood movies on HBO.

Dom never went far without Ralph Catalano, his chief of Studio Operations. The two of them talked like a couple of tough guys from Brooklyn, although I had no idea where they were really from. Whenever I ran into Ralph, he'd put his arm around me and say, "Whatever you need, Art, just ask me and *you got it*." He meant it as a promise of unconditional assistance, but it sounded vaguely threatening, to the point where I worried that one day he would come to my home and explain to me that it was payback time.

Dom and his people would be responsible for ensuring all the program elements (comedy clips and host segments) and commercials were broadcast quality, and then playing each piece of tape in the proper order with no gaps between them. This turned out to be much more difficult, unwieldy, and subject to error (if not outright catastrophe) than I had anticipated. But MTV had been doing virtually the same thing with their music-video channel for years, so I had no doubt that Dom could handle it.

One morning, Dom announced that he'd found a new gadget that would make Comedy Channel broadcasting simple. "It's a giant jukebox but for video," he explained. "Everything's on its own videocassette: your jokes, your commercials, your promos." (Dom always referred to the comedy clips as "jokes.") "You tell the computer what order you want them played, and then a robotic arm picks out the right videocassette and plays it automatically."

As he described it to us, I worried that we were being used to test some newfangled approach that wouldn't work. "Sounds cool," I said. "Two questions—where do we get all the quarters, and who pumps them into the jukebox?"

Everyone laughed but Dom. "It don't take quarters, Art," Dom said to me with a straight face. "You just get me the log and the jokes and the commercials on one-inch tape and I'll take care of the rest."

Dom was feeling the pressure. He explained to the group that the automated system he was planning to use for The Comedy Channel was new technology and one that he'd never used before.

95

Like any new system it was sure to have bugs, and his people would deal with that. This was critical to an on-time launch. If the new jukebox technology didn't work, Dom would be on the spot. When Dom didn't laugh at my joke, I flushed, not out of embarrassment, but from a sense of dread. Something was bound to go wrong. I just didn't know what it was.

I was about to find out.

CHAPTER 8

Clipped

We had only six months to get this channel fully formed and ready for its debut on November 1. I didn't realize how fast six months could fly by. Most of us were working flat out and everyone seemed to feel the time pressure. My vacations were cancelled, my weekends were workdays, and I was eating dinner late at night and often cold from the refrigerator. As our work continued, some things were ahead of schedule and some things behind, but I was starting to feel like we'd be ready. Stu had the comedians rehearsing on their mostly completed sets. The rest of the studio (Stu's office, the conference room, the greenroom where guests would wait before going on the air) was similarly undergoing the final stages of construction. The studio was down-town from HBO's offices, so whenever we went there we'd say, "We're going downtown." When it was time to name the studio, Eddie said, "Just call it what it is: Downtown." So we named it Downtown Productions.

Eddie Gorodetsky was instrumental in naming all the shows. Most involved the name of the comedian who hosted it. There was the *Sweet Life with Rachel Sweet* and *Night After Night with Allan Havey*. But my favorite was one everyone considered the least important. Eddie named the show *Short Attention Span Theater*, a name that perfectly described the format: it was light on hosting and heavy on clips. Since the hosts would have very little time for their own schtick, Stu wanted a male and a female comic to sit side by side at a desk, newscaster style, and trade the kind of playful banter made famous by local newscasters, only funnier. He teamed two young and relatively unknown comedians, Jon Stewart and Patty Rosborough.

Uptown, the Clip department was busy looking for funny scenes from movies, sitcoms, stand-up comedy specials, old television shows, and anything else we could get our hands on. The clip format was a breakthrough, and I felt confident it would work if we could find enough clips. The audience would tune in and watch a potpourri of funny stuff, never knowing exactly what was next. It was a radio format, and I hoped it would be like eating comedy popcorn. Maybe it would be addictive.

Reporters often asked about the clips. "Are you sure the clip format will work? How are you allowed to use clips from film and television? Doesn't that cost a fortune in license fees?"

"Good questions," I'd say, hoping to flatter the reporter. "And you're right. People usually have to pay expensive license fees if they want to use a piece of a movie in another movie, or on television." Then I'd explain how we would be able to use clips without paying license fees: If you show a clip from a movie that's available for sale or rental at your local video store and tell people it's available, then they might go rent the movie. We would put the name of the movie and the studio at the bottom of the television screen. The movie, the studio that distributed it, and ultimately, the video store would appreciate the free promotion.

The reporter might then ask, "You really think that'll work? You're using these clips to make a channel. Isn't somebody somewhere going to cry foul?"

"We're covered," I said. "We made sure we got permission from anyone who might object. We went to the movie studios, the Directors Guild, the Writers Guild, and a dozen other places and told them what we had in mind, and they all gave it their blessing." In fact those meetings had been my introduction to Hollywood. Neil Pennella, an HBO business affairs attorney, had escorted me to all the studios and the unions, and we made sure we had everyone's blessing in writing. It took months, and there were some potential holdouts, but in the end everyone agreed the promotion was a good thing. "Clever," the reporter would say as he wrote all this down. "Very, very clever." And it was. With those agreements in hand, we were confident we could find enough comedy clips for the channel, since we could use clips from any movie or television show that was available for sale or rental on videocassette. We'd never run out of clips from the existing material, and new movies and television were being produced every day, so the pile would just keep growing.

One day, just a couple of months before launch, Neil Pennella called. "We may have a small problem."

"How small?" I asked.

"Meet me in the conference room."

When I got there, I saw a bunch of HBO lawyers sitting around the table with Neil, including Hal "The Axe" Akselrad. Hal was a senior HBO lawyer known for taking tough stands. "If Hal's here," I said, "some shit must have hit the fan. Should I duck?"

"The Directors Guild just called," Hal said. "They changed their minds. They're withdrawing their approval. We can't use the clips." I grabbed a nearby chair and slumped into it, trying to make sense of what I was hearing. Hal explained that while we thought everything was "done," it apparently hadn't been "*done* done."

"The DGA put our clip request in front of their board of directors for final approval, just a formality they said, nothing to worry about," Hal said. "But one of the board members balked. We're not sure, but it's rumored to be Woody Allen. Sorry Art, but without the DGA, we're kinda screwed."

"Jesus, Hal, you're telling me we can't use any clips at all? We're supposed to launch this thing in like eight weeks! Can't we sue?"

"Nope. We're totally at their mercy."

"Woody Allen did this?"

"What's the difference? Somebody shut us down," Hal said. "You got some kind of plan B?"

"Cyanide?" I really wasn't sure what to do, or even who I should tell first.

Hal looked thoughtful for a moment. "Here's what we can do. The promotional exception still applies to movies we're showing on HBO. So you can take clips from any movie we're showing that month."

"Are you sure that's okay, Hal?" I asked.

"Absolutely. Our studio contracts give us promotional rights on all the movies. Anybody makes trouble about that, I *will* sue."

While it was better than nothing, I knew we were still screwed. We now had access to far fewer clips than we needed. Shaken, I thanked Hal and the rest of the lawyers for the information and returned to my office.

I dreaded breaking the news to my staff but felt I should do it immediately. As I walked down the hall toward my office, I shouted, "Everyone in my office, now." One by one, the ten people on my staff collected in my office and silently exchanged glances, trying to figure out what was wrong. When the last person came in, I stood up and closed the door. Then I went back to my desk and told them what I'd just heard from Hal the Axe.

Ben Zurier, my scheduling guy, looked stunned and asked, "What do we do now?"

"We figure it out," I said. "We're gonna have to go on the air with fewer clips."

"*Fewer* clips? We need more clips." Ben was rattled. "Art, this is a disaster."

"No, it isn't. First thing we do is check what's playing on HBO when we launch in November. Then we extract every clip we can from those movies, put together the schedule, and see where we are. We've got other stuff we can play, like *Mystery Science Theater 3000* and some old movies. We'll just repeat everything more."

"A lot more," Ben said. "A whole lot more."

"We'll make it work," I said, trying hard to say it like I believed it. But I wasn't sure we could.

• • •

This colossal setback meant we couldn't have the huge number of clips we needed, so I shifted my focus from producing comedy clips to finding other sources of comedy programming. I had almost no money for other programming. I'd sold this whole Comedy Channel idea by promising it would be inexpensive. That plan had just gone to hell. So, with only eight weeks before launch, I put my panic on hold and began looking for something to fill in for the missing clips, programming that would be cheap, plentiful, and immediately available.

The first place I looked was short films produced by students. When I first began working at HBO, a close friend of mine who was in NYU's Graduate Film Program had recruited me to perform in one of his classroom assignments. It was a comedy horror film called *Art's Garden* (I was Art). At that time HBO was running short films as filler between programs, and I pitched *Art's Garden* to the HBO department responsible for sourcing short films, and they put it on the air. There were hundreds of these shorts available, many of them made by students, and it turned out they were licensed for television by one small company in New York City. We licensed as much content as we could (which wasn't all that much, given that we were looking for hundreds of hours of short programming). Of course we needed more, so we contacted a guy named Rick Prelinger who had collected a vast library of short films. A few days later Rick was in my office showing me some of his collection.

Rick was about my age (early thirties), with straight blond hair, a crooked smile, and the quiet manner that you would expect of a librarian. "I collect what I call 'incidental footage,'" he said softly and deliberately. "I've been doing it for years. Some of it is film shot by the government for one reason or another. Like propaganda material during the 1950s, which is a big part of my collection."

"Propaganda?"

"During the 1950s," he explained, "somebody somewhere in the government concluded that people had been so focused on the war that they needed to be reminded how to behave." He put a videocassette into my machine. "Here, this one's called *How to Go on a Date*. It's hilarious." The narrator of this earnest how-to film described the right way and the wrong way to ask a girl on a date, what to wear, and how to behave. When that ended, Rick selected another one. "Here's a film made by an appliance manufacturer association. They wanted to promote the idea of a modern kitchen." In this slice of life, a couple goes to their friends' house and marvel at the brand-new kitchen, complete with all the modern conveniences. Back at her own house, the woman laments that her kitchen doesn't measure up and begs her husband to get her a new kitchen like her friend's. "This is how they introduced the idea of 'keeping up with the Joneses,'" Rick said, and I laughed.

We made a deal for access to Rick Prelinger's library. I asked him to put together some of the crazier ones, and we sent that reel to the producers of *Mystery Science Theater 3000*. They loved these short films and incorporated them into their show.

As much as I was working toward the goal of getting The Comedy Channel on the air, the closer we got to November, the less I felt we had any kind of a plan. Every day was an improvisation, and the days were flying by. I felt like we were trying to build a barn in a tornado—the noise was deafening, everything was spinning around, and the walls kept blowing away.

By the end of October, Stu Smiley and the producers had come up with several distinct shows hosted by the comedians and comic actors he'd hired. Some I'd heard of, like Rich Hall and Richard Belzer. Others, like Rachel Sweet, Tommy Sledge, The Higgins Boys and Gruber, and Allan Havey, were new to me. Stu had done a great job of finding the right talent, and the pilot host segments he'd produced were engaging and funny. Sets were completed, shows scripted, performers rehearsed and ready. The comedy clips we had by then were loaded into the jukebox.

It was time.

CHAPTER 9

Launch

The night before we launched, I lay in bed and thought, after tomorrow, nothing will be the same. I wondered how I'd feel. Maybe I'd be elated and walking on air; maybe I'd feel let down in a kind of postpartum-depression way.

I awoke at six in the morning. It was still dark out. D-Day, I thought, as I reached over to turn on the lamp on my night table. I showered, shaved, and tore the plastic off my best blue suit, just back from the cleaners. I began to wrestle my necktie into the perfect knot, then walked up to the mirror to make sure I hadn't botched it. I noticed my face was bleeding in half a dozen places. I returned to the bathroom, tore some toilet paper into tiny pieces, and placed one on each of the nicks. Satisfied that I wouldn't bleed out, I finished dressing and took the elevator down to the lobby.

Alonzo, the morning doorman, stopped me. "Package for you, Mr. Bell." It was a bottle of champagne from my brothers, Brian and Larry, wishing me good luck. I smiled as I read the card, and a little piece of toilet paper, red with blood, dropped from my face and landed on the card. I handed the bottle to Alonzo to hold until I got home from work.

It was very early and dead quiet when I got to the office. I'd kept my calendar clear in case I had to deal with any last-minute details, so I just sat at my desk and read the paper. People started wandering into my office around nine to wish me good luck, or to share their nervous energy with me. For my part, I tried to appear calm, afraid that if I showed even a little bit of excitement, the dam would break and I'd start laughing hysterically or crying uncontrollably, or maybe just faint. John Newton, my boss, called. "This is it, Art," he said. "If you wanna cut and run, maybe now's the time." I dug deep for an appropriate snappy comeback, but nothing surfaced. He suggested we have lunch and I was grateful that I now had something on my calendar. I glanced at my watch. It was only 9:40. I had three hours to kill before lunch.

Despite my avoidance of meaningful work, everyone else seemed busy. I was usually on top of things, but as people rushed back and forth past my office, I realized I wasn't sure what they were doing. My office seemed vaguely unfamiliar, like this was my first day at a new job. I noticed how tired I felt even though I was two coffees into my morning.

At 12:30 I went down to the cafeteria, grabbed a burger, and found John sitting with Stu Smiley. I sat down.

Stu said, "Here he is, Mr. Big Idea." I hated when Stu said that.

"We're about to find out how big an idea it really is," I said without enthusiasm.

"Art," John said, "I saw Fuchsy this morning." I wondered if Michael Fuchs knew that was John's nickname for him.

"Yeah? How's he doing?" I picked up my burger and took a bite.

"He's very excited, Art. All wound up, told me he's behind this one hundred percent."

Stu laughed. "Let's hope he stays at one hundred percent for more than a few days."

This conversation wasn't making me feel more relaxed on launch day. I took a bite of my burger and listened to Stu and John's banter like it was a morning radio show.

Stu stood up and announced he was going to the studio to make sure everything was ready; John said he would join him. It was only one o'clock. Launch wasn't until six o'clock. I went back to my office and pretended to be busy.

At around four I'd had enough of waiting. I grabbed a couple of the people who worked for me, and we walked the twenty-odd blocks to the studio. It was about forty degrees outside, and the dark and damp made it feel colder, but we walked quickly and didn't notice the chill. Nobody talked much on the walk; I said almost nothing. Funny—for six months we'd talked nonstop about launch day; now that it had arrived, we were out of things to say.

We arrived at the studio's building and took the elevator up. I thought we were early, but when the elevator doors opened, the place was already packed. Everybody who worked at the channel was there, and so were an assortment of HBO executives, press, and industry VIPs. At that point, only a couple million out of the sixty million cable homes across the country would be able to see The Comedy Channel, and my bet was very few viewers would actually tune in for it. Nevertheless, I felt that this was a moment in television history akin to...what, actually?

Everyone in the studio had been given champagne, and as I stood there waiting for the countdown to start, I thought about how much this felt like New Year's Eve. The room certainly had that kind of festive energy.

I walked over to Vinnie Favale who ran the Advertising Traffic department and was responsible for scheduling the ads that ran in our shows. Vinnie had a floppy head of hair and a baby face that would have been at home in a high-school yearbook photo. For some reason, Vinnie had brought his one-year-old kid to the launch party, so I chatted with them for a while and tried to relax. Then I turned to Vinnie and asked, "Is this thing ready to go?"

"Yep. Just finished the log. But I don't know, Art, we're running pretty thin here. We need more clips. We're repeating too much. And tomorrow's log looks a lot like today's. Same clips, different order."

I had been hoping for something a little more positive from Vinnie. I noticed my champagne glass was empty and felt the need for more. I raised the empty champagne glass and asked Vinnie if I could bring him a glass. "No, thanks." I felt I should shake hands with Vinnie before walking away. I shook his kid's hand, too. Vinnie said, "Don't worry, we'll make it all work."

I moved away from Vinnie, refilled my champagne glass, and stood alone watching the crowd. Michael Fuchs walked up to me. "Arrrrt." He put his hand on my shoulder. "You launch a channel and from that day on it never stops. It's on television forever." I nodded, and he walked away before I could say anything. I went back to watching the crowd and drinking my champagne.

I'd almost finished the glass when the studio lights came on. I squinted into the bright white light. The plan was for Stu Smiley to go on the air just before launch. He would be sitting at his desk with a comically oversized red button in front of him. Stu had made a ten-second countdown tape featuring ten famous comedians each saying a number. After the tape played, Stu would press the button and The Comedy Channel would go live, the television signal instantly transmitted to a waiting satellite, then beamed down to cable satellite dishes across the country, and finally sent across cable wires from the cable company to thousands of television sets.

How come Stu got to push the button, anyway? I wondered, not for the first time. Wasn't I the one with the "big idea"? Why hadn't I been asked to push the giant red button? True, Stu was better known in the comedy business than me, and he would make for a better press photo. I guess I could have suggested an alternate plan for the moment of launch that would have included me, but I hadn't. Now, with everyone looking at Stu sitting at his desk in front of the television camera, I was glad he was the center of attention rather than me. Still, would it have killed them to ask me?

The countdown started.

"Ten, nine, eight—" Oh my God, is this really happening? "Five, four—" What if it sucks? It's supposed to be funny. What if nobody thinks it's funny? What if my mother doesn't think it's funny? What if she does? "Four, three, two—" The room seemed to hold its breath. I held my breath and thought about how we'd promised everyone we'd make a great comedy channel, but in a couple of seconds the channel everyone had imagined, *the comedy channel I had imagined*, would be gone. In its place would be the real channel, right there on the television screen for everyone to see.

"ONE!" Stu hit the red button. The button was, of course, just a prop. Still, when he pushed it, the video monitors came to life, the TV announcer screamed, "You're watching The Comedy Channel," and I felt the channel's heartbeat for the very first time as the monitor showed the first comedy clip—a scene from Monty Python's *And Now for Something Completely Different.*

I started breathing again and looked around me. Everyone cheered. I cheered, too. We were on the air.

CHAPTER 10

After the Launch

After the launch, we all got down to work, doing everything we could to make adjustments and refinements, but the channel had problems. The hosts and the clips weren't seamlessly meshing, and the shows seemed disjointed and amateurish. We didn't have enough clips, so we were forced to play the same ones over and over. And the reviews were scathing. After we'd been on the air for only a week, *New York* magazine called us the "Gong Channel" and "the biggest cable flop in years."

Flop or no, we had a channel to run, and that required more than just propping up our programming. The HBO Affiliate Sales department hit the road in order to convince cable operators to carry the new channel. Our Marketing department started developing ads and sales materials. The Press department was working hard to convince newspapers and magazines to write about the fledgling channel without trashing it completely. And the Advertising Sales department was trying to convince advertisers that this new channel with only a couple million subscribers, and practically no viewers, was worth taking a chance on.

Immediately after the launch, I began going to meetings with cable affiliates and advertisers to explain our current programming and our "really big plans" for the future. Our Sales guys introduced me at these meetings as "the guy who started The Comedy Channel," a dubious credential given the channel's terrible reputation. At every Ad Sales meeting we heard the same thing: "MTV Networks' comedy channel, HA!, is launching in a few months. When they do, we'll buy you or we'll buy them. We won't buy both." HA! hadn't even launched, and it was already messing us up.

But nothing was going to go well with advertisers or cable affiliates or anyone if we didn't work on the programming.

John Newton, Stu Smiley, and I spent hours reviewing tapes of the channel looking for strengths and weaknesses. We knew we had to make some big changes, but we also kept our eye out for any adjustments that would improve the existing programming. One of our shows, *Short Attention Span Theater* (a perfect example of an Eddie Gorodetsky naming), was hosted by Jon Stewart and Patty Rosborough. The show was the closest incarnation to my original concept of the channel: a clip show with hosts that would introduce the clips and be interesting and funny in the process. We scheduled the clips in themed groups, so that when Jon and Patty introduced them, they could say, "Here are three clips featuring spit takes." This was taking a page out of FM radio's book, where DJs would find clever ways to organize their playlists based on subject matter ("here are three songs about gambling, starting with..."). We immediately recognized that Jon Stewart was, even in his minor role as host, a standout performer and destined for bigger things. His clip intros (which were scripted, but he ad-libbed a lot) were done perfectly. He and Patty were cute together, sitting behind a desk like a couple of news anchors, and their banter was usually fun. But Jon was the show. He was charismatic and funny and watchable, and as much as we all thought they would work well together, Patty was more often the audience for Jon's commentary, laughing along. I liked them together, but Stu thought we should make a change and let Jon Stewart do the show solo. My boss left it to Stu (or his producers) to let Patty know that she was being let go.

A few hours later I got a call from John Newton. "I just heard from Stu. After they finished taping *SAST*, they told Patty."

"Did it go okay?" I asked.

"Patty was very upset, as you would expect, Art. Getting fired is traumatic, as you know." Actually, I didn't know, having never been fired myself and having had very little experience with people being told to leave. And I liked Patty. I saw the wisdom in letting Jon do the show alone, but I felt bad for her.

"But," John continued, "that's not our biggest problem. It's Jon Stewart. He's ripshit."

"He doesn't want to do the show alone?"

"He says he's quitting out of loyalty to Patty."

"That's bad," I said. "Now what?"

"We go down to the studio, try and talk him out of it."

"Hold on. Did Stu offer him anything? Maybe he's just seeing this as a way to get more money."

"It's not about the money. I think Jon's just pissed that we fired his partner."

We took a cab to the studio and found Jon in the conference room waiting for us. He got right to the point.

"You can't do this!" he said, clearly upset and almost shouting. "You can't just fire Patty without even talking to me about it. We're partners, we've been working together for three months. It's outrageous!" I didn't say anything for a few seconds. Jon continued. "I'm quitting. If Patty goes, I go."

Before this, my experience with comedians was that they were in it for themselves, mostly, and I understood that. Comedy was a tough business, and comedians had to spend a lot of time and energy looking out for themselves. I never imagined anyone would get indignant over the fate of a fellow performer, but here was Jon Stewart, a young, relatively unknown comedian, taking a stand for his partner.

My boss spoke first. "Jon, you're right, we should have told you first."

"No," Jon said, "you should have *asked* me first."

"We did what we did for the good of the show, and the channel," I said. "None of us is happy to see Patty go."

"We're friends," Jon said. "If I don't take a stand for my friend, what does that say about me? About the kind of person I am?"

This went on for a while. Jon Stewart was upset about the unfairness to Patty. He was indignant that we'd not consulted him. And he was hell-bent on quitting to make his point.

In the end, Jon agreed to continue on the show "for a while... to be fair to you, and my commitment to *SAST*." But he'd made a stand for his coworker that went way beyond what I would have expected of someone in his position. I admired him for it, and I hoped we could find ways to keep him on The Comedy Channel for a long time.

•   •   •

As we slogged through the next couple of months, I kept looking for any glimmer of hope, any small success we could trumpet in order to drown out the criticism and break through the gloom. The National Cable Television Association (NCTA) annual conference was coming up in March, and everyone was starting to think we wouldn't even make it to that. Dick Beahrs, the president of The Comedy Channel, who was leading the effort with cable operators, was distraught.

"We got nothing," he moaned. "We don't even have a booth. I thought we could just hang around HBO's booth, but that's not gonna work. I don't think they want us there."

"We've got space, right?" I asked. The convention had offered to give us a small space on the floor if we wanted to set up our own booth.

"Yeah, but there's no time to get a booth built, and we don't have the money anyway."

It wasn't about the money. It was about putting our best foot forward, and our best foot at that moment was *Mystery Science Theater 3000*. We'd started hearing from viewers that they loved the show. And some reviewer had referred to it as a "cult hit." A cartoonist in the *Village Voice,* a major alternative weekly in New York City, had included the characters from *MST 3000* (Joel, Tom Servo, and Crow) in a comic strip. Clearly the show was starting to gain an audience and maybe even a cult following. Dick knew this but didn't see the opportunity I did. "What about *MST 3000*? We can make that the centerpiece of our booth." I wasn't sure how, but it sounded right. "Let me talk to the new Marketing guy."

Pete Danielsen was the Marketing guy I had hired from MTV. He claimed he was twenty-eight years old when I interviewed him, but with his shaggy blond pageboy haircut, he looked like he was sixteen. Not that I cared. As long as he had the goods. I told Pete what was going on.

"Simple," he said. "And it'll be great. We don't have a booth, right? So we just set up some chairs and posters and our logo on our space, and that's it—The Comedy Channel's un-booth!"

We took the idea back to Dick and the rest of the executives. "Sounds kinda crazy," Dick said. "The un-booth? With posters of *MST 3000*? Is that enough?"

"You gotta go with your strengths, and right now *MST 3000* is what we have," I said. "Let's make a big deal out of it. We'll put up some quotes from the reviews—we'll make *MST 3000* look like the biggest cable hit since..." For a second I was stumped. "I know...since *Biography* on A&E."

Dick was dubious, but our Ad Sales guy loved it and so did John Newton, my boss. Stu wasn't going to the cable show, so he didn't care what we did. With our heads held high we set up our un-booth at the NCTA conference. We were given a small location at the back of the conference hall. Since we didn't have the time or money to put up walls, we just spread some Mardi Gras–style plastic necklaces around the perimeter of the area (we were in New Orleans, and the necklaces were cheap and available by the truckload) and put the *MST 3000* posters on cheap poster stands that kept falling down when someone bumped them. Our booth looked so cheap, improvised, and unprofessional that everyone at the convention was talking about it. Even though we didn't get any new business, everyone knew that, despite its wobbly start, The Comedy Channel had made it to its first cable convention.

While The Comedy Channel team felt the cable show was a success for us (or at least not a failure, as Dick had anticipated), HA! was right behind us, breathing down our necks, waiting to strike. Months earlier, HA! had announced their programming strategy: they would build their channel around reruns of classic comedy sitcoms from the '60s, '70s, 'and 80s. They hired Fred Silverman, a legendary network programmer, to advise them. They declared The Comedy Channel's short-form comedy dead on arrival. But despite their bluster, a lineup consisting of old sitcoms (like *McHale's Navy, The Betty White Show,* and *Love, American Style*) didn't look too impressive.

However, HA! was about to upstage us. In March, around the same time as the NCTA conference, we convinced *Saturday Night Live* to license their library of old shows. HA! swooped in, forcing us to bid against them. We knew that *Saturday Night Live* would either supercharge our programming lineup or theirs, and both sides were hell bent on not losing it. The bidding was over in a matter of weeks. HA! had bid a whopping forty million dollars for the rights to air the show, far more than The Comedy Channel could afford.

HA! The TV Comedy Network launched on April Fools' Day, 1990. A lot of people thought the world didn't need even one all-comedy television channel. Suddenly there were two, each trying to convince cable operators that theirs was the better comedy network. Distribution was key. The channel with the most cable distribution would prevail. We had about four million subscribers out of the fifty million U.S. cable house-holds. HA! launched with just two million full-time subscribers (they claimed another two million part-time subscribers through channel sharing).

HA! went on the air with little more than a bunch of old sitcoms and the promise of *Saturday Night Live* reruns in June. The critics were as unkind to them at launch as they'd been to The Comedy Channel. The competition for the hearts and minds of comedy lovers everywhere was off to a lackluster start.

The press called it "the Cable Comedy Wars," and it sure felt like a war. Victory was far from guaranteed for either channel, and everyone assumed there was no scenario where both chan-nels could survive. A few powerful people in the cable industry were calling for the channels to merge so the war would end.

We fought the comedy war with advertising and propa-ganda, press releases, and dirty tricks. They bought a billboard across from our offices advertising HA! We reciprocated the psychological torture and bought a billboard across from their headquarters. We said we were the purest comedy vision; they said they were comedy for everyone. Top executives in the cable business took sides, and the press constantly kept score: who had better programming, who had the bigger audience, who had more subscribers.

Almost overnight, our task wasn't only to make a great comedy network, it was to beat the other comedy network to a pulp. I hadn't anticipated this. I should have.

I hated the idea of merging the channels, but I knew it was unlikely because Viacom (MTV's corporate parent) and Time Warner were fierce competitors. Viacom was suing HBO, alleging that Viacom's pay-TV service, Showtime, was being starved of first-run movies by HBO's aggressive bidding tactics. Not only that, but the competition between the two companies was personal. Viacom was headed by Frank Biondi. He and Michael Fuchs had both started at HBO in the mid-1970s, and they became close friends. They worked together to build the HBO brand; they played tennis together; and when Biondi's daughter was born, Fuchs became her godfather. But when Biondi was promoted to chairman of HBO over Fuchs, their relationship soured. Eight months later, when Biondi was ousted as chairman and Fuchs given the job, their friendship was over. I was certain there was no way HBO and Viacom could run a network together.

• • •

We had our successes, too. A few months after HA! launched, I ran an all-weekend marathon of stand-up clips, hosted by guest comedians. We called it *Stand-up Stand-up!*, and it was immensely popular. I learned that stand-up comedy could possibly be our trump card, especially in the war against HA! And I learned the value of marathons. Marathons had been used for years by radio (one enthusiastic San Francisco DJ played the three hundred versions of the hit single "Louie Louie" back to back for twelve hours and added live bands and guest appearances). Cable television was starting to learn that marathons offered an excuse to advertise and to concoct an event out of thin air by packaging programming around a theme, performer, or program.

Sensing that our short-form clip strategy was falling short, John Newton and I started looking for available comedy series. We'd lost *Saturday Night Live* to HA!, but there were other comedy series out there. HBO had produced a sketch comedy series with a group of Canadians called the *Kids in the Hall.* HBO allowed us to air reruns of the series, and we ran a marathon of the *Kids in the Hall* on Father's Day weekend in June 1990. We called it *Father's Day with the Kids*, and while ratings information was estimated, we knew we'd drawn one of our biggest audiences to date.

Both The Comedy Channel and HA! were too small to get audience ratings from Nielsen. But when HA! did a survey of viewers in a Rhode Island cable system and boasted that it showed HA! was a ratings success, we did our own survey in a Philadelphia cable system that showed our ratings were even higher. Both of these claims were a little ridiculous, manipulations of survey data for bragging and press-release purposes.

The Comedy Wars were exhausting. At the same time, I felt like the days and weeks were galloping by, because not only was I struggling to find ways to improve The Comedy Channel programming, but I also had to react to incoming bombshells (like the ratings survey from HA!). And there was plenty of unrest on the home front, too, as everyone had their own idea of what we should be doing to win the war and emerge as the last comedy network standing.

CHAPTER 11

Lunch with Eddie G.

A few months later the war was still grinding on. Some of the staff was getting burned out and dispirited. Eddie Gorodetsky had suggested several times that we have lunch together, but I kept ducking him, because I didn't need an additional earful of his criticism. But by August I couldn't avoid him any longer.

Even though it was miserably hot, I decided to walk to lunch. The eight-block walk through the city heat and humidity had steam-broiled me, but when I stepped through the door, I was freeze-dried by an enormous industrial air-conditioning unit hanging from the ceiling. I imagined the blast of cold air turning the perspiration under my shirt into ice crystals. I didn't know whether to loosen my necktie or wrap it around me like a scarf.

The place reeked of tobacco and sweat. I spotted Eddie at a table near the front and walked over to join him. Despite the fact that he wore a white tee shirt emblazoned with an image of a heavy-metal rock band, I kept my suit jacket on.

I sat down, slumped back in my chair, and took a deep breath. Five feet in front of me a nearly naked woman onstage was gyrating to a slow blues tune from the speakers. Her eyes were shut, as if she were sleeping through her act. I was close enough to see the goose bumps on her legs and the yellow-purple bruises on her thighs. Eddie caught me looking at the topless dancer. I quickly turned away and felt the blood rush to my face.

Immediately, Eddie started in on me. "Whadda you know about comedy?" When I didn't answer—I thought it was a rhetorical question—his meaty hand poked my chest, and he raised his sandpaper voice. "What do *you* know about comedy?" I wanted to get up and leave, but Eddie had been itching to have it out with me for a while. Let's get this over with, I thought.

"What do you want me to say, Eddie?" I said. "I'm stuck for a line here."

"Admit I'm right. Admit you don't know shit about comedy."

"I admit it. Okay? Compared to you, I don't know shit about comedy."

"And admit the channel sucks." I winced. He was right.

My own mother had phoned me to say that some of her friends had seen the channel. "They said it wasn't funny. Isn't it supposed to be funny?"

For months, as The Comedy Channel floundered, Eddie and I had been arguing about what a comedy channel should be and what should be on it. This was really just a continuation of that argument. But this time it felt different. Desperate. The worst moment for me had come when Michael Fuchs, our beloved leader, was asked in a press interview what he thought of The Comedy Channel's programming. He answered that the programming quality, on a scale of one to ten, was "maybe a two or a three." I couldn't believe he had condemned us so publicly. The comment ricocheted around the business, from potential advertisers, to cable operators, to the comedy community. It crushed staff morale. It crushed me. It felt like Michael had already decided our fate, but rather than tell us he was shutting down the channel, he dropped a giant hint. Was this the end of The Comedy Channel?

But none of us gave up. At least I didn't, and I could see most of the staff staying with it, as if they saw a bright future that the press and our small audience didn't. Eddie, however, seemed to be losing hope.

As head writer, Eddie had much more creative control than I did. He and his boss, Stu, shaped the original programming for the channel. They hired the hosts and worked with the producers on the host segments. They were in charge of the original comedy on The Comedy Channel. It wasn't me who was telling them what to do.

"You blaming me?" I asked. "You're the head writer. You're the one who's supposed to make it funny. I do the movies and the clips. So how is this totally my fault?"

Eddie didn't answer. Despite myself, I looked up at the stripper again. She was blond and had a pretty face. Her dancing, though languid, was uninhibited. I wondered whether she liked dancing half-naked for Eddie and me, or if she was just drifting quietly through the morning, enjoying the music, thinking of nothing in particular.

Eddie smiled. "Like this place?" he smirked.

"It's lovely," I said. "I just hope the food's as good as the entertainment."

Eddie snorted in response. I didn't really expect him to laugh, both because what I said wasn't all that funny and because nobody in the comedy business laughed much. The first time I'd hung out with the comedians and their agents at a comedy club, I noticed that none of them laughed. "That's funny," they'd comment to each other, deadpan. Comedy professionals apparently became desensitized to comedy the way soldiers were desensitized to violence. So far, I still laughed at funny stuff. Maybe if I stopped laughing, then Eddie would have more respect for me. Maybe he'd say that I *did* know shit about comedy.

Eddie looked up at the dancer. "I thought you'd like a break from your usual 'suit' restaurants."

No, I thought, Eddie brought me here because he knew it would disarm me. He chose this place so he could tell everyone that he took Art Bell, Mr. Doesn't-Know-Shit-About Comedy, to a strip club for lunch and watched him sweat through his suit. If I invited Eddie to lunch at the Four Seasons Restaurant, me in my blue suit and him in his tee shirt and flip-flops, he'd be the one squirming, not me. But Eddie knew I'd be disarmed, or dismayed, or disgusted, by the tawdry atmosphere, and he was right. Any minute I expected Mrs. Fish, my straitlaced piano teacher from when I was a kid, to appear out of nowhere, hands on hips, gleaming pearls tight around her throat, and say, "Arthur Bell, what are you doing in a horrid place like this? You should be ashamed of yourself." And I would burst into flames with embarrassment.

It's not like I hadn't been to clubs before. Strip clubs like this one, dance clubs with velvet ropes and a dusting of cocaine on the men's room floor, rock clubs on the Jersey Shore where

Springsteen was one of a dozen local bar bands that I thought were "pretty good."

And my first jazz club—Richard's Lounge.

.　　.　　.

I pulled into the parking lot of Richard's Lounge, a small, blue, one-story shack of a jazz club not far from my high school. A few days earlier, my friend Lenny had convinced me that we'd have no trouble getting in to hear some jazz even though we were both underage. I'd never been in a bar, let alone a lounge (whatever that was), and I was apprehensive, but I loved jazz, so I'd agreed to go. Besides, Lenny said he'd gotten in to Richard's before, and it wouldn't be a problem.

When I opened the car door, Lenny caught my arm. "Listen," he said. "I'll do the talking. You keep your mouth shut, got it?" I nodded. "And for chrissakes," he added, "don't fidget. It makes you look guilty."

I followed Lenny inside, and we stood facing a bar with a dozen barstools, half of them empty. Beyond the bar were about twenty small, wooden tables jammed closely together. The floor, walls, and ceiling were all painted black. A row of theatrical lights lit up a tiny stage against the back wall. I felt like we were walking into a furnished cave.

A guy holding a clipboard and dressed in black slacks and a black turtleneck stood near the bar. "Evening, gentlemen," he said, walking over, "can I see some ID?"

Lenny stepped forward before I could move. "Hi! You're Richard, right? I met you last time I was here, remember? We don't have any real ID and we're, like, too honest for fake ID."

"Too honest for fake ID? That's a new one," Richard said and gestured toward the door. "Sorry, boys."

"Please," Lenny said, "we'd really just like to hear the band."

Richard thought for a few seconds, then said, "Okay, I'm gonna let you in because you're here for the music. You can order some food and soda, but no booze."

Lenny said thank you, and Richard led us to a table near the stage. We wedged ourselves into our chairs at a round table the size of a bicycle tire. I stayed quiet and tried not to fidget, as instructed.

Lenny looked around and smiled. "How cool is this?" I agreed it was pretty cool.

A waitress in black tights and a turtleneck sidled up to our table. "Hi guys, something to drink?" She looked at me and I said, "I'll have a Coke."

She looked at Lenny and he said, "I'll have a gin and tonic."

"One Coke, one gin and tonic," she said. "Got it."

As she walked off, I whispered, "Lenny, what the fuck, man? You heard the guy...he said no booze!"

"Relax," Lenny whispered back. "The waitress took the order, right? I know what I'm doing."

I glanced at the bar and saw our waitress walk up to Richard. Then she gestured in our direction. Richard looked over, parked his drink on the bar, and started toward us. Three seconds later he was hulking over our table. "Okay," he said, "which one of you wise guys ordered the gin and tonic?"

"Sorry," Lenny said, "we're idiots and we messed up. Art here has never been to a jazz club before, and he's not sure what's what."

Richard looked at me. I felt my neck get hot, but I was too shocked to say anything. I just stared at Lenny, stunned that he would try to pin this on me. Richard turned back to Lenny and put his finger in his face. "You ordered the drink, you little shit. The waitress told me it was you." Richard waved his hand toward me without taking his eyes off Lenny. "He can stay. You get out." Lenny stood up. I didn't know what to do so I stayed seated.

Somebody motioned for Richard to get onstage, and as he walked away, the house lights went out. Three seconds later the stage lights came on, and Richard was onstage standing at the mike. "Please join me in welcoming, direct from their appearance at the Blue Note in New York City, the Three Sounds!" The audience applauded, and the band took the stage. Instead of coming back to our table, Richard walked over to the bar and picked up his drink.

Lenny sat down. "That was close," he said. The band started something fast and loud, and everything faded into the background but the musicians and the music.

Before the set was over, the waitresses came around with the checks and we paid right away. When the lights came on, I scanned the room. Richard was standing at the bar with his back to us talking to a customer. I stood up and zigzagged my way through the tables toward the door as quickly as I could, bumping into tables and patrons, hoping Richard wouldn't notice me.

I got to the parking lot, and Lenny finally straggled out. We'd escaped. How cool was that!

•　　•　　•

I decided I'd had enough of Eddie and I'd had enough of Jimmy's Topless. In fact, I was growing tired of all of this—tired of hearing from everyone that the channel sucked, tired of being told I knew nothing about comedy, tired of being made to feel like a fuckup. I glanced up at the dancer and wondered how she managed to keep dancing. Didn't she get tired?

"Whaddya want, Eddie? What can I do for you?"

"Stay out of my way. Let me make the comedy and stop putting on comedy shit that's old, tired, and not funny."

"Fine, but that would leave a lot of dead air. You and Stu can't pump out original comedy fast enough, which is why we need to fill it with other stuff. Movies, comedy clips, stand-up. Comedy shit, as you so graciously refer to it."

"I know comedy! You don't. Let me program the whole channel. I can do everything."

The waitress walked up to the table. "You mind if I sit? I'm beat." She was fully clothed on top but wearing such a short skirt that on first glance she looked naked from the waist down. She pulled out a chair at the next table and sat down, crossed her legs, and said, "What'll it be, boys?" Eddie and I ordered cheeseburgers and Cokes. The waitress scribbled on her pad and thanked Eddie by name.

Arguing was getting us nowhere. Eddie wasn't going to change his mind about me, and it had nothing to do with whether I did or didn't know anything about comedy. It was because I was not, in Eddie's eyes, a comedy professional like him. Like Stu. Like countless comedy writers and comedians and managers and agents and comedy club owners and all the others who were comedy professionals. And Eddie was right in that regard. I was an interloper, an upstart even, who had no previous professional comedy experience. I wasn't in the club.

Eddie wanted me to hand over my job responsibilities to him and walk away from programming the channel. I had no intention of doing that. Was there anything I could do to mollify Eddie and keep him working hard to make the channel a success? It sounded like he was on the verge of giving up entirely. But I knew we needed Eddie.

I decided to change my approach. "Eddie, let's look at what's happened over the last year, okay? What we've done together. Like the studio. We built the studio on Twenty-Third Street."

"So what," Eddie said, turning away, but I kept talking, more to myself than to him.

"We launched a twenty-four-hour comedy channel, the first one ever on TV. We named it The Comedy Channel, despite the fact that after we announced it, half a dozen lawsuits showed up from people who said *they* owned the name. And then we *kept* the name." Yeah, I thought, look at all we've done. Even if Eddie didn't care, I did. "We pissed off MTV so much they launched their own stupid-looking comedy channel to try and put us out of business."

"That channel sucks worse than we do," Eddie said in a muffled growl. "Their first mistake was calling it HA! They won't last a year."

"You're right, they won't last a year," I said. "And what about *MST 3000*?"

"What about it?"

"First off it's a hit. Second, if The Comedy Channel hadn't come along, that show would never have gotten on the air, right?"

"Yeah. Too weird for TV—we're the network of last resort."

"And we have you to thank for *MST 3000*."

"Me? They sent us the pilot in the mail," Eddie said. "I didn't do anything."

"C'mon, Eddie. You sat with their writers and helped pull it together. You got me that book on movies, the one that catalogs all the B movies ever made. Man, I love that book. What's it called?"

"*Psychotronics*."

"Yeah, *Psychotronics*. Where do you think we're finding all the *MST 3000* movies? I would have been totally lost without it."

"We still got a long way to go," Eddie said.

"We got nine million subscribers. Just fifty-one million more to go and we'll be in every home in the country."

My tirade about how much we'd accomplished coupled with my not-so-subtle attempt at flattery kept Eddie from barking at me for a minute, but I didn't kid myself that I'd changed his mind. He probably still felt The Comedy Channel was doomed unless I stepped aside and let him and the rest of the comedy professionals do their jobs. I was equally certain that the channel needed both of us to succeed.

The waitress brought our food, and we stopped to eat. Neither of us spoke. We were done arguing, and nothing had changed: I wasn't leaving my job, and Eddie wouldn't pretend to be happy about that. Was there anything I could say that would salvage this? I didn't think so, and I didn't try. Eddie gobbled his burger, wiped his hands and mouth on his napkin, and announced it was time to leave.

After we paid the check, I shot one more glance at the stage and the dancer caught my eye and smiled. I smiled back in spite of myself, then looked away. Eddie pulled out a twenty-dollar bill, stood up, and leaned toward her. She shimmied to the front of the stage to meet him. I stood up and walked away, not wanting to be sullied by the "money for sex" part of the lunch.

When I opened the door to leave, the summer sun momentarily blinded me. Since I was still chilled from the air conditioning, the blast of ninety-degree heat almost felt good. Eddie whipped out his aviator sunglasses; I just squinted into the bright light.

"Thanks for lunch," I said, shouting over the noontime din of the city.

"Any time." Eddie nodded his goodbye and walked away.

CHAPTER 12

Get Back

1. Temper Tantrum

A few weeks had passed since my lunch with Eddie and the topless dancer, and not much had changed. The summer was winding down. People were working as hard as ever to make the channel a success but hoping they could get some beach time before Labor Day. And Eddie wasn't the only one who thought that poor programming was killing the channel.

Dick Beahrs called me into his office, ostensibly to hear what I had to say about programming. I started talking about what we had coming up, trying to impress him with our plans. Before I finished, Dick stopped me with a question. "Art, do you think John knows what he's doing?"

I stiffened. John Newton was the head of programming for The Comedy Channel, and he was my boss. "I think he's working hard just like the rest of us," I said, hoping the conversation would end there.

Dick waved his hand and shook his head. "No, I know he's working hard, but do you think he knows what he's *doing*. I mean, we're dying here. Sometimes I'm not sure this thing's gonna make it. I mean, do *you* think it's working?"

"Jesus, Dick," I said, "you're the president of the channel. How can you sit there and ask me whether I think The Comedy Channel's going to be successful?" My voice was rising, and Dick appeared stricken by my reaction. "I've busted my ass on this thing for a year and a half, and what keeps me going is knowing that everyone else here is working hard, doing the best they can, trying to make the best comedy channel we know how." I was speaking louder than I had to, starting to lose control. "We're underfunded and shorthanded, and people are starting to burn out. Some of them think this whole thing is gonna crash and burn any minute. But it's not. We're here to make a comedy channel, the first one in the world, and there's no reason we can't. But if you, the president of The Comedy Channel, don't believe in it..." I hesitated, not because I didn't know what to say next, but because I was frightened by it. "Then maybe this whole thing is so fucked up I should just quit." Dick's eyes went wide. "Yeah, I quit." I pushed my chair back hard, stood up, and started to walk out.

"Wait, Art, sit down, I'm sorry, man, I didn't mean...Please... can you sit down?" I had reached the door but stopped. "Don't quit. I just was asking about John...C'mon, sit down." I was still angry, but I sat down again and crossed my arms. I couldn't even look at Dick, because I felt betrayed. Then, as I sat there brooding and trying to calm down, I wondered if the reason I felt so angry was because I was afraid, really afraid, that Dick might be right: The Comedy Channel wasn't working.

Both of us were quiet for a minute. I understood why I'd gotten so angry, but now I was embarrassed that I'd lost control. "I'm sorry for yelling," I said.

"I know you are," Dick said. "The stress around here's getting to us." He paused. "You're not really quitting, right?"

That night, as I lay in bed, in the dark, staring at the ceiling, I realized I had to try and pull the channel away from the edge of the abyss. Sure, our audience was small, distribution was slow, and we had hardly any revenue. But just because things weren't going well didn't mean that they couldn't be fixed. I had never considered the possibility that we would just say, "This is too hard," and give up. Despite my outburst, I didn't want to quit. I wanted to finish what we'd started.

I decided to write a plan to save The Comedy Channel.

2. Vacation Interruptus

I worked for a week straight on the plan. The memo ended up being forty-five pages, and I wasn't sure how it would be received. I passed it around to a few people on my staff and took their suggestions. Then I sent it off to Dick Beahrs and John Newton. I had no idea how it would be received, but rather than wait around to find out, I set out for Colorado with my fiancée, Carrie Livingston.

Carrie had invited me to Colorado to spend time with her parents (whom I'd met, of course, but didn't know very well), and her sister, brother-in-law, and their baby daughter, whom I'd not met. She had convinced me that spending a week with her family at a rented house in the mountains would be a great way for everyone to get to know each other; it would also be an overdue break from work. Two days after I arrived, my first vacation in two years was interrupted by a phone call.

"Art, Dick Beahrs. Sorry to interrupt your vacation. Is this a good time to talk?" Before I could answer, he said, "Fuchs is not happy. He thinks the channel is headed for the shitter, and he wants an off-site emergency meeting with us to review the situation. I think he might want to shut it down."

Shut it down? It was only ten months since we'd launched. Dick often made things sound worse than they were. I was hoping this was one of those times. Then Dick said, "The meeting's tomorrow and you have to be here. I read your memo on how to fix the channel. It's good. I want you to take Michael through it."

I'd been in Colorado for only two days. Carrie wanted me to relax and get to know her family. I owed it to her to try and talk my way out of this. So, in my calmest, most reasonable voice, I said, "Dick, I know this is important, but this is the first vacation I've had in a while. I've got something like thirty-five vacation days I haven't used. I don't want to be one of those guys who dies with three years' unused vacation time. That's like dying three years early." My calm voice turned into a whine. "Please, Dick, can't I just phone in to the meeting?"

But Dick was relentless. "Fly to New York tonight, do the meeting tomorrow, and you can fly back tomorrow night. You'll miss less than twenty-four hours with your in-laws. They'll barely notice you're gone."

Feigning capitulation, I said, "Let me call travel and see if I can even get flights," hoping that I couldn't. That's when Dick told me there was no need for me to call travel. His assistant had already booked my flights, and a car would pick me up in a couple hours and take me to the Denver airport.

I put the phone down, took a deep breath, and walked into the kitchen to break the news to Carrie and her parents. Carrie was disappointed but said she understood, as long as I could get back the next day. My father-in-law-to-be seemed both fascinated and sympathetic. He'd never worked in a corporation, opting instead for the family furniture business, so he didn't know if this was unusual. As I walked out of the room, I heard him say to Carrie, "He must be important if they're flying him back for a meeting." I smiled at the irony: my interrupted vacation impressed Carrie's dad, something I was hoping to do that week. But he was wrong about the circumstance. I was being called on the carpet. The Comedy Channel was circling the drain.

3. No Escape

I landed at LaGuardia that night, took a cab to my apartment, and tried to get some sleep. The meeting was scheduled for 8 a.m. the next morning. We were gathering at the Dorchester Hotel in midtown Manhattan. The lavishly appointed suite was leased by Time Inc. and sometimes used for "off-site meetings" like the one we were having. Being "off-site" meant holding the meeting away from the office. This was supposed to help everyone get out of the daily workflow in order to focus on something that needed extraordinary attention. I'd been to dozens of them. Sometimes they worked.

I got up, dressed, took the subway from my Upper East Side apartment to Midtown, and got to the hotel suite early.

When I arrived, Dick Beahrs was there, seated on one of the couches, legs crossed, writing something in his notebook. I knew from past experience that Dick had been busy primping the place for the meeting, arranging the chairs, turning various lamps on and off so the lighting would be right, fussing with the thermostat. There was a yellow legal pad and a freshly sharpened pencil on each seat in the room, probably placed there by Dick.

He looked up from his notebook. "Art, you're here, great. How ya doing?" Without waiting for an answer, he pointed to a stack of papers. "I made copies of your memo. I'll hand them out when everyone's here."

For some reason Dick's neurotic orchestration of these meetings always put me on edge. So when he asked how I planned to open the meeting, I shot back at him, "How am *I* gonna open the meeting? Isn't this Michael's meeting? He called it, right? Isn't he running the meeting?" Dick didn't notice my bad attitude. Try as I might, I could never successfully put an edge into my voice when speaking to my superiors.

Dick said, "Maybe, but he didn't exactly send out an agenda. I just think we should be ready in case he turns the whole thing back to us." Dick was right, of course. I told myself to stay calm.

As we waited for Michael and the others to arrive, I quickly reviewed the forty-five-page memo. It was divided into three sections. In the first section, I'd compiled everything I knew about the channel (research, early ratings information, feedback from viewers) to provide a snapshot of where things stood. The situation couldn't have been more dire. The Comedy Channel was off to a dismal start, and I took care not to sugarcoat it, other than to point out that since there were two comedy channels locked in a battle for dominance, the *idea* of an all-comedy channel could no longer be questioned.

In the second section, I identified the programming that was getting some traction and that had a chance to build an audience. This information came from a number of sources, including one of the HBO programming executives not working on the channel. Dave Baldwin was the head of Scheduling for HBO. He'd told me he'd been keeping The Comedy Channel on in his office over the last few weeks and that whenever there was stand-up comedy on, he'd look up from his desk. "It's a grabber, Art. Try scheduling more stand-up."

More stand-up comedy would be easy and an almost perfect fix. The proliferation of comedy clubs, many with their own television cameras, provided easy access to stand-up performances by hundreds of comedians. The relatively low cost of producing a stand-up show in a comedy club (add three cameras and book some decent acts) meant we would have access to a never-ending supply. And the best part: stand-up was repeatable, and since most comedians signed away the rights to the recordings of their acts, we could own them forever and play the sprockets off them. Even though HBO had elevated the stand-up show by taping with high production values, well-lit auditoriums, and A-list comedians, cheaply produced comedy still played.

I'd also gotten insight on how to sell the channel more effectively to the cable operators. It seemed that the cable guys, mostly middle-aged family men, weren't too excited about The Comedy Channel and didn't care about launching it. But one guy, the general manager of a small cable system near Green Bay, Wisconsin, told me he had seen the channel and hated it, but his teenage boys loved it. "I can't understand it," he said. "I don't know what they see in it, but they think it's great." When I checked with some of our Affiliate Sales guys, they said they'd heard the same thing from other cable operators. It was their teenage boys who were talking about the channel. MTV had done a famous campaign showing teens and rock stars screaming "I want my MTV" to get cable operators to launch MTV around the country. Maybe we needed something similar.

I'd taken these and other insights and written the third section of the memo, my recommendations. I urged patience, more stand-up comedy, a focus on the audience that seemed to appreciate us (teenage boys), and more marketing of our one cult hit show, *Mystery Science Theater 3000*, among other tactics.

As Dick and I flipped through the memo, John Newton walked in. "Art Bell, back from the mountains of Colorado!" He shook my hand and gave me a conspiratorial smile. "We'll make quick work of this meeting and then go out for a couple of pops," he said, referring to beer.

John's display of optimism did little to hide the trepidation I knew he felt. Like the rest of us, he'd never programmed a comedy channel, or any channel, before. He'd been minding his own business working in HBO's Film Acquisition department when Michael Fuchs tapped him to run Programming for The Comedy Channel. Some speculated that his key qualification for the job (other than knowing his way around Hollywood) was his great sense of humor. John was one of the funniest guys at HBO.

"When Dick's finished torturing you, come join me at the bagel spread for a quick strategy meeting," John said with a wink. I liked his optimism, which was a great counterweight to Dick's doom and gloom. And I had faith in John.

Dick finished telling me which parts of the plan I should emphasize during the meeting. I told him I'd do my best, then walked across the room to talk to John.

"Hey, bud," John said loudly and shook my hand. Then he said quietly, "I can't believe Dick made you come back for this meeting. It's employee abuse."

"You know that I was hanging out with my future in-laws for the first time," I said, reaching for a bagel. "Assuming the wedding's still on. Carrie wasn't too happy when I left yesterday." I shook my head. "But I'm here. Now what do we do?"

"Okay, here's the plan." John smiled, and I suspected he was about to try and break the tension with a plan that was stupid or funny or both. "You know that Russian submarine that just sunk off the coast of Norway?"

"Yeah. What about it?"

John leaned in and lowered his voice. "It was designed with an escape pod. In an emergency, everyone gets into the pod, you push a button that detonates explosive bolts, the pod detaches from the doomed submarine, and presto, it floats to the surface and saves everyone. I think we need one of those."

I nodded, pretending his nonsense was deadly serious. "An escape pod."

"Yeah, for when things get really rough. Like now. Me and you get into the pod and survive."

"Is this a metaphorical escape pod, or are you hoping to build something out of titanium we can actually climb into?"

"It started out metaphorical. But I like the sound of a titanium pod. Where can we get some titanium?"

Before I could answer, our fun conversation was interrupted by Dick, who'd wandered over to get some food. "What the hell are you guys talking about?"

"An escape pod. You in?" John asked.

"I don't know what it is, but it sounds like the right idea."

4. Waivers

An hour later Dick, John, and three other Comedy Channel executives were still sitting around waiting for Michael Fuchs to arrive.

"Just like Fuchsy to be late," John muttered to me, using his cute name for Chairman Fuchs that made him sound like a plush toy. "It's a power thing. He lets us all sweat, work ourselves into a frenzy of terror, before he even gets here." I nodded grimly.

Twenty minutes later Michael walked in without saying a word. We all watched him as he took off his jacket and hung it on the back of a chair near the window. Then he grabbed another chair, moved it into the circle, and stood behind it.

"It took The Comedy Channel to make me lose my sense of humor," Michael said. This wasn't a joke, and nobody laughed.

Then he said, "You're all on waivers."

I looked around the room. Everyone looked uncomfortable. I'm sure I did, too, but that's because I wasn't exactly sure what Michael meant when he said we were "on waivers." Then I recalled that it was some kind of term used in professional football, something about the players being free agents. So I guessed what he meant was that we were all up shit's creek unless, or until, we could tell him how to salvage the situation. Dick looked over at me, and our eyes locked. He gave me a slight nod that I took as my cue.

"Michael." I was surprised by the strength of my own voice. Everyone in the room turned to me, including Michael. "I have some ideas about what to do next."

With that, the meeting began in earnest. I began by methodically reviewing everything that had happened and the challenges we faced. Michael listened as we talked about all of it: the war with HA!, our anemic ratings, our lack of advertisers, the hostile cable affiliates, and what we thought we needed to make The Comedy Channel a success. By early afternoon, Michael had heard enough.

"Thank you, everyone. Unfortunately, I need to get back to the office." He stood up and put on his jacket. "It's clear to me that everyone's working hard, but The Comedy Channel is a disaster. We have to do better. I mean all of us, including me." Michael stood there for a few seconds, looking around the room, making sure he looked into the eyes of each one of us. "But mostly *you* have to do better."

After Michael left, Dick said he wouldn't be surprised if Michael shut us down before the end of the year. "This is about his reputation," Dick said.

"Yeah," John added, "this is humiliating for him. And the chairman hates to be humiliated."

"Hold on," I said. "We're still here, right? Michael didn't tell us it's over, he just said we had to do better."

"Art, we all think you did a great job with your memo and all," John said. "But do you think you changed Fuchsy's mind?"

"No," I admitted, "but at least he's giving us more time."

"More time, but not more money," Dick said. "That would make a difference."

Dick was right. Our biggest challenge, especially given our competition with HA!, was that the channel was underfunded. An increased budget could be used to produce and acquire programming—we'd lost *Saturday Night Live* to HA! because they outbid us. And the channel needed to advertise more. HA! could advertise for free on its sister channels, MTV and Nick at Nite. We had to buy advertising.

"Michael's pissed," Dick said. "He was expecting that by now we'd be showing more signs of success. Better press, more audience support, signs that we would be profitable."

"Profitable? It hasn't even been a year since we launched."

The room got quiet. Clearly, everyone but me thought that The Comedy Channel was sinking and that it was only a matter of time before we were shut down. The feeling of defeat in the room hung on me like a lead overcoat.

That night, on the plane back to Denver, I thought about whether they were right that if we didn't turn this around soon, Michael would shut us down.

It didn't matter. I wasn't ready to give up.

CHAPTER 13

All Over

The August off-site meeting and my multifaceted approach to fixing the channel formed a turning point for me, although I could have lived without Michael's threats. We had acknowledged the problems, reviewed the options, and identified a number of tactical changes to supercharge The Comedy Channel in a way that would guarantee our survival. We planned to program more stand-up comedy, we committed to more promotion and advertising to attract more fans, and since we had missed out on *Saturday Night Live,* we renewed our search for programming that would attract an audience.

The burst of energy inspired everyone, and the perception in the halls was that we were not only better than HA!, we were winning the Comedy Wars. We didn't believe they would shut us down if we were better than HA! For the next few months we worked like crazy, inspired by our sense that success was just around the corner.

• • •

Toward the end of October, thirty of us gathered in an HBO conference room for a champagne toast. I stood next to a flip chart that had "Congratulations, Art and Carrie" written in colorful magic marker. We were to be married that Sunday, October 28. The Comedy Channel had not yet reached its first birthday. That was still six weeks away.

John Newton, my boss, walked up to me. "One question, Art. Where did you find the time to find a girl and get married?"

"Have you met Carrie?"

"Yes I did, Art, and we had a nice chat. She's terrific. Good luck with the wedding."

"Thanks, John."

I looked around and saw Carrie in a corner talking to Pete Danielsen, our Marketing guy who'd come up with the un-booth concept. Just by chance, Pete had told me several weeks earlier that he, too, was getting married on October 28. "Where's the honeymoon?" I'd asked.

"Not sure yet. We're looking at Egypt, ya know, get married, see the pyramids. Very romantic."

I laughed. "Yeah, we're thinking about Tahiti." Pete and I hadn't discussed it since.

Now, watching Carrie and Pete talk, I saw Carrie laugh and Pete nod. He must have just told her about getting married the same day as us. Then Pete said something else, and Carrie immediately stopped laughing. She looked panic stricken. Pete looked uncharacteristically glum. Curious, I walked over.

"Hey, Pete, I see you met Carrie." He nodded. "Everything all right?"

"We have the same honeymoons," Carrie said.

"At the same time, you mean?"

"Well, yes. Same time, same place."

I looked at Pete. "We're going to Hawaii. I thought you were…"

"No," he said, "not Egypt. Hawaii. Maui. Hanna Ranch. Same place as you guys." Pete was looking worse and worse as he realized he was about to spend his honeymoon with his boss.

"Wait, same days?"

"Yep. And it's a really tiny place."

"Oh, no!"

"See you there, I guess."

Then, the three of us came up with a plan. Even though there was no way we wouldn't see each other on the beach at breakfast or strolling the grounds, we agreed we wouldn't talk, or smile, or acknowledge each other in any way. Each couple would treat the other as if they were complete strangers. Not even a nod of acknowledgement. We agreed that was a good plan and the best we could do.

That Sunday, Carrie and I were married in a hotel overlooking the Hudson River. It was a beautiful autumn morning and the wedding was perfect. After the reception, Carrie and I flew to Maui. Within the first ten minutes of arriving at our hotel, we ran into Pete and his new bride. We exchanged smiles then stuck to the plan, and it all worked out fine.

• • •

With my honeymoon behind me, I threw myself back into work. The sting of Michael's threat to shut down the channel had receded into the background. By Thanksgiving, I was starting to feel optimistic.

By Christmas, everything was turning to shit.

"Ho ho ho! Got a minute?" Josh said as he slouched into my office. His two-day beard was more scraggly than usual, and he looked like he'd slept in his clothes. But as always, regardless of circumstances, his chubby baby face seemed on the verge of laughter. Most of the guys in our office wore jackets and ties, but not Josh. He had on jeans and a white tee shirt with The Comedy Channel logo, one of several Comedy Channel tee shirts he wore on a rotating basis. (At least I hoped that's what he was doing.) Josh was one of the twenty-something-year-old guys who worked for me screening television shows and movies to look for funny scenes. He was the first cliptomaniac hired.

I often heard Josh laughing crazily as he screened hour after hour of comedy, watching on a small television so close to his face that his eyes seemed to cross. His small, windowless office was across from mine, and whenever I walked by, he'd grab me. "You gotta see this clip, it's hysterical," he'd say, and it usually was. Josh knew I loved comedy, and he was proud of his work. But in the year we'd worked together, he'd rarely come into my office.

"What's up, Josh?" I asked, looking up from my desk.

"Sorry to bother you, but I was just wondering what this 'super-big-everybody-at-the-channel's-invited-and-attendance-is-mandatory' meeting's about."

"Yeah, me, too." I actually knew but couldn't tell Josh. "Guess we'll find out when we get there."

"I heard some rumors. That the channel's being shut down."

"Well, they can fire us but they can't kill us," I said.

"Or can they?" said Josh as he walked out, happy to exit on a semi-funny line even if he had to forego finding out what I knew about the meeting.

In fact, I did know the reason Dick Beahrs, president of The Comedy Channel, had called the meeting of all 120 Comedy Channel employees. I knew because he'd called me into his office the night before to tell me the news: the Comedy Wars were over; we'd fought to a draw. HBO and MTV Networks had agreed to merge The Comedy Channel with MTV's HA! The TV Comedy Network.

I was devastated.

Never before had I put this much of myself into anything. My efforts to keep the channel going, to make it successful, were bound up with my sense of self from the beginning, even though Stu Smiley mocked me as "Mr. Big Idea." I felt responsible for the success of the channel. I'd sworn to myself that I would prove my big idea, a twenty-four-hour-a-day all-comedy network, could work, if for no other reason than to wipe that smirk off Stu Smiley's face. If The Comedy Channel didn't succeed, I would consider it a personal failure, one that would hang around my neck for the rest of my life. Deep down, I knew things weren't going well, but I thought that the memo I'd written and discussed at that meeting with Michael would convince him to support us, to keep funding us, and to stay solidly committed to our success until we beat those HA! guys into the ground.

"I thought we were gonna make it," I told Dick when he gave me the news. "I didn't think it would end like this. We deserved more of a chance."

Dick shrugged a miserable kind of shrug. "Yeah, well, I guess Michael got tired of it. He couldn't see how we could make this work as a business, not with the competition from HA! They were making us spend more money on programming and marketing than Michael wanted to spend. Who knows, maybe he was getting shit from corporate, too. The channel wasn't adding to Michael's reputation, that's for sure. In the end maybe it was just too hard on him." Dick paused. "At least it's a merger. Would have been worse if they shut us down and HA! became a brilliant success."

"That piece of shit channel would have shut down in a month. They only launched to piss us off."

While we sat quietly for a minute, I wondered if HA! would have prevailed, if it had actually been the better channel. No, I thought, we were better. They were still mostly a bunch of old sitcoms. We had made stand-up comedy a pillar of our channel. We had *MST 3000*. We had Eddie Gorodetsky and Stu Smiley. We would have been the successful channel. We would have won.

I asked Dick if he knew how this had happened, and he told me what he knew. Michael Fuchs and Frank Biondi had decided on a merger a few weeks earlier during their weekly tennis match. Biondi had been HBO's co-CEO with Michael when I first worked there in the mid-eighties, but he'd left HBO to become president of Viacom, owner of HA! He and Michael were apparently still tennis buddies.

"I always hated tennis," I said. "So what do you think will happen to all of us?"

Dick shrugged. "I'm probably fucked," he said. "No way they're keeping me around."

"And me?"

"No idea. But if it's a merger, they gotta keep somebody. I'm meeting with Michael at seven tonight. Maybe I'll find out more then."

I shook my head, got up, and started to walk out. Dick just sat there looking defeated. I'd never seen him so sad. I paused at the door. "Hey, we fought the good fight, Dick."

"Yeah, we did the best we could, I guess."

I went back to my office and called my wife.

"I'm coming home early. Just wanted to see if you were there."

"Where else would I be? Everything all right?"

"Maybe. Probably. I hope so," I said. Then I told her.

CHAPTER 14

Comedy Channel + HA! = ???

A corporate merger is like a marriage: The two companies are introduced with the highest hopes and the best intentions; the courtship has ups, downs, fits, and starts; there are occasional breakups, then things get worked out and patched up. When the special day finally arrives, both families gather to eyeball the new in-laws and whisper: Will the bride keep her name, take the groom's name, or will they hyphenate? Will the marriage last?

I thought that merging The Comedy Channel and HA! The TV Comedy Network was a bad idea that would come to a bad end. Viacom, the media behemoth that spawned HA! as a competitive response to The Comedy Channel, had no affection for HBO. In fact, Showtime (owned by Viacom) and HBO were sworn enemies. At one point, Showtime escalated the fight with a lawsuit alleging that HBO had illegally kept Showtime from licensing movies from the major studios. (I happened to be in my boss's office on the day HBO was notified of the lawsuit. Hal "The Axe" Akselrad, head of HBO's formidable legal team, burst into the office and practically screamed the news: "Viacom launched the nuclear missile! We're being sued!") With that as the back-drop, how were these two companies going to come together to make a single cable comedy network?

Those of us who had worked so hard on The Comedy Channel were now wandering the halls, commiserating with each other, and searching for clues about what was coming. Who would run it? Where would the offices be? And what would become of all of us? Everyone assumed they would be fired, but how could they fire everybody? Unless, of course, the actual plan was that HA! would prevail and their executives would run the new channel. They certainly had a successful group of cable channels. MTV owned teens and rock culture. Nickelodeon spoke to kids in their own language. These channels supplied the backdrop to a gener-ation and licensed their brands so that their audience could wear the channel, decorate with the channel, even eat the channel. We were doomed.

Worse yet, what if they insisted we call the merged channel HA! The Comedy Network? Could I work for a channel called HA!? *Rolling Stone* interviewed me right after HA! launched and asked me what I thought of the name. "I hope they keep it," I said.

After a few days the shock of the merger wore off, but I still felt angry and betrayed. Dreams die hard, and The Comedy Channel had been my dream for years. It seemed miraculous to me that I had gotten it as far as I had. Now it was dead, or at least dead to me, and I had no idea what would become of this channel we'd created. Probably it would be lost, gone, another footnote in the history of television, if that. And, worst of all, I had struggled and failed to make my mark.

On the other hand, The Comedy Channel had accomplished plenty. We had some good programming. We had a small but loyal audience. *Mystery Science Theater 3000* was creating buzz. (I remember the charge I got when I saw the characters Joel, Crow, and Tom Servo drawn into the margins of a comic strip published in the *Village Voice*.) The idea of a channel completely devoted to comedy no longer seemed ridiculous, because for a while there were *two* of them.

But to me our most remarkable accomplishment was this: we'd created a place for the comedy industry to hang out. Walking around the studio on any given day were the comedians who hosted our shows, comedians who were guests on our shows, writers, agents, girlfriends, boyfriends, managers, groupies, and an assortment of comedy wannabees. The Comedy Channel had become a clubhouse for the comedy industry, a role that previously belonged to comedy clubs, like Carolines, the Comedy Store, and the Comedy Cellar. The creation of a channel devoted to comedy not only promised a new television platform for comics, it legitimized the comedy business in a way that smoke-filled, alcohol-fueled comedy clubs didn't. We had created a place where comedy was the star, a place where young comedians and writers could gather to try new formats, to push the boundaries, to innovate.

I didn't want the channel to die. The merger was, if nothing else, a chance that some of what we'd started would continue in some form. I wasn't under any illusion that I was critical to its future success. I assumed my comedy adventure was over.

After the merger announcement, several days passed without any further revelations. We were told that our lawyers were huddled with their lawyers to hash out the details, but nobody saw any sign of a meeting in our building. It must have been over at Viacom's headquarters. I interpreted that as further proof that MTV was calling the shots and that HA! would emerge on top and in control.

I was wrong.

Three days after the announcement, Dick Beahrs learned what was going to happen. I met with him a short time later. He looked dejected.

"I was just in Michael's office with John Newton," Dick said. "Didn't go well for us. We're out. So's Stu Smiley. And the president of HA!, Debby Beece, she's out, too. They took out top management of both channels."

"Shit. I'm sorry, Dick." I wasn't surprised that they had lopped off the top of the org chart, and I braced for further bad news. "What else?"

"The new channel's gonna be run by Bob Kreek. Know him?"

I knew of him. He'd worked for a long time at HBO in Film Acquisitions, negotiating the big film rights deals with the studios. He'd worked closely with John Newton, and they were pals. But a few years earlier, Bob had left HBO for a job with Fox and moved to LA.

"He quit Fox?"

"Or got fired. That's the thing about Hollywood, right? Nobody quits a good job, but nobody owns up to being fired, either." He chuckled at his own observation. "Anyway, I guess Bob got the nod because he's a neutral choice–both Fuchs and Biondi know him. So he's the new president. He'll be reporting to Fuchs and Tom Freston, who works for Biondi as head of MTV Networks." Dick shook his head. "Jeez, it didn't take them long to tap Bob. They obviously didn't launch an exhaustive search for the perfect executive to run the channel."

Dick seemed heartbroken. He'd worked hard, and I knew how much he loved being president of The Comedy Channel.

I thought about standing up and putting a hand on his shoulder, but instead I just sat there, quietly looking down, waiting for Dick to continue, hoping that he'd continue. I still had no idea what was going to happen to me. Then I thought, maybe Dick doesn't know. Or maybe they hadn't decided.

Finally, after a long pause, he looked up at me and laid out my future in two sentences. "You're going with the new channel. You and their head programmer, Michael Klinghoffer, are staying on as coheads of Programming, reporting directly to Bob Kreek."

Dick stood up and held his hand out. "Good luck, Art. It was great working with you." We shook hands.

"You, too, Dick. You'll be okay here, right?"

"I guess so," he said as he let go of my hand. "Fuchs didn't fire me, not yet anyway. They'll probably find something for me to do around here. I guess I was hoping, you know, that they'd make me the head of the new channel." He shook his head again. We stood there for a minute, not saying anything. I knew what Dick was going through; minutes ago I'd been there myself. But hearing that I would be part of the new channel electrified me. I'd survived, and I'd be a part of whatever happened next.

Later, I thought about what would happen to Dick Beahrs, John Newton, Stu Smiley, and all the other people who worked at The Comedy Channel studio, the people who'd worked as hard as

I had to get The Comedy Channel up and running, and wondered what they were thinking as they lay in bed contemplating the future. I thought about what this guy Klinghoffer would be like and whether we'd get along. And I wondered what it would be like to work for Bob Kreek, my new boss.

CHAPTER 15

Meet the New Boss

The next morning I put on my best suit and sharpest red tie and headed for MTV headquarters to meet Michael Klinghoffer, my new partner in programming. I didn't love the idea of sharing the top programming job, but I told myself to make the best of it. I hoped this Klinghoffer guy would feel the same way.

As instructed, I took the elevator to the sixteenth floor and found the conference room. It was empty. According to my watch I was five minutes early. It was a small conference room with a round table and four chairs. I took a seat that allowed me to see the door. No sense letting the enemy sneak up behind me, I thought. Then I corrected myself: Not the enemy. My new coworker.

Ten minutes later a guy in jeans, a tee shirt, and white Converse sneakers (the low kind) quietly entered the room and sat down without a word. He had no briefcase, no pad or pencil. For a minute I thought one of us was in the wrong meeting. He put his hands on the table, interlaced his fingers, and looked down at them, as if he were praying.

"Hi," I said.

"Hello," he responded. An uncomfortable pause followed.

"Are you Michael Klinghoffer?"

"I am indeed," he said, smiling. I stood up and walked over to him with my hand outstretched. He stood up and shook my hand without meeting my gaze, like he was embarrassed to be shaking hands. I took a good look at him. He was medium height and stood stooped over a bit, like a teenager whose mother is constantly telling him to stand up straight. He looked to be about my age, and his thinning red hair and red beard showed pasty-white skin beneath. Even though he didn't really look at me, I could see his eyes darting around, taking in everything about me.

"I'm Art Bell. I'm here for the ten thirty meeting."

"I know. I recognize you from your picture," he said. His voice, high pitched and singsong, matched his look.

I returned to my seat. "How're you feeling about everything?" I asked.

"I guess I'm kind of in shock," Mike replied. "This all came down so fast and so...violently. Lots of people fired or in limbo. My boss was really pissed—she didn't see it coming."

"Neither did I."

"A wild ride off a cliff."

No, I thought, not off a cliff. Klinghoffer and I were somehow thrown clear before the plunge.

Just then another guy knocked on the doorframe to signal his presence. A tall, squarely built man filled the doorway. Like me, he wore a blue suit, white shirt, and red tie. He was clean shaven and wore his short brown hair parted on the side. His briefcase was one of those boxy-looking light-brown leather jobs that was scratched and scuffed, like it had been dragged along the sidewalk. The whole package screamed accountant or maybe financial advisor. "Hi," he said, "I'm Bob Kreek. You guys must be Bell and Klinghoffer."

Nobody had told us that Bob Kreek, the new president, our new boss, would be at this meeting. But here we were, the team that would devise an immediate future for the channel, including plans for who else stayed and who got fired, and what kind of channel would emerge from this mash-up of media giants, executives, and programming.

I looked at Klinghoffer and wondered if he was as committed to creating a successful cable comedy network as I was. Whether he would be able to compromise the soul of the channel he'd been building for the last nine months in favor of something new. I wondered about my own ability to compromise in order to make the merger work. And finally I looked at Bob Kreek as he stood in the doorway. I wondered if he was the right guy to oversee this mash-up.

Bob walked in, shook our hands, and started off with, "So—how's everyone doing?"

We chatted for a bit. Bob told us he'd heard good things about both of us. We said we were excited to be working for Bob. Then Bob told us some things about the terms of the merger that we already knew and some things that we didn't. Mike and I would run Programming. The other departments would be divided with a similar eye toward splitting the baby fairly: affiliate relations would be handled by MTV Networks Affiliate Relations, and Ad Sales would continue under The Comedy Channel team. We would find office space somewhere in the city but not in any HBO or MTV buildings.

Each channel would contribute programming they had licensed, bought, or produced. HA! had licensed hundreds of old episodes of *Saturday Night Live* from NBC. Now *SNL* would be on the new channel, and that would be, at least for a while, the jewel in our crown. I suggested we keep producing *MST 3000* and *Short Attention Span Theater* hosted by Jon Stewart; Mike hoped we would continue to play some old sitcoms HA! had licensed. So, out of this primordial soup made up of bits and pieces of each of the old comedy networks, a new all-comedy network was starting to emerge.

One detail left hanging was the name of the new channel. Bob repeated to us that the merger agreement specified that the combined channel couldn't be named The Comedy Channel or HA! The TV Comedy Network. But what else do you call a comedy channel other than The Comedy Channel? How could any name beat that?

•   •   •

In the years before I got to HBO, before The Comedy Channel was on its way to becoming a real channel, I looked forward to the day when a twenty-four-hour comedy channel finally made it to cable television. I'd been thinking about it since my time in graduate school in the early '80s, and I'd imagined it taking shape in lots of different ways. But the one constant as I sat around developing the concept in my head was the name: it had to be called The Comedy Channel. It was simple, descriptive, and told you everything you needed to know. The name promised a channel that would deliver laughs at any time of the day or night, a promise that most people in the cable-television business were convinced could not be kept. But comedy is about *trying* to be funny as much as it is about actually *being* funny. Ask any stand-up comedian who's been heckled mercilessly, or anyone who's sat through a stand-up routine that was only occasionally funny.

So when I first pitched the idea at HBO, I called it The Comedy Channel. After all, there were lots of channels called the [Subject] Channel: the Discovery Channel, the Learning Channel, the Arts and Entertainment Network (A&E), the Entertainment and Sports Programming Network (ESPN). And there were plenty more to come: the Sci Fi Channel, the Biography Channel, the National Geographic Channel, the Outdoor Channel, the History Channel. So everyone agreed it would be called The Comedy Channel. Everyone except Mitzi Shore.

Mitzi Shore owned a famous LA comedy club called the Comedy Store. She sometimes showed taped performances of comedians on a TV monitor in the club, and she called the tapes The Comedy Channel. We learned this in a letter sent by her lawyer suggesting that Mitzi would sue HBO for millions of dollars if we launched a channel by that name. Pandemonium ensued.

We called in HBO's crack team of attorneys, who advised us that we had three choices. One: we could find another name ("Out of the question!" I said). Two: we could fight the lawsuit on the grounds that the name was generic and couldn't be owned. A shoe company can't trademark and protect the word *Shoes* as the brand name for its product, since the term *shoes* is a common, generic word describing all kinds of footwear. By the same token, since there could be lots of comedy channels, no single all-comedy channel could claim *comedy channel* as its own exclusive brand name. This argument might have worked, but the downside would have been that anyone could use the name; the last thing HBO wanted was another Comedy Channel showing up. We needed to own the name exclusively. Three: we could just ignore Mitzi and launch as The Comedy Channel. If we ended up in court, we'd have already spent loads of money on a name we might not be able to keep, and we'd potentially have to spend a lot more to change it or buy it from Mitzi.

After a few weeks of handwringing, our lawyers told us they'd decided to see if Mitzi was willing to settle. Michael Fuchs authorized an offer to Mitzi of $100,000 to let us keep the name. I remember thinking, Shit, that's a lot of money! But our lawyers didn't want to fight it in court, because that might cost even more by delaying the launch of the network.

Days before we made the offer, Mitzi's lawyer phoned with a stunning announcement: she was dropping the lawsuit, just like that. "Life's too short," Mitzi said by way of explanation. We were relieved and a little mystified. Our lawyers huddled to figure out whether they could get some credit for this turn of events, but ultimately everyone chalked it up to Mitzi's being Mitzi, and we went back to the more quotidian challenge of how to actually launch our all-comedy cable network.

．　　　．　　　．

"So we need a new name," Bob said, "and fast. Any ideas?"

"Let's call it The Comedy Channel! with an exclamation mark," I suggested, hoping this would sidestep the merger requirement that we not call it either The Comedy Channel or HA!

Bob looked at me without smiling and said, "The only rule is we can't use either name."

"Yeah, I know. But this is a combination of both names, right? It's worth a try."

"No, it isn't," he said. "Suck it up and figure out a new name." Okay, this was my first lesson about Bob Kreek. He had no interest in challenging his new bosses. As if to emphasize this, he filled in some of his recent boss history. "The last guy I worked for was tough," Bob explained, "and if I learned one thing from him, it's 'Don't cross the boss.' I once saw him throw a phone at someone. I'm looking for a more peaceful relationship with Freston and Fuchs. We need a name they both like. Find one."

With that, Bob stood up and said he was on his way to check out some new office space. The three of us gathered our things, left the conference room, and took the elevator to the lobby but said nothing more about the channel, the name, or anything else. Other people got on and off the elevator on our way down to the lobby, and a few of them said hi to Mike and mumbled something like "Sorry to hear about HA!," which was a little unsettling to me. But I realized they probably were genuinely sorry to hear about HA!

When we reached the lobby, Bob said he'd be in touch and walked away, leaving Mike and me standing at the elevator banks, awkwardly listening to the elevator chimes and the opening and closing of elevator doors. Finally I said, "Well, here we go."

"Yeah, here we go," Mike said. "This ought to be interesting."

"I hate interesting," I said.

"Me, too," Mike said. "Lunch?"

"I should get back and report on the meeting."

"To whom?" Mike asked.

I thought about that for a second. "Jeez, you're right," I said. "Let's get some lunch."

CHAPTER 16

The Name Game

1. At the Cosmic Diner

A few weeks after meeting Bob, Mike Klinghoffer and I moved into adjacent offices on the fifteenth floor of 1775 Broadway and Fifty-Eighth Street, a 1920s-era twenty-six story brown building notable for its two ground floor tenants. The first was Cosmic Diner, an old-style Greek restaurant with fake leather booths, a countertop with round backless stools, and waiters shouting your order to the kitchen in Greek-accented restaurant-speak. Every morning when I stopped at the counter on my way upstairs and ordered rye toast, the waiter would scream "Whiskey down!" loud enough to alarm the tourists on the sidewalk gazing into the diner. Most of the time the same waiter who screamed actually put the rye bread into the toaster and pushed it down. That always left we wondering, What's with all the screaming? Cosmic would become our breakfast, lunch, and, on late nights, dinner place. Nobody loved the food, but it was cheap and hot and once you got used to the coffee, it almost tasted good.

On the opposite corner of the building, at Fifty-Seventh and Broadway, was Coliseum Books, one of the best independent bookstores in the city and a great place to browse after a Cosmic lunch before heading back to work.

I liked the new digs. The gloom that hung over me when The Comedy Channel died had dissipated. This was a new chance to make a comedy network. I was still involved, and I was excited by the challenge of creating a new channel out of the ruins of The Comedy Channel and HA! I looked forward to getting to know my new coworkers and making a success of it.

All of this felt different. I was no longer "the guy with the big idea," as Stu Smiley had put it. While I still hoped to make the channel successful, I no longer felt the crushing responsibility that came with championing the project at HBO, launching it, and then trying to keep it alive.

The first thing Mike Klinghoffer and I had to do was decide how to run the department together. I had no idea how good or competent a programmer Mike was. He'd been responsible for all the original programming at HA!, but I knew nothing about him other than I found him hard to read. His comedy sensibility (what comedy he liked, how he saw the channel developing) wasn't obvious, and he didn't reveal much in our conversations. He was kind of a cipher to me. While he laughed easily, seemed thoughtful, and had strong opinions, I realized my new partner was a stranger to me, and I was a stranger to him.

But rather than eyeing each other warily, or worse, arguing that all of Programming should be under one of us or the other, we quickly settled on how to divide programming responsibilities rather than share them. That felt right. Somebody had to be accountable when things went wrong, and, conversely, to get the credit for good decisions. Mike, having been a producer at MTV Networks for several years, took Original Programming. I would be responsible for Acquired Programming (old television series, movies, and other shows licensed for some period of time), along with On-Air Promotion, the department that produced the channel IDs, show opens, show promotions, and all the other visual flotsam and jetsam that appears between the actual programs. This department was important because it helped create the look, sound, texture, and personality of the channel.

While we were settling in and getting down to the business of running the channel, weeks went by and we'd yet to come up with a new name. According to our stationery the company was called Comedy Partners, but that was no name for a channel. So we hired a branding agency, Brandbuiders, to advise us. They came back with a list of about one hundred names, alphabetized, categorized, and available, meaning nobody else was using them as far as they could tell. They asked which ones we liked.

After caucusing for a week, Mike and I decided we needed more help. Mike suggested we ask Fred/Alan, HA!'s advertising agency, for help. Fred Seibert had been MTV's first creative director and had midwifed the first groundbreaking MTV logo, notable in that it could take on a multitude of colors and textures. (Logos were usually one specific, unchangeable color.) He and Alan Goodman formed an agency that worked on the Nickelodeon channel concept. They helped create and brand HA!, and they were still, technically, the merged channel's advertising and branding agency.

Fred and Alan were anxious to keep the business and eager to please, but to me they were the heart and soul of the MTV approach, and I still thought of them as being from the enemy camp. Mike had worked closely with them and wanted their help. "They've done a bunch of work for MTV and Nickelodeon, and they're a really creative agency. Let's meet with Fred—you'll like him!"

"Maybe," I said, "but you know I hate the name HA! If they came up with that, I'm not sure we should let them in the building."

"You got a better idea? Bob's all over us to get this thing named, and he's right. Look, if we don't like what these guys come up with, we'll try somebody else."

A few days later Mike and I sat across the table from Fred Seibert at the Cosmic Diner. "What's wrong with calling it HA! The Comedy Network?" Fred asked with a smile five seconds after we sat down and three seconds before our waiter threw three giant, plastic-encased menus at us. I'd never met Fred before but knew that he was considered one of the hippest advertising guys in New York City. He was tall, dressed in a button-down shirt and blue sport jacket, and seemed affable as all hell. I kept looking at him, trying to think whether I'd met him before or he reminded me of someone else.

"Can't call it that. Terms of the merger agreement," I said. "We can't call it either of the old names. Besides, I never liked the name HA!"

"Yeah, you made that clear in the *Rolling Stone* article," Fred said. "You didn't hurt my feelings. Well, maybe a little bit." Still smiling, Fred said, "Okay, how about a compromise? Call it HA! The Comedy Channel." That's when I realized who he looked like: the actor Harold Ramis from *Ghostbusters*.

Mike laughed and said, "We already tried something like that. Art wanted to call it Comedy Channel! with an exclamation mark. Didn't fly."

"Okay, it was worth a shot," Fred said. "I was hoping to solve all your problems before we looked at the menu, but if you want to make this difficult..." I didn't, but we really had no choice. I handed Fred the list of one hundred names that Brandbuilders came up with.

"Whoa!" Fred said, dropping the list on the table like it was radioactive. "Whaddya want me to do with this?"

"Use it as a starting point," I said. "Narrow it down for us and add some suggestions of your own. That work?"

"I guess. But first we need to understand what the channel wants to be. What kind of programming, who it's for, attitude, stuff like that."

Mike and I agreed that sounded like a place to start, so we ordered some burgers and told Fred our hopes and dreams for the channel.

It struck me then that Mike's conception of the channel wasn't all that different from mine. While we weren't totally in sync, I realized that Mike wanted this comedy network to be successful as much as I did. And I also realized that the people who came with Mike from HA! and the people who came with me from The Comedy Channel did, too. After a few days of eyeing each other suspiciously, everyone had gotten down to the hard work of making a programming schedule, developing a budget, and discussing the best way to relaunch a comedy network. Everyone seemed willing to put the past behind them, to sit side by side with people they had tried to put out of business just a few weeks earlier, and to make sure that whatever happened, we wouldn't let the dream die. There would be a comedy network for the foreseeable future, and we would make it successful. We just had to name the damn thing.

By the time the check came, Fred had promised to pull together some ideas. We agreed to meet the following week so that he and his partner, Alan, could present them.

"Hurry," I said, wiping the cheeseburger grease from my lips.

2. What's in a Name

"Oh my God, we're never gonna name this thing," I said as Mike and I took the elevator upstairs.

"They'll come back with something," Mike said. "They always do." He gave a little chuckle. I had noticed Mike almost always chuckled or even giggled after saying something to me. Was he nervous, or did he genuinely find everything amusing? He sure smiled a lot for no reason, a counterpoint to my continual look of dread that had people constantly asking me "Are you all right?" Well, no, these days I wasn't, but I didn't mask my trepidation with a smile or a laugh. The channel was teetering on the brink of extinction, and I felt it was my personal mission to keep it alive. If the channel failed, it would be a crushing disappointment to me, but I'd survive. On the other hand, I felt like I'd made a commitment, a promise that I'd find a way to bring a comedy network into the world, and I still felt that responsibility weighing on me—especially since I'd gotten tantalizingly close to making it happen. And despite my partnership with Mike, despite being surrounded by coworkers equally committed to the network's success, I still suffered the anxiety of a new parent constantly checking the nursery for signs of respiratory distress.

The next day I huddled with the Research guys to tell them about our meeting with Fred and express hope that we'd have some possible names by the next week. My instinct was to do some research on the name so that we'd be sure we didn't make some colossal mistake. One thing I'd learned by then was that consumer research provided insight that either confirmed your gut instinct or completely dashed your hopes. So when it came to the most important decisions, like launching an expensive ad campaign, or, in this case, naming the channel, making choices without research was like flying a plane blindfolded. Doable, but dangerous.

I asked Galen Jones, the head of Research, if we could do a survey and get the results quickly so we could make a decision.

"Well, fast is never best. But if that's what you want, we can take a bunch of names and do a survey. We'll ask people to choose their favorite name. Whole thing could be done in a week."

"You think it's worth doing?"

Galen nodded. "If nothing else, we'll find out which names *don't* resonate with the audience."

"Okay," I said. "Let's do the survey. At least we'll all sleep better. And maybe one of the names will pop."

"Unlikely," Galen said. "Usually when you're looking for black-and-white answers from this kind of research, you get gray. Or worse, mud."

The next week, as promised, Fred and Alan came ready to give us their take on a name. Mike, Galen, and I, along with a handful of others, assembled in the conference room. I hoped that in the next hour or so Fred would pull away the curtain to reveal "the name," and, following a collection of gasps, or maybe an astonished hush, the room would break into applause. Fred stood next to the blank white projection screen, ready to go. Alan turned on the overhead projector, and the Fred/Alan logo shot to the screen. We quieted down and stared at Fred as if he were about to tell us the meaning of life, or better yet, how to achieve immortality. Just as I nodded to Fred, signaling we were ready, the door to the conference room opened, and in walked the boss. "Hi, I'm Bob Kreek, president of the channel."

Bob closed the door, walked to the other side of the conference table, and leaned against the wall. In his right hand was a squishy rubber ball about the size of a baseball. Sticking out from the ball were hundreds of tentacles, and the whole thing was bright blue. Bob passed the thing back and forth from hand to hand. It was that kids' toy called a Koosh ball. As he squeezed the ball, I could feel nervous energy flowing from Bob to the ball and then radiating out into the room. This was the first time I saw him with the Koosh ball. It would become his trademark, a nervous tick masquerading as a power prop. It reminded me of the cat languishing in the lap of the evil Dr. No, the James Bond villain.

Bob looked menacingly at Fred. "Ready when you are."

Fred began the presentation. "I know you're all anxious to hear our recommended names, but please indulge me for a few minutes so I can give you some insight into our thinking and process." We indulged him for twenty-five minutes. Fred was an enthusiastic and animated presenter, but the crowd was starting to get restless. Finally, Bob, who was now seated but obviously losing patience, broke in. "You come up with any names, Fred, or are we gonna talk theoretically for the next hour, too?" He tossed the Koosh ball in the air and caught it, apparently pleased with what he'd said.

Fred laughed. "Okay, Bob, thank you for providing that great segue. Let me crystallize what I've been saying. We've heard from many of you, especially Mike and Art, about what the channel is and, more important, what it *aspires* to be. Alan and I believe that the best names suggest what we *want* to be, not what we are now." He scanned the room looking for acknowledgement and approval. "The best names are aspirational, right?" Everyone stared back at him.

Bob said, "That sounds right. Whaddya got?"

"What we've got is this, Bob. The network needs a name that emphasizes that we are the number-one, go-to place for comedy. And not just on television, but everywhere in the world, throughout the entire universe. We not only provide great comedy, we are the ultimate arbiter of comedy taste. Everyone will look to us as the comedy beacon, the comedy expert." He again paused for emphasis. "Does that sound right?" He looked at Bob, who said nothing.

"Sounds right," I said.

"Good." Fred looked around the room. Satisfied that we were all in agreement, he put both hands on the conference table, leaned in, and said, "So, what we need to be is comedy central." He paused, then stood up again and, with a wave of his hand, said, "Of course we'd never suggest using that as the name."

"Why not?" I asked. "Comedy Central? Sounds like it does all the stuff you're talking about."

Fred shook his head. "No, you see, comedy central is the brand positioning—the unifying idea that inspires everything you do, from your programming to your advertising, your on-air promotion, your logo. Everything. But as a name it's too 'on the nose.'" He put his finger on his nose. "And, we would never recommend using comedy in the name, because what if you want to do something else? Something that's not comedy?"

"Like what, girls' field hockey?" I asked, and a couple of people laughed. "This is a comedy network. That's what we aspire to be. Why hide it?"

"Too risky," Fred explained. "Comedy may not be the focus of the channel forever. But I take your point. Let's look at some names, and I think you'll see that they say comedy, and all the other things I talked about, without using the word." With that, Fred placed a slide on the overhead projector. It had one word on it: *BIG*. Fred said, with pride and finality, "Big."

"Big what?" Bob asked.

"Just BIG." He went on to praise the name *BIG* as perfect for our channel, explaining that it had balls, chutzpah, gravitas. "It makes a statement. And it says what you want to be: big." He looked around and saw that despite his enthusiasm, this name wasn't giving anyone chills or palpitations. Undaunted, he removed the BIG slide without further comment and put up the next one. This, too, had one word on it: *ACME.*

"Like the grocery store?" somebody asked.

"No, acme, like apex, like the top, like the best. And it screams comedy."

Bob snorted. "Screams comedy? How?"

"I think I get it," I said. "You're talking about Acme, from the Road Runner cartoons, right?"

"Yes, Art! Yes, that's it!" Fred pointed at me with both hands, excited that I'd made the connection. "Everyone knows the famous Chuck Jones cartoons made for Warner Brothers with Wile E. Coyote chasing Road Runner around the desert, right? And the Coyote tries to capture Road Runner using explosives and other stuff manufactured and delivered by a company called...Acme!"

"Does everybody know that?" Bob asked, looking around the room, and we all nodded. Bob looked surprised. "Really? Yeah, I guess I knew it, but I forgot." Bob didn't seem to be enjoying any of this. "Are there more names, or is that it?"

The meeting continued through a few more names, each spectacularly introduced and then quietly set aside. When he was finished, Fred, exhausted but still upbeat, asked us what he should do next. Bob looked at me and then Mike with raised eyebrows, suggesting that since Mike and I got us into this, we should decide what to do.

Mike stayed quiet, so I fielded the question. "I think it's safe to say that none of the names seems like the perfect solution." That got a laugh. "Give us a day or two to get back to you." The meeting broke up, and Mike and I stayed behind to thank Fred and Alan.

3. We've Got a Name!

Later that day I met with the Research team. We decided we might as well take the names Fred had presented and start testing them in the survey. There were four names in all, including BIG and ACME, which were worth considering. The plan was to describe a generic comedy network and ask which of the names fit the network best. Then Galen said, "Ya know, we need some more names. We can't go out with just these four in the survey. Let's face it—none of these names really says anything about comedy."

"Yeah, you're right," I agreed, but I didn't have any more suggestions.

"Too bad we can't use Comedy Channel," he said. Galen was from The Comedy Channel team and, like me, lamented the loss of the name. Then he thought for a minute. "Hey, remember when Fred said the positioning for the channel was to make it comedy central? Let's use that. Comedy Central. What the hell."

So we threw that one in, and Galen and the Research guys got the survey out in record time.

Two days later Galen walked into my office waving a sheet of paper. "Just got the survey results."

"Yeah? Any of the names pop?"

"Well, you could say that. Hands down, the favorite name by a huge margin? Comedy Central."

"You're kidding me. I thought we were just throwing that in."

"We were. Now the question is, are we throwing it out? I've never seen results like this." Galen, usually analytical and thoughtful, was as excited as I'd ever seen him. "I mean, this couldn't be clearer! It does a great job of describing who we are.

And these surveys don't often end up with a definitive favorite. We've gotta take this seriously."

"Fred Seibert's not gonna like it." I said. "And we need him to like it. He's the guru, and MTV loves him. Fred was pretty clear that he'd never use Comedy Central as the name."

"So give him the credit," Galen suggested. "Tell him he *did* come up with the name—he just didn't know it. That'll get him on board."

I nodded. "Let's see what Klinghoffer thinks."

Mike liked it, too, so he, Galen, and I went straight to Bob's office to share the good news. We sat down on the couch across from his desk and described the results of the survey. Bob leaned back in his chair, put his feet on his desk, and looked at me. "Sounds a little like Comedy Channel, doesn't it?" He then asked each of us individually if we liked the name, and we all said yes. "Lemme run it by Fuchs and Freston and see what they think. I'll let you know." That signaled the end of the meeting, but Mike had a question.

"Bob, are you gonna tell them you like the name, or are you just getting their reaction?" Bob glared at Mike for a long time before answering. Galen and I shifted uncomfortably on the couch. Mike didn't squirm at all. He just sat there waiting patiently for Bob's response.

"They are my bosses. I'll tell them what you guys came up with and ask whether they approve. If they both say yes, we've got a name." I looked at Mike. He didn't seem bothered by what was clearly a rebuke. Maybe Bob saw that, too, because he repeated the last part with a touch more menace. *"If they both say yes, Mike, we've got a name."*

We scrambled off the couch and out of the office.

A few days later Bob told us that both Michael Fuchs and Tom Freston had approved the name, although he didn't say what they thought of it. But Bob seemed to be warming to Comedy Central now that it was official. The best part about it, I thought, was that it kept the word *comedy* front and center. And as Fred Seibert had said, it was aspirational. It was March 1991, three months after the channel merger, and we had a name.

Now, all we had to do was mash the two channels into one and build a Comedy Central that lived up to its name. A Comedy Central that would become the center of the comedy universe.

CHAPTER 17

Tagline

On April 1, 1991, we premiered the newly named Comedy Central channel. Six months later, in the fall of 1991, I felt that the channel needed a tagline that would further define Comedy Central's attitude. I knew just the guy for the job. Danny Abelson was someone I'd worked with before who had, among other things, written for *National Lampoon* in its heyday. I considered that the ultimate comedy-writer pedigree. Danny was a magician, the guy you called when you wanted it brilliant and fast and you didn't have time to fool around. He'd never failed me, so I looked forward to hearing his ideas and getting Comedy Central an effective tagline.

A tagline could do a lot for a company or a product. It could be a short phrase that introduced a new product; a statement of a company's mission (like General Electric's "We Bring Good Things to Life"); a way to define a product (like BMW's "BMW: The Ultimate Driving Machine"); or aspirational (like IBM's "Think Big" and Apple's rejoinder, "Think Different"). I asked

Danny to come up with a tagline that would do all of these things, and he took the challenge.

After working on it for a couple of weeks, Danny sat with me in my office, itching to unveil the new slogan and the campaign that would launch the name *Comedy Central* to the world. Like so many advertising guys, he sat with a piece of paper face down, hiding the payoff. Then he began telling me how hard he'd worked, how he'd tried and discarded hundreds of taglines, and how this one finally came to him like a gift from God and he couldn't stop thinking about how perfect it was for the channel. I interrupted him. "Can I just see it now?" That was my role, to keep asking that he cut the preamble and show me the damn thing. Danny's role was to ignore me. We hadn't invented these roles. Creative ad guys always explained first and revealed last, and the client just wanted to see what was behind the curtain and make a snap judgement: I love it! Or, I hate it!

Danny, ignoring me, continued the preamble. "It's important for you to understand the creative underpinning, armature, and superstructure of the line, and to understand my process. Over the last two weeks I spent hundreds of hours pacing, thinking, trying out taglines on my wife, my son, my cat, listening to their feedback. If you don't appreciate this, you'll never be able to appreciate the final product. So listen up, boychik."

I sat back in my chair, knowing from past experience that this would take a while.

"There are few certainties in the world," Danny began, "but as I'm sure you are aware, death comes to us all. The younger you are, the more likely you are to feel immortal, and thoughts of death only intrude once in a blue moon, like when your parrot dies, or when your high school has an assembly to memorialize a classmate who just overdosed on Quaaludes. But the older you get—and I speak from experience because I'm older than you, Arturo—"

"No, you're not." I said this quickly, to ensure that I got all three words in.

"No? Well, I'm wiser than you, and that's what's critical. The older you get, the wiser you get, the more death is on your mind, until at middle age it's a constant drumbeat, like an unshakable pounding migraine. And then, desperate for relief, you start the quest for meaning, which is really just a way to massage your temples during that migraine so that the thought of death doesn't completely consume you. And don't forget religion."

"Religion?"

"Religion also supplies some relief by convincing us that when we die, that's only stage one of a multi-stage existence..."

As Danny waxed philosophical, my mind drifted to my first encounter with death at the age of five, courtesy of Fern Levin's grandmother.

• • •

"Arrrrthur. Arrrthur!" Fern Levin's full-throated yell echoed through the neighborhood. I was two houses away, sitting on the floor of my room with a toy truck, but really just waiting for Fern to summon me. At six, she was only a year older than me but that extra year carried with it a world of sophistication. I jumped up and bolted out the front door.

"Don't get too dirty; we're eating soon," my mother said as I left.

I ran to Fern's backyard and climbed onto the swing next to hers. "Guess what?" she said, her long black hair flying as she swung by me.

"What?"

"My nana died today. She's going to heaven."

"What's heaven?"

"That's where you go when you're dead," she said happily, her face skyward as her swing reached the top of its arc and paused. "Heaven's way up there, past the clouds."

I looked when I reached the top of my arc but saw nothing but sky. "When's she coming back?"

"Never." Fern was smart. She spoke with the confidence of a ten-year-old. I believed everything she said. "You don't come back when you're dead," Fern explained. "You stay there forever."

"Forever?" So far, I didn't like this dead thing at all.

I launched myself off the swing, rolled like a paratrooper, stood up, and started running home.

"Where're you going?" Fern called from her swing.

"Home. See you tomorrow."

As soon as I got to my house, I found my mom and said, "Fern's nana got dead and went to heaven." Then I asked, "Are you going to heaven?"

"Arthur, you don't die until you're old. Fern's nana was old."

"How old are you when you die?"

"Very old."

"Like twenty?"

"No, like eighty."

I was five. I could count to five in a few seconds. Counting to eighty would take me forever. "Oh, okay, good."

A few minutes later my dad's car pulled into the driveway where I was waiting for him. When he got out of the car I asked, "Dad, how old are you?"

"How old am I? I'm old."

"I know you're old, but how old are you?"

"Very old." My father laughed. "I'm eighty."

Without saying anything, I walked into the house, went to my room, and fell onto my bed. I stared at the ceiling and felt sad that my dad was going to be dead soon because he was eighty. I'd never felt so sad before. That night I said I had a stomachache and skipped dinner. The next day I sat on the curb and threw stones into the road. I didn't talk much. I didn't run when Fern called.

The day after that was another sad day.

My parents became concerned.

After meticulously reviewing the events of the previous several days, they figured out what had happened. They came into my bedroom as I was putting on my pajamas and explained that my father was only joking. He wasn't eighty, he had just said that to be funny. He was thirty-one years old, and my mother was thirty. My dad was just making a joke about being old and dead. There was no need for me to worry.

I worried.

．　•　•

It had been over a half hour since Danny first sat down, and he was still preamble-ing. As much as I enjoyed Danny and his philosophizing, I was getting more and more anxious to see the tagline he'd come up with. Nevertheless, Danny was on a roll. Who was I to stop him?

"Death is a subject that people will go to great lengths to avoid," Danny said.

"Because it's unsettling?" I offered.

"Exactly. So...for many of us the only thing that keeps us from thinking about death is...what?" Danny paused. "Arturo, I'm asking you what keeps you from thinking about death?"

"Oh. Um...chocolate?"

"Really? No, not what I had in mind, but interesting. No, what keeps you from thinking about death is...comedy. We tell each other funny stories, we hang out with funny people, we watch stand-up comedy. Why? Because it distracts us from the fact that we are going to die. Right?"

"Okay. Right. So what's the tagline?"

"I thought you'd never ask." Danny starts to turn over the piece of paper then stops. "Are you ready for this, Arturo? Here it is."

"We're all gonna die. Watch Comedy Central."

After Danny read the line aloud to me, he said, "Arturo, is it not perfect?"

No, I thought, it's not perfect, but something about it excited me. Was it because, as Danny said, it illuminated an essential truth about comedy? Was it because it finally allowed me to understand Eddie Gorodetsky's boast to me that he had cracked jokes at his mother's funeral? Maybe it was this: ever since my first experience with the concept of death, my father's joke that he was eighty years old, I had had a special appreciation for the nexus between death and comedy.

"It's good," I said. "It's really good."

Then Danny showed me some storyboards that outlined the television campaign. Each spot featured a famous person who, according to Danny, "knew a little something about dying." The celebrity would look into the camera, talk frankly and authoritatively about death, then say, "We're all gonna die." And then the lettering on the screen would say, "We're all gonna die. Watch Comedy Central." Danny had approached a bunch of people about appearing in the spot, including the novelist Stephen King. King had already agreed to do it.

That night my father called me just to see how I was doing, and before he hung up, I asked him what he thought of Danny's tagline. "You can't say that! It's horrible and morbid."

For a few minutes I wondered whether the new slogan went too far, so I called my younger brother Larry and asked him what he thought.

"I love it," he said, laughing. "Use that one." That's when I knew it was perfect. This tagline not only appealed to our target audience (young men) but it offended and alienated everyone outside the target (including older guys like my dad). It was brash and edgy and slightly horrifying.

I showed the tagline to my boss. He laughed out loud.

I was glad Bob got on board with the tagline so quickly. He liked it enough that he didn't even mention reviewing it with his bosses. Maybe he was starting to feel more confident. Maybe we all were.

CHAPTER 18

Cracking Wise

By December 1991, with our first year as Comedy Central coming to an end, I felt that the merger had been a success. Distribution was climbing, with Comedy Central available in twenty-two million homes, seven million more than we'd started the year with. Our programming was getting noticed—we'd been nominated for ten CableACE Awards for excellence in cable programming. Thanks to our tagline, we were becoming known as a comedy network that was brash and unafraid. And, after sharing the experience of naming the new channel and giving it life, we were starting to feel like a team rather than two groups from two different companies and cultures thrown together by circumstance. I felt like Comedy Central was on its way to success, and I went to the final Comedy Central board meeting of the year expecting to hear the board say to all of us, "Good job. The channel's doing great. Keep it up." Or something like that. Instead, our board made it clear they expected more. After all, we weren't profitable yet, and we were costing our partners, MTV and HBO, loads of money. The board fired suggestions at us, but there was one suggestion that had all the board members nodding their heads.

"You know what the channel needs? More press. More people talking about you," Tom Freston, chairman of MTV Networks, said, banging the table. "You've gotta stir the pot, do something crazy, make some noise."

"Yes, exactly," another board member agreed. "You're a comedy network, and you're fading into the background. Get into some trouble."

A third offered this advice: "Everybody loves lists!" she said. "*People* magazine does the world's ten most beautiful people, and they get huge press. Do lists," she said. And then she added, waving her arms and shrieking it like an incantation, "Lists! Lists!"

My boss confronted me after the board meeting. "You've gotta do something to create some buzz around this channel. Come up with some ideas. And for God's sake, no 'lists, lists!'" he said, voice shrieking and arms waving. Bob suggested I put some people in a room and brainstorm. "And not the usual suspects from Programming," he said. "There's lots of good ideas floating around the halls. Find them and make something happen."

It wasn't completely true that we weren't getting noticed. We got press, and the channel was starting to develop a devoted audience, but the board was right: Buzz was more than just press. Buzz was about injecting Comedy Central into the zeitgeist, becoming part of the cultural landscape, getting talked about around the water cooler.

Over the last few months we'd done some of the usual stuff that channels did, like programming marathons, stunts, and contests. One of my favorite stunts took place at Christmas. We encouraged viewers to perform and videotape their favorite scenes from the Jimmy Stewart Christmas classic *It's a Wonderful Life* and then send in the videos. Then we strung them all together and played it as *It's a Wonderful Life, the Home Version.* It was hilarious (or maybe just weird), and it got some press. But now we had to go from a small network with a cult following to a big, successful channel. That required bigger thinking.

I gathered a small, eclectic group, plucked from several departments including Press, On-Air Promotion, and Marketing, for a brainstorming session. Nobody from Programming was included, as per Bob's directive. I also invited Vinnie Favale. Even though he ran the Advertising Traffic department, everyone knew Vinnie as a guy who loved comedy and who constantly came up with crazy ideas for the channel. We needed some now. I also invited Steve Mark, our chief counsel, for two reasons. First, I knew he longed to be part of this kind of creative endeavor. Steve loved comedy and the channel, and he was always looking for an opportunity to be creative. Second, I wanted him to tell us when he thought we were crossing the line and could get in trouble. I also tapped Ken Olshansky, head writer for On-Air Promotions; two On-Air Promo producers, both named Chris, who I knew were full of ideas; and Tony Fox, head of Public Relations.

I started the meeting and addressed the six scattered around my office. "You all know why we're here, right?"

"No idea, Art," Vinnie said from his seat on the windowsill. "I didn't read the memo. I just heard you called a meeting, so I came. I figured you'd tell us."

Ken was sitting cross-legged on the couch. "I like that. Why waste precious time reading memos?" Everyone laughed. "I'm taking a page out of Vinnie's book: no more reading memos."

Vinnie grinned proudly and addressed the room. "You know I'm right, right? Art always starts his meeting by telling us what's up. Why read? I should get a prize for streamlining the bullshit corporate process around here."

"You get the prize all right," I deadpanned. "Did anybody here read the memo?"

Everyone shook their heads. They were playing with me now. "Does anybody actually know how to read?" I asked.

"Not really," said Ken. "Why do you think we went into television?"

Vinnie said, "Whatever it's about, I think we're off to a great start."

This is what working with a bunch of wise guys was like. I knew I had the right people in the room for the job. When I explained that we needed to get buzz for the channel and our job was to toss around some ideas, Vinnie said, "Oh—we're the 'Buzz Committee.'" And so we were.

The Buzz Committee met frequently and never failed to come up with ideas. They were often rejected as impractical, bad for advertising sales, dangerously over the line of good taste, or just plain dangerous. But all of the ideas made us laugh, and that seemed as important as coming up with something useful. One day, Vinnie walked in with a truly transformational idea.

"Check this out," he said, screaming and bouncing up and down like a kid who can't wait to tell you something if only you'd listen. "January's when the president does the State of the Union

Address, right? All the networks carry it, right? So...we carry it, too! We put the State of the Union Address on Comedy Central, like we're a news channel or a big network." He stood there wide eyed and waiting for me to get excited.

"Yeah?" I said. "That it?"

"No, that's *not* it. *This* is it. Look at me." I was looking at him, but I tried to look harder. "We get a comedian to make wiseass comments during the speech. Live. While it's happening."

"So we show President George Bush making his speech to Congress, and some guy's offscreen wisecracking *during* the speech? He talks *over* the president?"

"With all that applause after every line? Plenty of time for the jokes. And I've got the perfect name." Vinnie always had a great name for stunts. "The *State of the Union: Undressed*. Now give me a hug and tell me how much you love the idea."

CHAPTER 19

Undressed Rehearsal

Programming loved the idea, and they began looking for a comedian who would do it. Most stand-up comedians work for months or years on forty minutes of material, crafting, re-crafting, trying out new bits in clubs; every word, phrase, and pause is carefully arranged for maximum comic effect. Even the *Mystery Science Theater 3000* writers spent hours coming up with their "ad-libbed" wisecracks. Not every comedian relished the idea of going on live television without a script, but we knew someone would, and our talent department took on the challenge of finding that someone. The additional challenge was finding someone willing to do this who was at least moderately famous and whose name could attract an audience.

In the meantime, we had to clear the way for the State of the Union speech to be shown live on Comedy Central. Nobody thought that would be a problem, since networks, cable news channels, and radio stations carried the speech live. All you had to do was ask, right? Steve Mark, Buzz Committee member, in-house counsel, and my favorite lawyer, loved the idea. He said he'd make a few calls and see what was involved. I heard from him a few hours later.

"They won't let us carry the speech live." Steve went on to explain that every year one network is given access to the live feed on the condition that they provide the broadcast, called the "pool feed," to the other channels. The network in charge has some say over who gets the feed. "We're not a bona fide news organization, and we don't have a news department. So they said, 'No dice.'"

"Shit, really?" I asked. "If we can't get the live feed, the whole *State of the Union: Undressed* idea goes down the drain. Now what do we do?"

Steve smiled, put his hands on the wheels of his wheelchair, and propelled himself from behind his desk to where I stood.

"Art, my boy, we have not yet begun to fight," he said. "First I call the legal eagles at Time Warner and Viacom. Our corporate parents should be able to help. Who knows, we may have to file a lawsuit. And you know something?" Steve grinned. "I'm gonna enjoy this. And don't worry, I'll get us the feed. Worse comes to worse, I've got a backup plan that can't fail."

The Talent department came up with gold: Al Franken, the writer and occasional performer on *Saturday Night Live*, had agreed to do it. They also recruited Billy Kimball to be his sidekick and to produce the show. Both Al and Billy had worked with Comedy Central before. Al had produced a bunch of *SNL* promos for us, and Billy was the star and producer of a game show for us. We liked and trusted Billy, he seemed to have a good handle on what we wanted, and he was easy to work with.

Al was a little quirky. Ken Olshansky, our head writer, had worked with him on the *SNL* promos, and while Ken wasn't a professional actor, he'd agreed to be in one of them. Ken recounted the story: "Al was directing the shoot, but every time I said my line, he'd stop the cameras and tell me my line reading was wrong. Then Al would read it the way he wanted me to do it. We did three more takes, but the same thing kept happening. Finally, exasperated, I read the line with my best Al Franken impression, mimicking his flat midwestern accent, sarcasm, and monotonic delivery. 'Perfect,' he said, and that was that."

•   •   •

With a couple of weeks to go, we still didn't have the feed, but Steve was giving it his all. The networks were using every excuse and legal maneuver at their disposal to keep us from getting the State of the Union live feed. I guessed they were scared of the precedent they were setting and maybe worried we'd take some of their precious audience. Tony Fox, our head of PR, made certain that the press knew what was going on and got us lots of coverage. "This is David and Goliath," he told me. "The big ugly networks send in their team of lawyers to fight us, and we send in Steve, our one measly lawyer." Steve kept telling us not to worry; the feed would be there by the time we went live. The press coverage exceeded our expectations, and everyone was pumped up. We were making comedy history. But we were past the point of no return, having announced the show and the talent. We had to get the feed, or the whole thing would crash. I was worried.

Meanwhile, we outfitted a studio with a realistic-looking news desk and all the accoutrements. Billy and Al worked with writers to prepare their opening comments for the show. They learned as much as they could about the event, like who would be in the gallery and what exactly would take place before the president began his address. With a week to go, Al and Billy went into rehearsal, using videotapes of previous State of the Union Addresses to practice ad-libbing remarks. But two days before the event, we still had no feed. Now everyone was worried.

I dropped by the studio. Billy Kimball and Al Franken were putting in as many hours as they could rehearsing. Al seemed subdued. He didn't laugh much, and I never saw him smile. I wondered whether he was getting nervous about the show. Why shouldn't he be nervous? Even though he had experience in front of live television audiences on *Saturday Night Live,* and even though he and Billy had made sure they had enough pre-written material to keep things going during the speech, this was live improvisational comedy and they were working without a net. When I asked Billy, "How do you know when you're ready for something like this?" he replied, "You don't."

The day before the speech, Steve rolled into my office, parked his wheelchair, and put on the brake. "We got the pool feed. Don't ask what I had to do."

"Nothing illegal or immoral, I hope."

"I told you not to ask. But worst case, it'll be me going to jail, not you."

"That's why you're my favorite lawyer." I gave him a high five.

Steve was kidding, of course. He'd gotten some of the other networks to take our side. CNN apparently didn't like the idea that we couldn't have the feed, and they made that clear. It became a first-amendment issue. Somehow that made the difference.

Now all we had to do was put on a great show.

•　•　•

The next day was the day of the speech. At 7 p.m., with two hours to go before the start of the show, Vinnie, Steve, and I went to the studio to see how things were going. Al and Billy were doing some last-minute rehearsing. The set looked great. Al was standing behind the anchor desk, and Billy was talking to one of the camera operators. Billy walked back to the desk and said loudly, "All right, everybody, let's get ready." Everyone in the studio started talking at once, electrified by the live show they were about to do.

Billy turned to Al and said, "Al, you need to get to makeup. We go live in two hours."

Al looked at Billy. Then his low monotonic midwestern voice cut through the din. "Did you just say, 'We go live?'" He looked around the studio. All eyes were on him. "You expect me to do this live? I thought we were taping it. No way I'm doing this live." He started walking toward the studio door and said to nobody in particular, "I'm calling my manager."

I thought he was kidding, but Al continued to walk off the set. How could he not know this was to be done live? Whose job was it to tell him that? Didn't it come up in rehearsal? Steve, Vinnie, and I watched in confused horror. So did Billy, the production crew, and Al's assistant.

For a second nobody moved or said a word. For Al to walk away from the show now was so completely unexpected that it took time for everyone's brains to process what was happening. Even Billy, usually unflappable while in producing mode, seemed flapped. Then, the silence was broken by the sound of high heels on the hard, cement studio floor. Laurie Zaks, Comedy Central's vice president of Talent, was on the move, her shoulder-length, jet-black hair bouncing on her white blouse as she walked, a look of quiet determination on her face. She was following Al, but clearly wasn't going to get to him before he left the room. Suddenly she stopped and stood calmly, hands by her side. "Al. Wait a minute." He didn't even turn around, so she followed him out the door.

The studio was suddenly quiet. The crew was whispering to each other about what had just happened. They knew that the show was scheduled, that we were committed to a live broadcast. They knew we'd look totally lame if we showed up at 9 p.m. with an announcement that "The *State of the Union: Undressed*, previously scheduled for this time, will not be seen." No, we couldn't do that. Our backup plan was obvious: Billy Kimball would go on, note that Al had food poisoning or something, and continue the show alone. I wondered if Billy was up to that. I glanced over at him. He still hadn't moved.

The studio door opened. Laurie Zaks scanned the room, located Billy, then gestured for him to come with her. They disappeared into the hall. I took that as a positive development. A few minutes later, Billy and Laurie came back. "Okay, people, everything's fine. Al just needed a moment, but he's doing the show as planned." It seemed like a good place for a shout of joy, or a hooray, or something. Instead, everyone just seemed relieved and went back to doing what they were supposed to, as if this were all part of the pre-show plan. Vinnie, Steve, and I left the studio to watch the show from a conference room with a monitor.

As we walked out, Vinnie looked over at me. "That was a close one." He had a lot riding on this. *Undressed* was his idea, and he wanted it to be great. I smiled and patted him on the shoulder. "I wasn't worried for a second," I said.

"Bullshit, Bell. You looked like you were about to throw up," Vinnie said.

"But I didn't throw up, did I? I knew Laurie would work it out with him."

"Yeah. What'd she do, throw money at him?"

"No idea, and right now I don't care."

A few minutes later I found Laurie and asked her what had happened. She looked remarkably calm given the circumstance. "Al either forgot it was live," she said, "or he didn't understand it in the first place. Or maybe he was just being a jerk. Honestly, I have no idea."

"Well, I'm glad whatever you said to him worked." I paused. "What *did* you say to him, anyway?"

"That's confidential," she said with a smile. "Let's go watch the show."

We sat down to wait for the show to start. At 9 p.m. sharp, NBC, ABC, CBS, and PBS announced the start of their coverage of President Bush's State of the Union Address with all the gravitas they could muster. And we were right there with them, but with a lot less gravitas and a lot more fun.

Al Franken and Billy Kimball were terrific. They were respectful and irreverent at the same time. My favorite Al line: "I should have prepared more. This is a long speech." And once Al asked, "What's he talking about now, Billy?" Billy replied, "I have no idea, Al."

As I watched, I felt we were entering unclaimed comedy territory and planting our flag. Lots of comedy took advantage of politics and the news, but nobody had done anything as audacious as this. It combined "watch-us-watch" comedy with smart, irreverent commentary. And now that we'd done it, there was nothing to stop us from doing it again. It was our first foray into using news and politics as a platform for our comedy. That night was a turning point: by taking a huge risk, we discovered what we were good at.

The television critics seemed as delighted by it as we were:

"Comedy Central's *State of the Union: Undressed* was groundbreaking—embodying the lack of respect for authority that is part of the proud tradition of the United States. A real TV alternative, like it or not. Unsportsmanlike, yes. Nihilistic, yes—reflecting a serious cynicism toward the politicians of any major party. But, primarily because of the sophisticated, witty comments of Comedy Central's two chief correspondents for the speech—Al Franken and Billy Kimball—the surreal takeoff also embodied some of the best elements of humor: rebellion and a healthy lack of conventional taste when it was called for. The success of the broadcast as a lampoon was chiefly attributable to the choice of Franken and Kimball to carry the experiment." (Steve DuBrow, *Los Angeles Times*, January 30, 1992)

That night finally established us as the comedy network we wanted to be.

CHAPTER 20

Bill Maher and Me

That first *State of the Union: Undressed* in January 1992 was a success with the press and the audience. But it was more than that. That show helped Comedy Central define who we were and what we were to become. The show inspired everyone at the channel. It was audacious. It was historic. And it opened up new possibilities in comedy. For us, it was like NASA's first suborbital flight, inaugurating some sort of new frontier for Comedy Central. We didn't quite know where it was going, but it was thrilling.

The *State of the Union: Undressed* set the programming agenda for the rest of 1992. We capitalized on our "watch us watch politicians" success by covering the Republican and Democratic National Conventions. We called our coverage *InDecision '92*. MTV had Rock the Vote, their bad-boy rocker version of being part of the election. But while they encouraged their teen audience to join the revolution, we preferred to watch from the sidelines with a jaundiced and comedic viewpoint.

We had locked on to something that defined us. It was a continuation of *MST 3000*'s wisecracking about movies. This time the show was politics. Franken was perfect for it: smart, observant, and funny. *SNL* was doing some of this with "Weekend Update," but we had our own style. This was a great coming-of-age for Comedy Central just one year after launch.

In the fall of 1992, during a break at an all-day meeting of Comedy Central's top management, Mike Klinghoffer walked up to me, his never-ending smile still there but somehow off-kilter. "I'm no longer a part of Comedy Central," he said. When I looked at him quizzically, he laid it out for me. "Bob just fired me."

"Are you serious?" I asked, and then seeing that he was, I said, "Jesus. What happened?" But I knew what had happened. Despite Mike's many programming successes since the merger, it was no secret that Bob was painfully uncomfortable with Mike. In the end, Bob felt he couldn't work with him anymore. As Bob explained later to me, "Mike just didn't fit in."

With Mike gone, I was the presumptive head of Programming, and for a few weeks I was in charge without being told to take charge. But Bob wanted someone with "Hollywood street cred" to run Programming, and after a short, intensive search, he found Mitch Semel. "Mitch is an LA programmer, and that's what we need," Bob told me. "He even dresses the part. He wore funny shoes to the interview." Clearly, Bob hadn't even considered letting me run the Programming department alone, and that hurt me. I didn't know Mitch, but I pictured him wearing clown shoes. I would have worn clown shoes if that's what Bob wanted. Mitch started in October of 1992.

Several weeks later, I stood outside a convention center in Southern California next to our new head of Original Programming. We were both dressed in conference clothes, but Mitch, in a lightweight blue blazer, camel khakis, and no tie, more easily blended into the Southern California backdrop of foothills, highways, and strip mall sprawl. I, on the other hand, looked like a banker in blue pinstripes who'd flown in that morning to close a deal, have a few drinks, and catch a flight back to New York City. Mitch looked very LA. He had lived and worked in LA for years as president of Gary Goldberg's production company (producer of *Family Ties*). Despite our differences, I found Mitch charismatic, easygoing, and likable. We immediately hit it off.

I turned to Mitch. "How can this guy be late? It's quarter after. Isn't he supposed to be on time if he's pitching *us* a show?"

"He's talent," Mitch said. "Talent's allowed to be late. And driving in Southern California means never being on time. But you can't beat the weather." He held his arms out to show me the weather. "Seventy degrees, no humidity, bright sunshine, not a cloud in the sky. What's it like in New York today?" he asked, then answered: "Miserably cold."

"Okay," I said, "the weather's great, and he's talent, but he's still late. And Bill Maher's not exactly a movie star. Last time I checked, nobody ever heard of him but us."

"Doesn't matter. Talent is talent. We're the suits. It's the talent who go out every day and perform for millions of people. It's the talent who put food on our table. Without them, we're just a couple of bookkeepers."

Mitch had a point.

"But it takes talent and guys like us to make it work," I said, unwilling to let this go. "Talent's got their own problems, and I don't blame them for being crazy sometimes. I just wish Bill wasn't late, because I hate waiting. I'm from New York."

I stood there watching the hotel buses disgorge enthusiastic conventioneers who walked past us into the convention hall, each one wearing a name tag that included their company name and location. Every now and then one of the conventioneers would glance at Mitch and then do a double take as if they recognized him. I couldn't blame them: Mitch was a dead ringer for Jerry Seinfeld, the most famous comedian in the country since NBC's *Seinfeld* had become a hit comedy three years earlier. Millions of fans were dying to catch a glimpse of Seinfeld in airports, fancy restaurants, comedy clubs, or just tooling around Manhattan, and Mitch was out there doubling their chances. "Hey, Jerry!" was a cry that followed Mitch around like an excited puppy.

In the short time I'd known him, I'd seen Mitch cringe through dozens of mistaken identity calamities. It had happened the previous day as we sat in first class on the flight to LA. Twenty minutes into the flight, a boy of about nine or ten walked up the aisle to our row and, eyes wide, said, "Mr. Seinfeld, can I please have your autograph?" Mitch gently explained that he wasn't Mr. Seinfeld but a lot of people thought he looked just like him. For a second the kid looked confused. Not knowing what else to do, he returned to his seat.

"I'm really getting sick of this," Mitch said to me after we heard the kid bitterly tell his mother why he'd returned empty handed. "I feel terrible, but it's not my fault. The world insists I'm Seinfeld."

"And who are you to argue with the fans?"

A minute later the kid's mother sent him back for another try. This time the boy held out a paper napkin and pen, his jaw set, and dared Mitch to refuse. Mitch shrugged, took the pen and napkin from the boy, and said, "Okay, pal, what's your name?" Then he wrote, "To Billy, Great flying with you, Best, Jerry Seinfeld." The kid grabbed the napkin and tore back to his seat. Mitch turned to me shaking his head. "What have I done?"

"C'mon, it's no worse than what millions of fake Santas do every Christmas." Just then, the woman across the aisle and two seats ahead of us turned around.

"Hi Jerry!"

•   •   •

Mitch and I had been waiting in front of the convention center for over half an hour when a blue sports car, mid-1980s vintage with a dented front-left fender, pulled up to the curb not far from where we were standing. The driver got out and yelled, "Mitch."

"That's him," Mitch said, and we started walking to the car, where Mitch introduced me to Bill Maher.

"Hi, Bill. We met before, when you were sitting in for Jon Stewart on *Short Attention Span Theater* a couple months ago."

"Oh, yeah, that's right, I remember you." I suspected he didn't, but he clapped me on the shoulder as if we were old pals. "You guys want to get some breakfast? I passed a diner on the way here."

"Sure, but can we all fit?" Mitch asked, eyeing Bill's tiny sports car.

"What are you talking about?" Bill replied. "There's plenty of room. Art, you mind riding in the back? Mitch needs the front seat." I bent down and looked into the car. The back was, in fact, the back and not a back seat. Mitch was a good six inches taller than me; the back seat might cripple me, but it would kill him for sure.

"Yeah, no problem." I took off my jacket and handed it to Mitch, then pushed the passenger seat forward and climbed in. I pulled myself in and turned over so that I was lying on my back with my knees up and my shoes placed just below the rear window. "I'm good," I said. "But I can't find the seat belt." Mitch laughed, and Bill gave a little snort.

"I'll drive carefully," Bill said, "but if there's a horrific fiery crash, you're toast."

"Sounds good to me," I said. Bill and Mitch climbed in and put on their seat belts, and we pulled away from the curb, leaving the cable convention behind us.

Mitch turned in his seat to look at me. "You okay back there, Art?"

"Yeah, I'm fine. I just hope this diner is worth it."

"It's breakfast," Bill said. "What could possibly go wrong? Couple eggs, some bacon, a stack of pancakes with fake maple syrup, and a wiseass, gum-snapping waitress as old as my mother with a face like my father."

The car lurched crazily to the left and screeched to a stop. Mitch opened his door and gave me a hand getting out. I looked up and saw the giant sign: Bright Stars Diner. There was one of those big plastic letter boards under it that read "Welcome National Cable Television Conference."

"Give me a second while I un-crumple myself," I said, brushing dust off my suit. "Shit, my leg's asleep."

Bill took charge as soon as we walked in the door. "Three for breakfast," he said to the guy sitting at the cash register, who in turn told us to sit anywhere we liked. Then Bill pointed to a pretty blond waitress and asked, "That waitress, which table's she working? She seems nice." The cash register guy looked over and gestured to a booth by the bathroom. "That's perfect," Bill said, and we walked over and sat down, Mitch and me on one side, Bill on the other. The waitress was there in an instant.

"Hi, boys." She looked at Mitch. "Hey, are you Jerry Seinfeld?"

"At this point I might as well be. But no, I'm not."

"His name's Mitch, this is Art, and I'm Bill. I'm a comedian, if that helps."

"Why would that help?" She passed out the giant diner menus. "Everyone want coffee?"

After we ordered, Mitch set up the conversation. "Okay, Bill. You've been working on a talk show idea, and your timing is good. Art and I have been looking for some kind of talk show."

Bill straightened up and ran both hands through his dirty-blond, shoulder-length hair, moving some stray locks back behind his ears. "You know what's wrong with talk shows?"

"They're boring," I said, and I immediately regretted it. Bill glanced at me and continued without acknowledging my response. I shifted uncomfortably in the booth and waited.

"The trouble with talk shows," Bill continued, "is that nobody talks. I mean, the host talks, the guests talk, their lips move, and sound comes out, but what are they talking about? Anything important? No. Usually the guests are just there to hype their new movie or book. And who cares what they have to say? The guests are mostly celebrities without a fucking clue. I want to do a talk show where the people actually talk." He stopped for emphasis, but I wasn't sure yet what he was emphasizing. "You know, about *the issues*. And I am gonna tell it like it is. No pulling my punches, no pussyfooting around the guests, no playing to their egos, no stroking them so they just sit there and beam at the audience. We'll have real conversations about real issues, and I'm gonna get nasty when I have to, call out the hypocrisy, nail the bullshitters. The show's called *Politically Incorrect*, and that's what it'll be."

"I think I got it," Mitch said. "Question: Where's the funny?"

"I'm the funny. But I won't compete with my guests. I won't dive in with a joke at every opportunity just to get a laugh. I want the audience to get something out of this other than just me being funny."

"Are all the guests comics?" I asked. "You put five comics on a panel on TV, and they all talk at the same time, you can't hear a thing. Preschoolers would do better."

"Yeah, good point," Bill said, "but I'm not gonna let that happen. Of course we'll have comics on, but we'll talk about real stuff. And not all the guests will be comics. I want interesting people who can hold up their end of a conversation. Politicians, novelists, futurists, tattoo artists..." Our breakfast arrived, and Bill kept talking for another twenty minutes, answering our questions. When he excused himself to go to the men's room, I looked at Mitch.

"Whaddya think?"

"He's smart and he's funny. I think he can pull it off."

"I do, too," I said, "but we'll have to start with a small order, maybe two months' worth of shows. We don't have much of a budget."

Mitch nodded. "I never bought a show this fast. You think we're making a mistake?"

"No," I said. "It feels right. And how long have we been saying we need a show like this?"

Bill came back and sat down. We told him we'd like to do the show, and he smiled. "I knew you would. You don't have a lot of good programs on that channel of yours. But this is a start." He looked around for the waitress. "Check!"

Mitch and I had only been working together for three weeks, but in that diner we made our first programming decision together. The show wasn't another comedian talkfest, and Bill seemed capable of striking the right tone. And, bonus, Bill seemed like a guy who would be easy to work with. At least he and I had an easy rapport. Maybe we'd become friends.

CHAPTER 21

What...and Leave Programming?*

Mitch and I returned to New York excited to get *Politically Incorrect* on the air as soon as possible. We knew the show would be good for us, if only because Bill was planning to book as many A-list guests as he could and the publicity of having comedians on the show would get Comedy Central some much-needed press.

A few months after *Politically Incorrect* debuted, my boss called me into his office. "Art," Bob said after I settled into his couch. He sat down in the big leather chair across from me and began lobbing his Koosh ball from hand to hand. This one was bright orange with blue mixed in. Bob's Koosh ball collection had grown impressively, and he had mastered the art of juggling one ball. Bob continued: "I thought a lot about what we talked about a couple of weeks ago." Bob had asked how things were going with Mitch, and I told him that I got along fine with Mitch but that I had less to do in my job than before and would like to take on additional responsibility. What I didn't say was that while I

---

* Two guys are shoveling elephant dung at a circus. One says to the other, "Why don't we get out of here and find some real jobs?" The other guys says, "What ... and leave show business?"

liked and respected Mitch, he had kept me from being made sole head of Programming. "You've done a good job of getting Mitch up to speed, but it's his department now. He can handle it, or not, on his own. So I'm pulling you out of Programming to be the new head of Marketing."

"Marketing? But I don't know much about marketing."

"What do you have to know? It can't be that hard. Lots of marketers I know are idiots." Bob had a knack for belittling just about anyone. "And Divney's just not doing a great job with it." Larry Divney was currently head of Ad Sales and Marketing. "Divney's an Ad Sales guy. That's what he does, and nobody's better at it. But he has to concentrate on Ad Sales if he's gonna get anywhere near hitting his budget. So I'm moving the Marketing department under you." He threw the Koosh ball straight up in the air, almost to the ceiling, and caught it. Then he stood up. "Don't fuck this up," he said and walked back to his desk.

"Does Divney know about this?"

"Yeah, I just told him," Bob said. "He wasn't real happy about it. He loved marketing." And I loved programming. It seemed that nobody was happy about this except Bob.

I went back to my office and sulked for a few minutes until I realized I needed a crash course in television marketing. The giant bookstore downstairs must have books on marketing, I thought, and I can have lunch with the head of Marketing at HBO. That ought to do it.

I read some books, had lunch with every marketing guy I knew, and hired a veteran marketer from a packaged goods company as my number two. None of this helped very much in my quest for marketing enlightenment. It wasn't until we started searching for a new ad agency that I met my marketing mentor during a visit to Korey Kay & Partners, a New York City–based agency. I'd seen some of their work and liked it. I hoped the office visit would give me a better sense of what they were all about and what kind of work they did.

"Hi Art, I'm Allen Kay, president of Korey Kay & Partners." I shook Allen's hand. "Allen, with two L's and an E." He was older than me but wore his hair slicked back and almost to his shoulders. He looked like an old surfer in a tailored suit and tie. He had a great laugh and a kind face, and I could tell he approached everything with a lot of humor.

"Well, Allen," I said, immediately enjoying myself, "other than the spelling of your name, is there anything else I should know about you and your advertising agency?"

"Like what?"

"Like where's Korey?" I asked. "And how'd he get top billing?"

"Not he—she. Lois Korey died a while ago. She was a great ad writer, very funny, started in TV writing for Ernie Kovacs and Lucille Ball. I miss her."

I felt like an idiot. "Oh, sorry, I didn't know."

"Nothing to be sorry about," Allen said. "Anyway, Lois got top billing because it sounded better than Kay, Korey...plus, she insisted."

With the preliminaries out of the way, the agency started their pitch. While Allen's team presented an impressive array of advertising, he sat there, alternately beaming with pride and drawing pictures on his notepad. His agency was known for its oddball creativity, and I sensed that Allen was the source of both the oddball and the creativity. I decided that whether or not we chose his agency, Allen was a guy I'd like to get to know better. I mentioned this to him as he was leaving. He took the compliment with a smile. "You want to get to know me better? Hire us. Otherwise, sayonara."

The meeting at Korey Kay had been set up for us by our agency consultant, a former advertising executive who was an expert on helping companies choose the right ad agency. He set up preliminary pitches from nearly twenty New York ad agencies, and I was impressed by all of them. Narrowing the field would not be easy. *New York* magazine found out that we were conducting an agency search and asked if they could follow me around. The reporter wanted to witness the entire process, from the agency pitches to my final decision. With the reporter, the agency consultant, and my marketing staff, we were a pretty big posse.

Despite the distractions of the constant journalistic scrutiny and the back-and-forth with my staff and the consultant, we managed after a few weeks to narrow the search to three agencies. The final step was to give each agency an "assignment," a set of tasks they all had to do so that we could compare their work. One of the tasks was to come up with a new slogan or tagline for the channel. It had been over a year since the launch slogan, "We're all gonna die, watch Comedy Central," and I felt we should explore something new. Our consultant cautioned me: "Don't expect any of the agencies to come up with anything useful. It's really just a chance for them to strut their creative stuff."

Korey Kay was the first agency to present. As everyone took a seat, Allen Kay walked up to me and said, "We got this. We win. You'll agree when you see your new tagline." I admired his confidence, but I was skeptical. Twenty minutes into the presentation, Allen proudly unveiled his work. It was an ad campaign for Comedy Central that would end with: *"Comedy Central. What the hell is going on here?"*

It really didn't need further explanation, but Allen couldn't resist. "This is about how comedy throws everything and everyone down a flight of stairs for a laugh. It's about enjoying the anarchy. It's the Marx Brothers, Lenny Bruce, and Jerry Lewis rolled into one."

I hired Korey Kay & Partners to be Comedy Central's advertising agency.

CHAPTER 22

Advertising Politically Incorrectly

I looked forward to working with Korey Kay not only because I knew the agency would create great advertising for us, but also because I felt that I had a lot to learn from Allen Kay himself. After all, he was something of a legend in the advertising business, having created an iconic television commercial for Xerox in 1977.*

One day, while sitting in his office, I confessed to him that I knew very little about advertising. "Don't worry," he said, "I'll teach you everything you need to know. Are you ready?"

"Oh, we're starting now?"

"We are. Take out a blank sheet of paper and write down what I'm about to tell you." I wasn't sure if he was serious. "Listen, if I'm gonna teach you everything you have to know, the least you can do is take notes." I scrambled for a pen and a pad of paper from my briefcase and indicated that I was ready.

---

* The spot featured Brother Dominic, a monk who painstakingly hand copied a sacred manuscript. His superior commends him on his work and asks for five hundred more copies. Brother Dominic uses a Xerox 500 instead of hand copying. When he returns with the copies a short time later, his superior looks to heaven and says, "It's a miracle!"

"Okay, here it is: *First, figure out exactly what you want to say. Then say it in a memorable way.*" I took that down, then looked at him, waiting for more. "That's all you have to know." When I got back to my office, I pinned it to the bulletin board. From that moment on, I evaluated all the advertising I saw, and all the advertising we did, based on this simple rule. What was it trying to say? And did it say it in a way that people would remember?

Our first big advertising campaign was for Bill Maher's *Politically Incorrect.* The show had started to gain an audience and deserved wider attention. The team at Korey Kay came up with a campaign for New York City bus sides that we thought would work. It featured "politically incorrect" comments written on the side of the bus and directed at the bus riders sitting next to the windows. One said, "Does this guy's head look pointy to you?" Each window had a comment. When we launched the campaign and it started appearing on bus sides all over New York City, it created buzz and got some favorable press, just as we'd hoped.

The day after the campaign launched, my assistant came in to tell me that Bill Maher was on the phone. Bill never called me. In fact, I rarely spoke to him except when I was showing visitors around the set.

"Hi Bill. Everything okay?"

"No, everything's not okay. What the fuck were you thinking with those bus ads?"

I guess I'd expected this reaction from Bill, which is why I hadn't shown him the ads in the first place. I did preview the campaign to Mitch Semel, his Programming staff, and the show's producers. They approved. I knew that Bill wasn't likely to just nod and smile, and since we all loved the campaign, I just pressed ahead. Not showing Bill the ads in advance might have been a mistake. Possibly a very big mistake.

I wiped the sweat beads off my upper lip, squeezed the receiver tightly, and hoped my fight-or-flight response would provide some guidance. I could just fall into an orgy of apology, beg Bill to forgive me, and swear that I'd never try a lame-brained stunt like this again. Or, I could stand up to him, defend our ad campaign, and tell him to get back to making his show.

I decided to start with orgy. "Bill, you're probably right, I should have—"

He interrupted. "If you think this is good advertising, then you obviously don't know what the fuck you're doing. I think I do my job well. But if I fucked up, my show would be cancelled, right? And if you fuck up, I think you should be fired. Doesn't that sound fair?

"Um, Bill, I don't think—"

"I'm letting you know that I've already made some calls, and I'm trying to get you fired."

Did I hear him right? As if responding to my thought, he said, "That's right, Art, I'm working on getting you fired. And I won't be sorry to see you go."

"Nobody's firing me for this campaign," I said, my voice taut. "If you don't like the campaign, that's your business, but like you, Bill, I'm doing the best I can. If nothing else, I thought you'd be flattered that we decided to advertise your show. That was my decision. We could have done any of the other shows, but I decided that getting behind *Politically Incorrect* was important and would work for you, for the show, and for the channel."

"I'm going to get you fired," he repeated and hung up.

I pulled the phone away from my ear and glared at it, hoping if I glared hard enough Bill would feel the heat of my anger radiating from his phone. Then I slumped in my chair and thought about how this had happened. I briefly considered that maybe Bill was right, that maybe I did fuck up by not showing him the campaign in advance. But no. He would've killed it, and then we would have spun our wheels for weeks trying to come up with something he liked.

The phone rang and I answered it. "Art, it's Nancy." Nancy Geller was the executive in charge of producing Bill's show. "Bill's so upset about that advertising, you have no idea."

"I just got off the phone with him. I have some idea."

"He's talking about getting you fired. Jesus, Art, you should have shown it to him before it went out." She stopped and waited for me to respond. "Art, are you there?"

"Yeah, I'm here."

"Art, for everyone's sake, you have to include Bill in any decision involving the show." She scolded me for another five minutes. I asked if she was, like Bill, working on getting me fired. "Oh, Art, honey, I would never do that!" She was dripping with sincerity, but it might as well have been sarcasm. "And if I did try to get you fired, I would never tell you. That would just be mean."

Later that day my boss told me that Bill had, in fact, called him and said I should be fired immediately. "I told Bill I had no intention of firing you just because he told me to. But he was insistent, so I said I'd think about it." I laughed a little, but I didn't find much of this funny.

This was my first major ad campaign as head of Marketing. Not only did Bill weigh in with criticism, lots of other people did, too. Everyone had an opinion. That's when I realized that being head of Marketing was different from being head of Programming. Programming required skills and talents that most people felt they didn't have; it was a little mysterious to non-programmers. Marketing was different. Everyone thought they knew what made a good magazine ad, a good billboard, or a good television spot. They felt they had expertise in marketing. Not only that, but my marketing was seen by one hundred times as many people as had seen my programming. As head of Marketing, my work was much more visible and much more open to criticism. And everyone was a critic.

At first, my thin skin was flayed raw by the constant criticism. But eventually I learned to be less defensive. I learned to focus on the next campaign rather than the last one. I learned that while mistakes are inevitable, there's no reason to make the same mistake twice.

CHAPTER 23

And the Winner Is...

Bill may have hated the campaign, but it worked. In the weeks that followed, lots of people saw the ads. The advertising trade press reacted favorably with reviews lauding the creativity and the audacity of the bus sides. And, most importantly, *Politically Incorrect*'s ratings climbed.

A few months later, Allen Kay called with some good news. One of our campaigns had been nominated for an Effie Award. He explained over the phone that an Effie was an advertising industry award that wasn't just about how the ads were written and produced. They also took into account the *effectiveness* of the advertising. I asked him which campaign was nominated, and he told me it was the bus-side campaign for *Politically Incorrect*. I nearly dropped the phone. "Couldn't they have nominated something else we did? Bill Maher gave me so much shit over that campaign. He told me it sucked, remember?"

"Well," Allen said, "looks like you might get the last laugh."

"How? Bill won't even know about the nomination."

Allen laughed. "I can pretty much guarantee he'll know. Bill Maher's hosting the Effie Awards dinner. Maybe we'll get lucky and win the award—in his face! Come to the dinner and we'll see what happens."

A few days before the dinner, I called Allen and told him I was having second thoughts about going, because Bill would be there. Bill and I had been doing a good job of avoiding each other since he'd told me he was trying to get me fired. The idea of seeing Bill at an awards dinner, where people would expect us to be cordial given that we supposedly worked together, made me uncomfortable. "What if he becomes irate all over again? What if he stands onstage and shits on our campaign in front of the entire advertising industry? What if we don't win and he says into the microphone, 'Art, remember when I told you the campaign sucked?' and then asks me to stand so everyone can see me?"

"If he does," Allen said, "I'll stand up with you, and we'll wave to the crowd, heads held high. Okay? See you at the dinner."

On the night of the dinner I walked into the ballroom of the Marriott Marquis hotel in Times Square and scanned the room, hoping to find my assigned table. Allen waved me over to the seat next to him. As the lights dimmed for the award presentations, he whispered to me, "I've got a really good feeling about this."

"Hope you're right," I said. The lights came up on the stage, and there was Bill Maher, looking dapper in a dark suit and blue tie. As the audience applauded, Bill acknowledged them with a smirk.

Bill opened with a short monologue and then started presenting the awards. An hour into the proceedings, our category came up (Best Outdoor Campaign), and I felt my body tense and my palms start to sweat. I never told Bill the campaign was up for an award, so he probably had no idea. He was seeing the nominees for the first time as he read them off the teleprompter. What would Bill Maher say when he learned that the *Politically Incorrect* campaign was in the running?

"And the nominees are...," he began, and as he listed them, a picture of each of the nominated campaigns appeared on the screen behind him. Bill announced our nomination with the same disinterest he'd shown all evening: "Comedy Central's *Politically Incorrect* tune-in campaign; Korey Kay and Partners." Then he paused, turned around, and looked at the picture of our ad on the screen. He turned to the audience. "Now *that's* advertising."

The crowd laughed, and so did Bill, but I knew the crowd didn't really get the joke the way I got it. The laughter subsided, and Bill started to open the envelope. "And the winner is..." My heart was pounding as Bill pulled the card from the envelope, read it, then looked up and smiled. "Korey Kay and Partners for *Politically Incorrect.*" I closed my eyes and said "Yes," then started clapping with the rest of the audience.

Allen patted me on the shoulder and walked briskly to the stage to accept the award. He shook Bill's hand, took the gold statuette, and began his acceptance speech while Bill stood off to one side. "Great advertising happens when a first-rate creative team collaborates with a terrific client," he said, and I took the compliment with a smile. When he finished, Allen bounded back to the table and placed the Effie Award in front of me. "I told you I had a good feeling about this," he said.

At the end of the awards ceremony the lights came up. People started to leave, but our table stayed seated. We stuck around, finishing our coffee and congratulating each other over and over. I didn't want this to end. I felt vindicated. Bill was wrong—it wasn't a terrible campaign. As of that night, it was an award-winning campaign.

From the corner of my eye I saw Bill walking through the crowd toward our table. "Here he comes," I thought. I started to stand up. When he reached our table, Bill looked right at me, nodded slightly, and continued walking without saying a word.

As much as I regretted my tussle with Bill Maher, being acknowledged for my newly acquired marketing chops made the whole thing worth it. At the same time, I knew how important Bill and the show were to Comedy Central. *Politically Incorrect with Bill Maher* had a growing audience, and critics were writing about it. His notoriety helped shine a light on our other signature shows, including *Mystery Science Theater 3000*, which was well on its way to cult status. Bill hated the campaign and that was his prerogative. I still felt that I'd made the right decision by not showing it to him first. I put the Effie Award (a six-inch statue of a shiny gold *E*) on my desk to remind myself, or convince myself, that I'd done the right thing. But it also reminded me of Bill's indignation. Maybe there was something I might have done differently.

CHAPTER 24

From Lemmings to Lemmings

Launching Bill Maher's *Politically Incorrect* was probably the Comedy Central highlight of 1993, although Bill Maher trying to get me fired for our award-winning advertising campaign was, for me, the lowlight. In the meantime, the network was cooking. Comedy Central was becoming a force in stand-up comedy with a stand-up show called *The A-List*, hosted by comedian Richard Lewis. In August, Jerry Seinfeld hosted a ten-hour tribute to his comedy heroes, Abbott and Costello. The network acquired the show *Soap*, starring Billy Crystal.

In April 1994, *Mystery Science Theater 3000* won a Peabody Award for excellence in television. And in July, the British comedy hit *Absolutely Fabulous* premiered on Comedy Central in a twelve-hour marathon to record ratings and critical acclaim.

Behind the scenes, the Buzz Committee continued to stir the comedy pot. At our weekly meeting in mid-July 1993, the seven members of the Comedy Central Buzz Committee were scattered haphazardly around the conference room, trying to come up with the next cool stunt, promotion, contest, or television show that would get us noticed. Two people had their feet on the table, one guy had his head down and appeared to be napping, and none of us had any ideas. Rather than call it quits and go back to our offices, I got up and grabbed yesterday's *New York Post* out of a nearby wastebasket. "Hey, look," I said, "the twenty-fifth anniversary of Woodstock's coming up. Everyone's climbing all over themselves to celebrate."

Vinnie perked up. "They say if everyone who said they were at Woodstock was actually *at* Woodstock, there would have been, like, fifty million people. It's one of the great lies of all time. The check is in the mail, my dog ate my homework, I was at Woodstock."

"I was like fourteen at the time," I added. "My friends and I decided to hitchhike to Woodstock because we loved Jimi Hendrix. We only made it as far as Paramus before we got scared, so we hitched back. It's really only half a lie—I tried to get there, right? For years I told everyone I hitchhiked to Woodstock but didn't make it because they closed the New York Thruway."

"They closed the Thruway?"

"I think so. Actually, I got that from the movie. Then once, at a party, I changed the story and told everyone that I hitchhiked all the way to Woodstock. They were totally impressed, but I immediately felt guilty."

Vinnie said, "Maybe you should find those people at the party and apologize."

"I did. Took me two years, but I tracked everyone down...I'm lying, I didn't do that."

Nobody said anything. Then I had a thought. "Hey, anybody remember the off-Broadway show called *Lemmings*? It was a comedy revue that made fun of Woodstock. I saw it my senior year of high school at some club in Greenwich Village. Some friends and I took the bus into the city, and—"

"Hold on," Vinnie said, "You took a bus into the city to see a comedy show at a club? I thought you told me you were a nerd in high school."

"Yeah, I was," I admitted, "but I was a *comedy* nerd."

•   •   •

Being a nerd in high school meant that I read books that weren't assigned, I played classical piano, and I was in the marching band. That didn't mean I couldn't make people laugh. Being funny enabled me to transcend nerdiness enough to keep me from fading into the gray hallway lockers. Lots of guys were funny. I wasn't sure how well it served everyone else, but I knew what it did for me. It was a way to get the attention of girls. Making the girls laugh was a way to get on their radar. This didn't get me dates or anything, but it gave me hope.

I never consciously attempted to hone my sense of humor, but I listened day and night to comedy albums (Bill Cosby, Nichols and May, Robert Klein, George Carlin) and soon enough found myself using some of their inflections. I liked to tell jokes even though they weren't very popular, except for the dead-baby jokes that enjoyed a renaissance during my high school years.

I didn't repeat dead-baby jokes: too gruesome. Dirty jokes made me laugh, but I felt like I was breaking a commandment if

I told one. My jokes were taken from an old Myron Cohen album I found in my parents' record collection. Cohen's jokes worked for me for two reasons: they were clean, and I could tell these jokes with a Yiddish accent, which I'd perfected thanks to my Russian-born grandmother. My grandmother told me stories with a deeply inflected Yiddish accent that would make Mel Brooks proud. She told me how she had nearly starved during the Great Depression; she told me how the Jews were the chosen people; she cursed the name of Adolf Hitler, spitting on the floor as she said it. Through all of this, the Yiddish accent always made me smile. She ended every story the same way, with a sigh and this small prayer: "As long as you have what to eat." While this never made sense to me because I found my food supply to be at least adequate, I appreciated the syntax and the Yiddish inflection that made *fut* out of *what* and *yeet* out of *eat*. The first joke I ever told with a Yiddish accent was this:

> *Two little old Jewish ladies discussing world politics:*
> *"So, Fut do you tink of Red China?"*
> *"Nice! 'Special if you got a yellow table-clought."*

Telling jokes, and making people laugh in any way I could, allowed me to communicate with people who wouldn't otherwise pay attention to me, starting with girls, but including the jocks, the druggies, the bullies, and anyone who thought it might be a good idea to beat me up for sport. Being funny kept the bullies off my back and let me settle into a safer, more comfortable, and more social high-school experience.

Nothing did more to shape the humor gestalt in those days than *National Lampoon: The Humor Magazine.* The satire and humor were the best I'd ever read. I needed to try writing like that, so a bunch of friends and I started an "underground" satirical news-paper. We called it *The Tongue* because it was one of the few things Kevin Friedland, our "art director," could draw convincingly—and since it was a body part with some relationship to sex, we thought it sounded irreverent enough to nail our underground status. *The Tongue* was dedicated to ridiculing everything about our high school. We took apart the teachers for not giving a shit about their students and the administration for building a bureaucracy that crushed our souls. We railed against in-school suspension. We questioned why the football players got all the girls; that got us in a lot of trouble. Apparently, the football team didn't share our sophisticated philosophy and humor, but fortu-nately we talked our way out of getting beaten up. We published a song called "In-School Suspension Blues." Glenn Harrison and I wrote it in study hall, and it went something like this:

Once I was the winner, the guy with plenty to lose
Now I've lost near all
Got those in-school suspension blues

My tale it is a sad one, I was once Joe Cool
Now my dues I am a-payin'
Got those in-school suspension blues

(Chorus)
I cut class once too often
They picked up all the clues
And now my life's a wastin'
Got those in-school suspension blues

The principal said, "Boy, I heard you like to cruise
Round the hallways during classes"
Got them in-school suspension blues

He said, "Three doors and to the right
Is where you gotta go"
And now I'm in that hellhole
And I'm feeling mighty low

National Lampoon's writing set the standard for our writing, and it was a very high bar. I paid attention to everything they wrote. When they did a record album, I bought it. And when they put on an Off-Broadway show in New York City in the fall of 1973, I alerted *The Tongue* staff. Kevin and Glenn agreed we couldn't miss this. We took an afternoon bus to New York, wandered around Times Square, then took the subway to Greenwich Village. We walked over to the Village Gate and read the poster out front. "Tonight: *National Lampoon's Lemmings*, starring John Belushi and Chevy Chase."

None of us had heard of either Belushi or Chase, but who cared? We bought our tickets and took our seats.

•　　•　　•

"Now I understand what a comedy nerd is," Vinnie said.

"Based on your definition," Ken said, "I was a comedy nerd, too."

Vinnie said, "Enough with high school. We were talking about Woodstock and *Lemmings*."

"Right. It was a show written by the *National Lampoon* guys, and the cast was John Belushi, Chevy Chase, and Christopher Guest.

"It took place at 'Woodshuck, the rock festival of love, peace, and death.' Great songs, takeoffs on Joan Baez, Richie Havens, Dylan. They did an impression of James Taylor singing that makes me laugh just thinking about it. I went home and memorized the words."

"Sing it! I wanna hear James Taylor."

So I started to sing the few verses I remembered:

I'm stuck in this old city now, where living ain't no fun,
Where steel and glass and concrete cancel out the wind and sun,
But I'm thinking of last winter, when we walked hand in hand,
By the trails of the Colorado Rockies.

We had space and love and freedom, We had love enough to spare,
Though we ran out of things to eat and say and do and wear
And the morning of the avalanche,
The Yeti kidnapped Blanche,
And took her to his home up in the Rockies

The baby didn't die until we used up all the wood,
Considering we ate it raw, she tasted pretty good...

"Stop—that's disgusting," Vinnie said. "But funny."

"Yeah," I said. "Everyone at the festival dies at the end... funny."

Then Steve said, "Maybe there's a video or audio recording we could put on."

"What if we produce a revival?" Ken suggested. "Comedy Central presents *National Lampoon's Lemmings*. One night only. That's our tribute to Woodstock. Kind of an anti-tribute."

There it was, the moment I'd been waiting for. Reaching back twenty years to pay tribute to the *National Lampoon,* to Belushi's memory, to my comedy awakening.

We had to get this done quickly if it was going to catch the Woodstock anniversary wave. First, we had to find the script. It turned out that Lorne Michaels, producer of *Saturday Night Live,* had optioned it for television, so we had to get his permission to stage it live. Next, I had to find a way to pay for the production. We were always short of money in those days, and I knew there wasn't any extra lying around, so I removed some planned marketing from my list and scraped up enough money for production. And finally, we needed a star, someone to play the John Belushi role.

I asked Laurie Zaks, our head of Talent, if she had a suggestion. "Chris Farley. He's a star on *SNL,* he's fat like Belushi, and he's a slob like Belushi. He is, for all practical purposes, Belushi. Question is, does he want to do it?" The next day Laurie called to tell me Chris would do it, and he was bringing along two other *SNL* stars, Andy Richter and Tim Meadows.

Finally, we needed a venue. Our first choice was the Village Gate, where the original *Lemmings* had been staged, but we couldn't get it. The next best thing was The Bottom Line, a similarly storied and popular West Village club.

The project, which just a few weeks ago had been a crazy idea, was starting to become real. And people in the business recognized this for what it was—a tribute. John Belushi had died twelve years earlier at the height of his career, and the comedy business missed him. *Lemmings* was a part of comedy history and had launched Belushi and Chevy Chase. The original *Lemmings* writers were flattered by our efforts. Everybody wanted to be a part of it. Everyone wanted to remember and to pay homage.

On the night of the show, I left my office, hailed a taxi, and headed to the Village. From the back of the cab, I looked out the window at Times Square. It didn't seem so different from when Kevin, Glenn, and I had walked through it on our way to the Village Gate in 1973. I told the cab to pull over. I opened the cab door and jumped out into the river of Times Square tourists flowing into the subway, just like we'd done that night twenty years ago.

I arrived a couple of hours before the start of the show. I walked into The Bottom Line, sat down at a table, and tried to appear calm as I watched the crew put some finishing touches on the set. Ken spotted me and came over. "You ready?" I asked him.

"Not even close. But it sure is fun working on a show that opens and closes the same night."

An hour later the audience started arriving and taking their seats. I took a table way in the back in order to give the best seats to the press and other invited notables. We'd sent invitations to all of the old *National Lampoon* writers and the original *Lemmings* cast. I assumed none of them would show up, but I kept glancing at the door to see if I recognized anyone. I told myself it didn't really matter if the *Lampoon* guys came, but deep down I wanted them there.

At ten minutes to show time the house was full. Tom Freston, chairman of MTV Networks, walked in. Several people walked up to greet him, but when he saw me, he stopped talking to them and edged his way through the standing crowd. "Art," he said, "this is really cool." I nodded my agreement and acknowledgement. Tom pointed to the door. "Look, see that tall guy with the long hair walking in? That's Tony Hendra. He wrote this show." Tony didn't sit, he just backed up against the wall and said hello to people who recognized him. A few minutes later I saw Sean Kelly, one of my favorite *Lampoon* writers, talking to Hendra.

Then the lights went down and the show started. Chris Farley lumbered out onto the stage and spoke his first line. Everyone laughed and applauded. They were applauding him, but they were also cheering the way the night brought us all back to that moment in time when John Belushi and Chevy Chase were just a couple of kids doing a show in Greenwich Village. Some people knew the words to the songs and started singing along. Everyone was having a great time, especially Chris Farley and the rest of the performers. I sat in the back, craning my neck to see them.

After the show, I met Hendra, Kelly, and some of the other *National Lampoon* writers whom I'd idolized as a kid. They thanked me, and I thanked them. *New York* magazine did a feature story on the show. When I read it, I felt that we had finally lived up to our name. We were, on that night, Comedy Central.

CHAPTER 25

Spectacular

The phone rang.

It was Sunday morning at eleven. An unlikely time for a phone call, I thought. I looked over at my wife, who was, like me, sitting on the floor, wrapping holiday presents, totally absorbed in trying to tie a ribbon on a freshly gift-wrapped box. She made no move for the phone. It was completely impossible for her not to have heard it, because Carrie's hearing was so much better than mine that I regularly accused her of having spidey senses rather than hearing.

"I'll get it," I said drily.

"Let it ring. It's probably Debbie." This was true. Her friend Debbie called every day with no apparent reason other than to insert herself into the flow of our lives. She started every phone call with the same question: "What's doing?" She said it low and fast, and it came out sounding like "Stuin'." I imagined that even if she were calling to tell us that nuclear war had been declared and we would hear the whistle of Russia's ICBMs any minute, she'd start with "Stuin'?" I liked talking to Debbie. She made me laugh.

I got up and started for the phone in the kitchen. Sitting on the floor was uncomfortable for me, and I noticed as I got up that my knee ached. Maybe I'd kill a few minutes talking to Debbie about nothing before handing the phone to Carrie. But when I picked up the phone, instead of "Stuin'?," it was my boss. "Art."

"Bob. Everything all right?" My grandmother taught me when I was four that if someone called unexpectedly, somebody was dead. She started every phone call with me by asking if everyone in my family was accounted for.

"No, everything isn't all right," Bob said. "We need to talk. Right now."

"Okay..."

"Art, Michael Fuchs doesn't like what you're doing. He thinks your marketing stinks."

"Really? Was he specific? I mean, the last campaign? Our on-air promos, our radio spots? What doesn't he like?"

"He's the chairman of the board. He doesn't have to get specific."

"He told you this?"

"Pretty much in those words. I started to defend you, and our marketing, but you know Michael. He just cut me off."

"Well, maybe we should try to get a better sense of what it is he doesn't like?"

It was at this point that I wondered why Bob was telling me this on a Sunday morning a week before Christmas. Michael Fuchs saying he didn't like something—our programming, our marketing, this show, that show—wasn't exactly unusual or even cause for alarm. Michael's carping about practically everything we did had become part of our working environment. Not that anyone wanted to hear that he was unhappy, but it was a constant drumbeat, and we had learned to live with it.

Bob said, "Michael wants you fired."

Before I spoke again, even though Carrie was out of earshot, I closed the door.

"He told you that? Michael actually said, 'I want Art fired?'"

"Yes."

"I'm stunned. I mean, he never mentioned anything to me at the board meetings. I thought he liked our stuff when we presented it to him. He laughed at the radio spot I played last month, you know, the one where the plane's about to crash and the pilot says, 'Watch Comedy Central, you'll feel better.'"

Bob didn't say anything. He seemed to be letting me get my arms around the enormity of the situation.

"When? I mean, does he want me out tomorrow, or what?" Then it crept up on me, like an uncomfortable feeling that turns out to be a boa constrictor wrapping itself around you. "Bob, are you calling to fire me?"

That's when I started thinking about what being fired would be like. We had one child and planned to have more, so we'd given up our one-bedroom apartment on the Upper East Side and bought a four-bedroom house in the suburbs. A house with a nice piece of property and a thirty-year mortgage. This could be bad.

"Actually, what Michael said was, 'If Art doesn't do something spectacular in the next couple months, I want him out.'"

"Oh. Okay. What does he mean, spectacular?"

"No idea. But I'm pretty sure it means that you ought to spend Christmas coming up with a world-class marketing idea that'll save your job."

Bob and I stayed on the phone for a few more minutes, but nothing he said made me feel any better about this. I was in deep shit, and I had very little time to dig myself out. There was nothing he could do for me, and he wasn't capable of helping me come up with something that would save my hide. I was on my own.

"Thanks for the call, Bob. Merry Christmas."

I opened the door and walked back into the family room. Carrie was still on the floor, surrounded by presents wrapped and yet to be wrapped. The floor was littered with bits of blue paper with menorahs on them and a big sheet of red paper with Santa's disembodied head repeated hundreds of times. Carrie didn't look up. "Who was that?"

"Bob."

"Your boss?" She stopped what she was doing and looked up. "What'd *he* want? Don't tell me you have to go in to work today." For a split second I wondered whether I should spare Carrie by making something up. Maybe I'd do something spectacular, and this would all blow over. "What's the matter? You don't look so good. Did Bob tell you something bad?" I nodded. "What? Tell me."

"He said Michael told him that unless I did something spectacular in the next couple months, I was out."

"Out? What, fired? How can they do that? They can't do that, can they? I mean, you started the channel. I thought you said Michael liked you."

"Yeah," I said, "guess I got that wrong. And yes, they can fire me. Look at all the other people who've gone down in the last couple years. It's like the Russian revolution around Comedy Central. People come to power, and a few months later they get dragged out of the office in the middle of the night and shot. Most of the time they don't see it coming. At least I'm being warned."

Carrie put the present she was holding on the floor next to her. "I hate that place. I hate that they take you for granted, that they treat you like shit." I cleared the present away and sat down next to her, my back against the couch, my head back, my eyes closed.

"I'll just have to come up with 'spectacular.'"

Carrie moved over and put her head on my shoulder and her arm across my chest, and we stayed that way for a few minutes. Then the baby started crying, and Carrie let go of me. I wanted to pull her back, to tell her everything would be okay, not to worry. Instead, I sat where I was. She left the room and hustled upstairs.

•　　•　　•

That night I lay in bed, too agitated to fall asleep.

"You up?" Carrie said in the dark.

"No." I rolled over, away from her.

"What's gonna happen?" she asked. "Are you scared?"

I took a breath, letting my nasal passages and throat emit a subtle vibration that I hoped she would interpret as a legitimate snore. "I know you're up," Carrie said. "I just asked if you were scared."

I didn't try to fake snore my way out this time. "Honey, I've been scared for the last five years. Ever since this whole comedy thing started, I've felt like I was on a roller coaster with nobody else on it. I was screaming, but nobody could hear me."

Carrie took my hand and squeezed it. "The last five years were scary and crazy, but you've done great. You're doing great. What you've built is spectacular."

I winced. "We're gonna have to avoid the word *spectacular* for the next few weeks." Carrie laughed, and I laughed with her. I needed that laugh; it was nice to know that I could still laugh.

"No, really. You've done something great."

But I wondered. "Sleep time," I said, closing my eyes and hoping the world would quietly slide away, like a big wave after it breaks on the beach. Slide away and leave me safe and dry.

Carrie said, "One more thing. Whatever happens, I'm with you."

I smiled and drifted off.

CHAPTER 26

Get Me the Buzz Committee

The next morning I woke up exhausted and considered calling in sick, but I decided it would be better to go to work than to mope around the house stewing about Bob's phone call.

Bob held a staff meeting, our last one before the Christmas break. He came in late and sat at the head of the table. I sat next to him as usual, my notebook open, my pen poised, hoping I wasn't telegraphing my anxiety to anyone in the room. Bob was handling an orange Koosh ball. I sometimes tried to divine Bob's mood from the size and color of the Koosh ball, but I had learned that what was more telling was how he handled it. He squeezed it when he was nervous or upset. He tossed it when he felt in control. Today he was alternately tossing and squeezing.

Laurie Zaks started talking before she even sat down. "Guess what? We got Dennis." She didn't have to say Dennis Miller. Everyone knew she'd been after him for months to host the upcoming *State of the Union: Undressed,* our third. Getting him was a big deal.

We all looked at Bob to see if he approved. "How much?"

"Bob, aren't you gonna say, 'Good job getting Dennis?' He's on fire since his HBO special." Listening to Laurie talk to Bob was always a treat, because no matter how edgy Bob was, Laurie kept talking to him like they were flirting. She stood there with her hands on her hips, tall in her black high heels, looking sideways at Bob and smiling.

Bob said, "I'll say good job when you tell me how much."

"You're no fun," she said and sat down, scowling. "Just a little over budget, but Bob, he's so worth it."

"Okay, we'll come back to this. Let's hear what else is going on."

During the meeting Bob didn't mention our weekend conversation, and he didn't say anything about it when we stood up to leave. He looked over at me and tossed me the Koosh ball. "How ya doing, kiddo?" I tossed it back.

"Fine," I said. I was confused by Bob's change in tone from yesterday's phone call. Maybe he felt sorry for me. It was hard for me to tell whether Bob was a great guy or not. I wanted him to be a great guy all the time. When our baby was born, he sent over a huge black-and-white panda, four feet tall. He ran a crawl on Comedy Central announcing the birth, so that our thirty million subscribers would share in my joy. Bob could be so warm and generous sometimes, and so off-putting other times, that I was constantly trying to figure out where I stood with him.

"Good," he said and walked away. I watched as Bob, and everyone else, walked out of the conference room.

I had ten minutes until my next meeting, and it was in the same conference room. No sense going back to my office, so I just sat there, swiveling in the chair, waiting for the people to come in. Vinnie, recently made a vice president of Programming, showed up first.

"Art! Hey, you look like shit. This is the Buzz Committee, right? Or is this a funeral?"

I smiled. "Funeral. Possibly mine. But first, Buzz Committee."

This was my favorite meeting of the week, because it was fun. Two years had passed since the Buzz Committee first convened to make more noise, get more press, and make Comedy Central famous. Since then, the Committee had never missed an opportunity to insert Comedy Central's point of view into the national conversation. Like the time NBC announced that after some thirty-plus years on the air, Johnny Carson would end his run as the king of late night. Millions of people were expected to tune in to Johnny Carson's last show, and everyone was talking about it. The Buzz Committee got right on it. The meeting went like this:

Me: *Hey, Carson's last show's coming up. We doing anything for that?*

Vinnie: *Yeah, we gotta do something. He is comedy. We gotta honor him.*

Ken: *How about a special. Feature all the comedians he showcased for the first time, who got their start on* The Tonight Show. *Joan Rivers, Richard Pryor, Seinfeld.*

Steve: *Yeah, great idea, but how we gonna pull that off? It sounds like a clip show, and those clips are expensive.*

Vinnie: *Thanks, Steve. Who invited a lawyer to this meeting anyway? Mr. Cold Bucket of Water, Attorney at Law…*

Steve: *I keep your ass out of jail, remember?*

Ken: *Everyone in the country's gonna be watching.*

Me: *Yeah, including the guys in our control room. They'll be so absorbed they'll probably forget to run our programming.*

Ken: *Right. We'll all be watching. What if we don't run anything that night?*

Me: *Go dark? No signal? Test pattern?*

Vinnie: *No, we put up a sign that says nobody's here at Comedy Central because we're watching Johnny.*

Ken: *Love it. A sign. Like a big card, with Magic Marker on it standing on a stool. Perfect.*

Me: *What does it say?*

Ken: *How about: "We're all watching Johnny Carson's last show. You should, too." Something like that.*

Me: *Great. Let's do it. Who's gonna break this to Ad Sales?*

We figured Ad Sales would hate it because it meant that they'd have no advertising spots for a couple of hours. But they surprised us: they went out and sold a sponsorship to McIlhenny Tabasco sauce. So we put out a press release saying Comedy Central was going dark to honor Johnny Carson on the night of his last show. The press loved it; we were the sidebar to every Johnny Carson article leading up to the finale. And that night while his last show aired, all that was on Comedy Central was the sign saying, "We're all watching Johnny Carson's last show. You should be, too!" propped up on a stool with a spotlight on it. Beside the sign was a bottle of Tabasco sauce.

The best part was that during his show, Johnny said, "I'd like to thank Comedy Central for going dark tonight in honor of my last show."

That was spectacular. Now I needed the Buzz Committee to come up with something spectacular that would keep me from getting fired. And fast.

. . .

Vinnie sat down at the conference table. He wore a checked shirt and a red tie with gold stars on it that looked like it had been tied in the dark. Nobody massacred an outfit like Vinnie. He was like a little kid who'd landed in corporate.

Vinnie said, "Whatsa matter? Somebody yell at you? C'mon, this is Buzz Committee, we gotta get loose and have some fun."

"Fun's off my list," I said.

Ken walked in and said, "Fun's off your list? At least you have a list. Some people don't even have that, you lucky dog, you." I managed a small laugh, but it was immediately crushed by circumstances. Ken noticed. "Uh-oh. Something's seriously wrong."

I sat up straight in my chair and said, "No, just didn't sleep much last night. The baby kept us up. I'm just cranky. Give me a minute to rally."

Steve Mark, our lawyer, came in and positioned his wheelchair next to me. "Art, you look like shit. Bob on your case about something?"

"Okay, I look like shit, I got that. Now we'll go around the room and comment on how everyone else looks. Let's start with Steve."

"Steve looks like shit!" Ken said. "All right, I see your point, Art. We all look like shit."

"Thank you, Ken. Now, does anybody have any ideas?"

Nobody did. Like most Buzz Committee meetings, there was lots of talk, lots of laughs, but nothing concrete to show for it. That was the nature of the game. On top of everything else, it was a few days before Christmas and nobody really felt like starting anything that might involve working through the holiday. While I understood, I needed these guys to come up with a breakthrough idea, but I didn't know how to get them to focus. If I recounted my phone call with Bob, they'd probably rally around me, but I knew I couldn't.

That phone call had to stay between Bob and me. Unless...

"Hey, before everybody goes, I need to tell you something."

"Is this when you say how much you love us?" Vinnie asked.

"Sort of. I've been doing some thinking, you know, about how great things are going and how you guys are such a big part of that. And it's gotten where I can always count on this group to come up with The Big Idea. But now it's time for us to really show off."

"Whaddya mean, show off?"

Where was I going with this? I hoped something would come to me.

"I want us to explode into next year with something...*spectacular*. Even if it's crazy or costs a boatload of money. I need a Buzz Committee blue-ribbon special we can look back on in thirty years and say, 'Remember that? How cool was that? That was us. We did that.'" For the first time at a Buzz Committee meeting, nobody came back with a snappy remark.

Finally, Ken said, "Jesus, could you set the bar a little higher?"

"No, I think that'll do it. See you guys around campus." Everyone filed out of the room, and nobody was talking.

When I walked into the hall, the head of Ad Sales walked by. "Hey, Art. What's wrong? You look like shit."

I dragged myself home that night. The train was late, I couldn't get a seat, and some idiot was so drunk from his office Christmas party that he puked all over the guy next to him. When I walked in the door, I realized how good it felt to be there. I dropped my briefcase next to the couch. Carrie was sitting there with the baby on her lap. I sat down next to them and gave them both a hug at the same time. Carrie asked if I was okay, and I said I was fine, just tired. I really didn't feel like talking. As I stood up and headed for the stairs, Carrie asked if I'd come up with any ideas.

"Nope." I continued up the stairs to my bedroom. When I got there, I took off my tie and jacket and flopped face down on the bed. It was dark, soft, and soothing, so I stayed that way until Carrie called me down to dinner.

CHAPTER 27

Emergency!

One week later, Ken knocked on my office doorframe.

"Hey," he said. "I think we need an emergency meeting of the Buzz Committee."

"What's the emergency?"

"I have something. A big idea. Maybe."

I checked my watch. "Okay, round up the usual suspects." A few minutes later, Vinnie, Steve, and the rest of the Buzz Committee were in my office. I said, "Ken's got an idea. Ken?"

Ken stood up and he was excited. "It's the germ of an idea, anyway. I was watching the news last night, and that idiot Newt Gingrich—"

"What idiot Newt Gingrich?" somebody asked.

"You know, the guy who wrote the Contract with America a few weeks ago?"

I nodded. "I remember. There were full-page ads with the headline 'Contract with America,' like it was the Declaration of Independence or something, saying what the Republicans would do if they got elected."

Ken pulled out a piece of newsprint from his pocket and unfolded it on my desk. "I got a copy here. Check it out," Ken said, as we huddled around the desk to look at it. Ken started reading aloud. "'A Contract with America. As Republican Members of the House of Representatives and as citizens seeking to join that body we propose not just to change its policies, but even more important, to restore the bonds of trust between the people and their elected representatives. That is why, in this era of official evasion and posturing, we offer instead a detailed agenda for national renewal...'"

Vinnie was getting impatient. "Enough with the civics lesson. Is there an idea here or what?"

"Yes, there's an idea here," Ken said. "We do our own 'Comedy Central Contract with America.' Like, we say, 'The Republicans' Contract was a good start, but we have a few policy prescriptions of our own that'll *really* make a difference.' Kinda like Swift's 'Modest Proposal.'"

"Whaddya mean, Swift's 'Modest Proposal?'"

Ken let out a sigh. "Vinnie, couldn't you have just paid attention in English class? Jonathan Swift wrote "A Modest Proposal," which suggested that poor Irishmen should consider selling their children to the upper classes to use as food. Then they wouldn't be poor anymore."

The room was quiet. Somebody said, "I like it. We write our own 'Contract with America' that makes fun of the Republicans' Contract with America—but what do we do with it after it's written?"

"Full-page ad in the *New York Times*," I said. *Right in Michael's face.* "But it's gotta be really good, really funny. Can we do that, Ken?"

"As the head writer for Comedy Central, I have every confidence in the world that there's a pretty good chance we'll fuck it up."

"That's the spirit!" Vinnie said. Everyone started to leave.

"Wait." They stopped and gave me a "now what?" kind of look. "Why are we putting the 'Comedy Contract' out there? I mean, is it just a satire? A full page in the *Times*, that's, I don't know, a hundred thousand dollars?"

Steve said, "Make it an ad for the channel. Watch Comedy Central."

"Yes! YES!" Vinnie was screaming. "Dennis Miller's doing the *State of the Union: Undressed* end of January. We make it a full-page tune-in ad for *Undressed*!"

Everyone looked at me. Was this it? Was it big enough? Could we make it funny? Would it work? I nodded slowly and started to smile. "Let's do it. Ken, you're in charge." Not only would this be a great ad, but it would be another irreverent political satire courtesy of Comedy Central. It was perfect.

Ken's work was brilliant. We all helped, but he did most of it. The real Contract with America listed ten laws Republicans promised to pass in their first hundred days in office, and while some of them probably sounded pretty funny to the Democrats, they weren't nearly as funny as the six Ken came up with. We sent the whole thing over to our ad agency, and they did the full-page ad mock-up for the *Times*. The mock-up came back with a note from the agency's creative team: "We love this."

Ken and Vinnie sat in my office and stared at the mock-up of the ad on the coffee table.

"Is it funny?" Ken asked. "I thought it was funny, but the more I look at it the less funny it gets."

"No, it's funny." Vinnie said. "My wife thought it was funny. And she never laughs at anything."

"Being married to you? Yeah, I can see that," Ken said.

"Now we have to sell it to Bob," I said.

Vinnie gave me a look. "Whaddya mean *we* have to sell it? Isn't that your job?" Vinnie was right. It was my job to sell it to Bob, and I was on my own.

Bob's office was on the other side of the building, so it took a few minutes to walk over. I was hoping an opening line would come to me before I got there, but nothing seemed right. I knocked on his open door and stuck my head in. "Got a minute for me?"

"Sure, c'mon in." He picked up a green-and-red Koosh ball, and I wondered if he'd chosen Christmas colors for the holidays. He threw it up in the air, which meant he was feeling confident. I waited to see if he squeezed it. He threw it up in the air again. Perfect.

"I think I have something that will impress Michael."

"Really? That was fast. Is that it?" He gestured at the ad mock-up in my hand. I took a look at it, as if I were making sure I'd brought the right one. I knew that if there was one spelling error or anything else wrong, Bob would crucify me. I suddenly realized I hadn't proofread the damn thing. "Yes, this is it."

Bob held out his hand. I looked at the ad again. Bob said, "Art, are you gonna let me see it?"

"Give me one more minute, I'm just checking something," I said and gave it a quick read. It was perfect. A weight lifted from me. Whether Bob liked it or not, I was proud of it. I walked over to his desk and as I handed it to him, I said, "The Buzz Committee did this. I think it's great."

Bob took it from me and started reading. Then he smiled. Then he laughed. Then he really laughed, loud and hard. "This is hilarious," he said.

"I think we should do this as a full-page ad in the *Times*. That way Michael won't miss it. We'll get noticed, and we may even get some press."

Bob thought about it for a second and then nodded. "Yeah. I think that's good. I think that's real good. C'mon, let's go show it around."

Bob got up and walked the halls, showing it to anyone who passed. He went over to Ad Sales and showed them. Everyone agreed it was a great way to advertise our upcoming "State of the Union" show with Dennis Miller.

Maybe I was saved.

A Comedy Central Contract with America

HERE AT COMEDY CENTRAL, WE THINK THE CONTRACT WITH AMERICA WAS A GOOD START—IF YOU LIKE HALFWAY MEASURES. THAT'S WHY WE PLEDGE, IN WRITING, TO WORK FOR THESE *COMMON SENSE REFORMS*:

1. **Stop violent criminals before they commit their first crime.** We all know who breaks the law in this country. As soon as they're too old for orphanages, let's get 'em into the prisons where they belong.

2. **Get back to work, grampa.** Enough with this Social Security foolishness. Either you old people start earning a living like the hard-working middle class, or it's off to prison for you.

3. **Build a strong national defense with really big weapons and death rays and stuff.** If there's one thing we like more than prisons, it's really big weapons.

4. **Give American industry a break.** What is it that makes waste "toxic"? Just how low is a "minimum" wage? When do working conditions become "dangerous"? Do these questions really need to be answered?

5. **Combine congressional term limits with the death penalty.** Congressman may run for as many terms as they wish. But should they run for re-election and lose, they die.

6. **Three strikes and you're out.** Well, *duh!*

We further pledge to once again bring you
**"STATE OF THE UNION: UNDRESSED" hosted by
Dennis Miller**—ruthlessly live play-by-play commentary during
the President's speech. **JANUARY 24TH, 9 PM
EASTERN, 6 PM PACIFIC, ON COMEDY CENTRAL.**
Followed by a special live edition, direct from our nation's capital
(Washington D.C.), of "Politically Incorrect with Bill Maher."

DOING OUR PART FOR A NEW AMERICA.

CHAPTER 28

The Board Meeting

Christmas came and went and so did New Year's. Having put a plan in place, Carrie and I could enjoy the holidays with family and friends as we'd planned. The ad was scheduled to run on January 18, and just by chance there was a Comedy Central board meeting the following day. Michael would be at the board meeting, so I would get, at the very least, an indication of whether my gambit had worked. But my fantasy was that Michael wouldn't wait until the board meeting to heap praise upon me.

In my fantasy, I pictured Michael, Italian loafers perched on his vast glass sheet of a desk, little gold shoe buckles casting sparkles of light on the beige wall of his office, putting his cup of coffee down and turning the page to find...our "Contract with America!" And then laughing so hard he would yell to his assistant, "Merav, did you see this in today's *Times*?" And Merav (always so proper and refined, I'm sure she had a graduate degree in English from Oxford or something) saying, "Yes, Michael, it's quite funny, isn't it?" And Michael responding, when his laughter stopped, "Get Bob Kreek on the phone. I want to find out who did this so I can congratulate them." That was my little success fantasy. I replayed it in my mind hundreds of times before the ad ran.

Nobody at Comedy Central took board meetings lightly. We prepared weeks in advance, and the entire company was involved. The first half of the board meeting was our chance to show off our recent programming and marketing, our press and promotion, our revenues, and our myriad successes since the previous board meeting. Bob was the emcee who introduced his department heads, then sat down and hoped for the best. We would put our trepidation aside, stand up and show off our accomplishments as if every promo was life-changing, every advertisement was transcendent, and every new program a surefire hit. The board then took the second half of the meeting to offer their views, pointing out that try as we might, we just weren't blowing them away with our genius and hard work.

While everyone on the board was a big-deal executive from either Viacom or HBO, there was only one person we all hoped to impress: Michael. Like for Liberace and Garbo before him, a single name was sufficient. There was only one Michael in the business, and everyone knew who he was. Actually, I liked him. Even after I heard from Bob that Michael had it in for me, I couldn't bring myself to call him names or get angry with him. Mostly I just wanted him to think I was doing a decent job.

Comedy Central had two conference rooms, the small one and the big one, and, naturally, the board met in the big one. It had lush, dark-green carpeting; dark, wood-paneled walls; and a long dark mahogany conference table polished to a spit-shine that seemed to glow warmly even under the fluorescent lights. The day before, several of us made sure the room was ready. With the enthusiasm of the decorating committee the night before the senior prom, we dressed the conference room with Comedy Central posters, banners, charts, and graphs. We rolled in a couple of TV monitors and made sure the flip chart wouldn't fall over just because someone jabbed at it to make a point. Sometimes we placed gifts for the board members at each of their seats. As this was post-Christmas, they'd each already received a gift from us (delivered to their offices by messenger), so we thought having another gift at the meeting might be misinterpreted as brown-nosing. Nevertheless, we put a small gift (a framed production cell from a recent animated cartoon we'd done) at each of their places before we left for the evening.

The next morning I went to the conference room at 9:30 to make sure that everything was ready and that nothing had fallen off the walls. The meeting was scheduled for ten. I dropped my notebook, budget, and presentation materials on the conference table and waited for everyone else to arrive. Moments later Bob and the rest of the Comedy Central execs came in and sat down. Board members trickled in. When Michael arrived, you could feel the power dynamic change, as if the whole room just tilted his way.

I watched Michael as he entered. He was trim, fit, and well dressed. He smiled, a genuine smile that said he enjoyed what he did most of the time, and that he genuinely appreciated people. While he was said to be capable of eviscerating those who had failed him, I had never witnessed this personally.

Michael greeted the other board members and Bob. When he sat down at the head of the table, I noticed for the first time that he had a copy of the *New York Times* with him. He unfolded the newspaper and opened it to our full-page ad. "Everyone see this?"

Most people at the table nodded, but nobody ventured an opinion. "Pretty good," he said. Then he looked over at me.

"I'm glad you like it," I said.

Michael wasn't done. "Art, when you do something like this, when you take out a full-page ad in the *Times*, you could give me the courtesy of a preview, or at least a phone call, so I can be ready. I had no idea this was coming."

He held my gaze. I could feel the blood rising through my torso, my neck, my ears, my face, as I flushed with...embarrassment? Humiliation? But then, despite the intensity threatening to ignite the room, despite the urgent need to respond to Michael in a way that defused the situation, I just sat there and held Michael's gaze. I was confused: Why was Michael so pissed at me? After all, it wasn't my job to call Michael and tell him something was coming. It was Bob's responsibility. He was the president. Bob should have been the one playing stare-down with Michael, not me.

On the other hand, maybe I should have asked Bob whether he thought it would be prudent to check with Michael about taking out a full-page ad in the *New York Times*. But—no—I wanted it to take everyone by surprise. Surprise would make it funnier. And there was another point in my favor: this was essentially a tune-in ad for a Comedy Central special. Why would anyone tell Michael about it in advance? Hasn't he got more important things to do than preview a Comedy Central tune-in ad? No, I decided, there was no reason for anyone to give Michael a heads up about the ad. I was being unjustly thrashed in front of the board and in front of my boss.

And where was Bob in all this? If I were Bob watching a stare-down contest between the chairman and one of my devoted and most valued employees, I hoped I would say, "Sorry, Michael, that was *my* oversight, not Art's. I should have called. Lesson learned."

I would say that if I were Bob, wouldn't I? I mean, *what the fuck*!

"Sorry, Michael," I said.

Michael gave me an almost imperceptible nod before looking away. Then he turned to Bob. "Can we get started?"

As soon as Michael broke off his stare, I dropped my gaze to the table. My presentation notes were in front of me, and I started shuffling them like a TV news anchor during the credits. Nobody was looking at me, but everyone was watching.

"Well," said Bob, "we might as well start with Art's presentation." Start with me? I wanted to scream back, Can we *please* swing the spotlight to someone else? Give my flop sweat a few minutes to evaporate? Instead, I stood up, buttoned my jacket, and carried my notes and my presentation slides to the head of the conference table. I stood there for a moment looking at the fifteen or so people gazing back at me, frozen in their seats, giving the room an eerie quiet, like I was looking at a photograph of the meeting, not the actual meeting. When I turned on the overhead slide projector, the click of the switch sounded like a gunshot. "Thanks, Bob," I said, fighting to keep the sarcasm and snottiness from leaking into my voice. I must have failed, because as soon as I said it, everyone started laughing. Except me.

I put up my first slide, which showed my budget for the coming year and roughly how I planned to spend it. Nobody asked any questions, so I moved on to the entertainment portion of my presentation, the television commercials for the upcoming Dennis Miller *State of the Union: Undressed* special. I popped the videotape into the machine and pressed play. Even though I'd checked everything to make sure the television and the VCR were hooked up properly and operating smoothly, I knew there was no guarantee it would work now. "Don't fuck me," I said to the video equipment under my breath, and two seconds later Dennis Miller's face filled the screen and his voice took over the room. Phew. When the commercials ended, everyone clapped. I said thank you and sat down, relieved that my part of this was over and had gone well. I looked up, and Bob caught my eye. He mouthed, "Good job." I mouthed "Thanks" back.

I settled into my chair and waited for the meeting to end. When it did, instead of hanging around and chatting, I just collected my stuff and walked back to my office.

The rest of the week went by without drama. Bob said nothing more about Michael's "spectacular" directive. Finally I asked Bob if he'd gotten any signal from Michael regarding my fate. "Michael hasn't said anything more about it," Bob said. "Let's just enjoy the quiet." Maybe the storm had passed.

In the meantime, we were busy with the upcoming *State of the Union: Undressed*, the special advertised in the Comedy Contract ad. We usually broadcast live from our New York studio, but Dennis Miller wanted to stay in LA, so a bunch of us were going to fly out to oversee things. I was glad to get on a plane and concentrate on making television. I could put the events of the last few weeks behind me. Normally I wasn't an LA fan, but the mere thought of trading the battleship-gray gloom of mid-January New York City for a couple of warm, sunny days in a town where nobody knew the meaning of the word stress (well, pretended not to know) made me feel just a bit better.

CHAPTER 29

Dennis Miller: "Yer in trouble."*

"Okay, people, we go live in five, four, three...Cue graphic open."

The director's voice was calm as everyone in the television control room watched the monitor. Whatever the director commanded actually happened a split second later, so the animated show title swept over the newsroom-style set, visible on the giant monitor in front of him. The voice of Penn Jillette, the talking half of the famous magic act Penn & Teller, and also the official voice of Comedy Central, boomed from the speakers. "Welcome to Comedy Central's *State of the Union: Undressed...* with your host, Dennis Miller."

Laurie Zaks sat next to me at a long table in the back of the darkened control room on the fourth floor of an unassuming building in Burbank, California. In front of us sat rows of people at their long tables, some with headphones, all with schedules and notepads in front of them, all intensely focused on the big television screen on the wall. The large screen was surrounded by lots of smaller monitors, each with a different camera shot on them. One monitor showed the live feed of President Bill

* Get it? Urine trouble.

Clinton's upcoming State of the Union Address to Congress. President Clinton had yet to appear. The news feed, the same one showing on all the networks, showed the senators and congressmen talking, laughing, and waving at each other in the House of Representatives chamber as they waited for the big entrance. The nervous excitement in the Capitol building was nothing compared to the tension in the control room.

"Ready camera two...go camera two." The shot that had been on the small monitor labeled "Camera Two" was now on the large screen. Dennis Miller, a comedian with several HBO specials under his belt, sat at the anchor desk. And proudly pasted to the anchor desk was the Comedy Central logo, like we were NBC News or something.

"Hello everyone, I'm Dennis Miller, and this is the *State of the Union: Undressed, '96.*"

This was the first time Dennis was hosting the *State of the Union: Undressed.* The host had to provide a running comedic commentary on the president's speech live as it was being delivered, something even the most quick-witted comics found challenging. But Al Franken's performance in our first *State of the Union: Undressed* was so good we had decided to attempt this high wire act annually. The show got better every year.

Given our track record, I was nervous and excited. I wanted this to be our best *Undressed* ever. I whispered to Laurie, "I hope this works."

"Don't worry," she whispered back. "Dennis is great. The rehearsals were funny. When I talked to him a few minutes ago in makeup he was totally psyched."

"Yeah, but it's live." I knew that doing live television was working without a net—anything could happen, and a lot of times it did.

"Relax, Art. We've done this before. What could go wrong?"

The history of live television offered countless examples of what could go wrong. One of my favorite disasters was a live TV commercial for a Timex waterproof watch. It began with an onscreen announcer in a trench coat earnestly describing the action as technicians fastened the watch to the blade of an outboard motor propeller, dunked the propeller into a clear tank of water, and started the motor. What better way to bring to life the Timex slogan "It takes a licking but keeps on ticking!" When they stopped the engine and lifted it out of the tank, the watch had disappeared. The poor announcer sputtered into the microphone about how it must have flown out of the tank; how he'd witnessed it work several times in rehearsal; how he was sure wherever it was, the watch was still ticking. Hilarious. But still, a cautionary tale.

Dennis was on the air warming up the television audience while everyone waited for President Clinton to show up. His commentary stayed close to what he had written and rehearsed until President Clinton came into the chamber and began making his way toward the podium. "Here comes the president," Dennis said. "He's shaking hands with the senator from Iowa...Whoa, look at that bald spot...might want to get some minoxidil on that, Senator..."

Laurie stood up and smoothed her trademark black pencil skirt with her hands. "C'mon, let's watch from the other room." We walked across the hall. There was a couch and chairs arranged in front of a television mounted high on the wall. When we sat down the president was still walking down the aisle, laughing, shaking hands, and occasionally hugging someone, and Dennis jumped on every opportunity with something cynical, sarcastic, or just silly.

"Whoa, Mr. President, you're supposed to shake her hand, not hold on to it and ask her what she's doing later. You've got an address to give. Focus."

Dennis was doing fine. His style, confident with a touch of wonder and a dash of sarcasm, was perfect for the *State of the Union: Undressed*. I sat back and relaxed.

I watched the show as a television executive, observing the shots, keeping an eye on pacing, noting the minor gaffes and how they were resolved by the professionals in the control room. I looked at my watch and wondered if Clinton would set a record for longest State of the Union Address ever. We'd been on the air, live, with no breaks, for well over an hour. It's gotta end soon, I thought.

"Oh, shit," Laurie said.

"What...what's wrong?"

"You didn't hear what Dennis just said?"

"No, I kinda drifted off. What happened?"

"He said, 'I have to take a leak real bad.'"

"What? On the air? The audience heard him say he has to take a leak?"

"Oh, shit." She got up and flew out of the room. I watched Dennis get up and leave the set, but the camera didn't follow him out. Fortunately, or unfortunately (it wasn't yet clear), his headset stayed on, and Dennis kept talking. The viewers were hearing every word Dennis said even after he left the studio.

"Oh, man, where's the bathroom?" Dennis had stopped the comedy rant. Like me, he seemed to be fighting back panic. "There's gotta be a men's room around here somewhere. Or a women's room, I'd settle for that."

I watched the TV monitor, hoping Dennis wouldn't say anything else about this on the air, but his voice continued to crackle from the speaker.

"I can't find a bathroom. Hold on...hold on. This'll have to do. Sorry, everybody, I'll be back to the president's speech in just a few...seconds."

All I could do was hope Laurie came through again and fixed this, even though I wasn't quite sure yet what had to be fixed. Dennis said nothing for a few moments while the president spoke and the dignitaries applauded. The speech sounded hollow without Dennis's commentary filling in the pauses. I was still in my seat, leaning forward, my fingers digging into the armrest, waiting for Dennis to say something. Finally his voice-over resumed.

"Ahhh, that's better. My bladder lives to fight another day."

I opened the door and looked down the hall in time to see Dennis disappear into the studio. Laurie walked back to where I was standing. She was looking right at me, but I couldn't tell if she was calm or just trying to hold it together.

"See that garbage can?" I looked past her, then nodded. "Dennis just peed into that garbage can. On national television."

"Audio only," I said. "Nobody saw anything. Audio only."

I stood there and looked at the unassuming garbage can down the hall, sitting right outside the studio. It was gray plastic and waist high, one of those trash cans with a domed top and a plastic swinging door you pushed open to throw away the garbage.

"How exactly did he pee into that thing?" I whispered.

"You don't wanna know," Laurie said.

I wondered if I should do anything. Like maybe take out the garbage.

Someone pushed open the control room door. "Laurie, phone call for you."

Laurie looked at me, rolled her eyes, and said, "I better take this. It's probably his manager."

Better you than me, I thought, and followed her in.

President Clinton continued for another twenty minutes, and Dennis kept going like the peeing thing had never happened. It had to be on his mind, but he didn't mention it. He'd just slid back into his seat and picked up where he'd left off.

Finally the speech ended, and Dennis wrapped the show with a very funny "analysis" of the address. Laurie was already on her way to the studio to tell Dennis he had done great. Dennis, still on the monitor during the credit roll, pretended to read his notes the way a real television news anchor would. The broadcast ended, and we were off the air. All of us in the control room clapped, the way people on an airline clap on landing after a turbulent flight. Dennis, still visible on the monitor, ripped off his headset, slammed it onto the desk, and stormed out of the camera frame.

I jumped up and raced into the hall just in time to see the studio door fly open. Laurie was waiting for him with her biggest smile.

"Dennis, that was—"

"Fuck!" Dennis screamed, "Oh, God, what have I done? Fuck, fuck, fuck."

"No, you were great," Laurie said, but Dennis was gone. He rushed down the hall past Laurie and me and ducked into the men's room. Laurie and I followed him and stood outside the men's room door.

"Dennis?" Laurie said.

"Go away," was the petulant reply from within the men's room. "Leave me alone."

"Dennis, just come out," Laurie said, her voice calm. "It's fine, really. I talked to your manager. Everything's fine, you were fantastic, really funny." That got no response. Laurie looked over at me and said, "You have to go in there and talk to him."

"Me? You're the head of Talent—why me?"

"Because it's a fucking men's room, and I draw the line there." Laurie backed up and gestured toward the men's room door. "Go on. Talk to him. Get him to calm down."

I muttered "I don't believe this" under my breath and pushed open the men's room door.

Dennis was sitting on the floor between the row of sinks and the stalls, his back against the wall, his head down, and his hands over his face.

"Fuck, what have I done? I just killed my career. It's over." His head hung down.

"C'mon, Dennis, don't turn this into a catastrophe," I said.

"Catastrophe, yes, yes, that's the word. This is a catastrophe."

"You were great out there."

"Art, I took a leak into a garbage can. On TV. In front of what, two, three million people?"

"*Audio only*," I said, hoping he was right and there had been three million viewers. I was head of Marketing, so three million viewers would mean my advertising campaign had hit it out of the park.

"C'mon, Dennis. Stand up, wash your face, and let's get out of here and get a drink. Really, it was fine. It went by so fast probably no one even noticed."

"I took a leak in a garbage can on national television. My career is FUCKED."

"You guys okay in there?" Laurie was still standing outside the door.

"We're fine," I shouted. "We're coming out." I knelt down and looked at Dennis. He took his face out of his hands. "Dennis, time to go, man."

I stood up, and he pushed himself off the men's room floor. "You sure it wasn't that bad?"

I clapped a hand on his shoulder, buddy like. "I guarantee it."

Dennis slapped some water on his face, grabbed a paper towel, and mopped his face dry. We walked into the hallway. "Dennis." Laurie gave him a hug. "You feel better now?"

"I guess. Yeah, a little better. You think it was okay? Peeing didn't torpedo my career?"

"Not a chance," she answered, smiling. "Most people probably didn't even notice. It was a great performance. You killed."

Just then, a young woman who worked for Laurie hurried toward us. "Guess what? The switchboard's lighting up like a Christmas tree—tons of people are calling about Dennis peeing!"

CHAPTER 30

What the Hell Is Going On Here?

I returned to New York from LA feeling good about the *State of the Union: Undressed with Dennis Miller*: the ratings were great, the critics were kind, and Dennis Miller's career was not derailed by peeing on TV in front of millions of people (audio only). And so far, my career hadn't been derailed, either. Before I left for LA, Bob had suggested we enjoy the "quiet" and settle back into work assuming the worst had passed and I would be keeping my job.

But I soon realized I couldn't recover my equilibrium without knowing for sure. Michael wasn't one to traffic in idle threats. He'd been unhappy with one of the programmers several months earlier, and that programmer was swiftly dispatched. Had I been spared or just given a temporary reprieve?

The mood at Comedy Central seemed to be darkening. Something ominous was afoot. Nothing anyone could put a finger on. Maybe it was the increase in hushed hallway conversations and closed doors. Or the exchange of glances around the table at staff meetings when Bob seemed more agitated than usual. It was starting to drive me crazy.

I decided to ask Steve Mark what he thought. I had to talk to him about a contract anyway, so I walked down the hall to his office.

He was on the phone but signaled for me to wait. When he hung up, I started badgering him about a contract I needed. It was good-natured badgering, because I loved Steve. Not only was he a good lawyer, he was always willing to back me up whenever I wanted to push the boundaries of contracts or good taste. And he and I talked a lot about almost everything: his life, my life, his kids, my kids, his hopes and dreams, my hopes and dreams.

Steve traveled by wheelchair, but that didn't slow him down in any arena. He drove his car through midtown Manhattan with the ease and skill of a veteran cab driver. His driving scared the shit out of me and he knew it, but he always told me to relax.

While Steve's demeanor was usually calm, he often looked physically uncomfortable. He would shift constantly in his wheelchair, alternately sitting up straight and slouching, raising himself up with his hands on the arms of the wheelchair and moving his hips back and forth, then repositioning himself. He never complained.

I started to ask Steve if he'd noticed the same darkening mood at the channel as I had, but then he shifted again, and this time I noticed him grimace. "Hey Steve, how'd you end up in a wheelchair? You mind my asking?"

He smiled at me and shrugged. "I was a football star in college. Colgate. Star quarterback."

"My wife went to Colgate," I said.

"I'm older than she is. It was way before her time." He stopped and eyed me looking at him. "I know, hard to believe that this body once played football. I was over six feet tall and fast as hell. Anyway, usual story. I took the snap, dropped back, and got creamed. When I came to, I was in a hospital."

I nodded because I didn't know how else to acknowledge what he was telling me. No embellishment. No emotion. No wistfulness or regret. He looked down at his legs.

"I was in my hospital bed and didn't really know what was going on. Nobody was talking to me. Nurses, doctors, everyone just kept asking me how I felt, but they didn't say anything else. Finally, a doctor came in and sat down in the chair next to my bed. He said, 'Son, I don't know how to tell you this, so I'll just say it. We've done everything we can, but your spinal cord is a mess. You'll never be able to walk again.' I said to the doctor, 'Really? You mean I'm not going to die?' I was so relieved I started crying."

I don't know why I asked him on that day. I'd intended to ask him if he thought something was going on at Comedy Central, if he felt the mood in the office. I never did ask him that. Steve switched the subject, started talking about another project we were working on. I left his office a few minutes later, trying to imagine him crying tears of joy at the moment of his most profound tragedy. But I couldn't.

That night my brother Brian called. Brian was younger than me, but because I went to grad school while he jumped right into work, I felt he knew his way around the business world better than I did. He worked at Lotus Software and had risen through the ranks, mostly because he was smart and hardworking, but also because he had a keen understanding of how business, and the people in business, operated. His call seemed a good opportunity to ask his opinion. For twenty minutes I talked nonstop, explaining every nuance and every detail about my situation—Bob, the phone call, the spectacular project, the "Contract with America," the board meeting, and how nothing seemed resolved, just suspended over an abyss, hanging by a thread.

Brian said, "Here's what you do: strap on your biggest balls and go see Michael."

"Go see Michael. Just like that, just walk right in and…and what, confront him? Say, 'Hey Michael, what the fuck's going on?' Or, no, I got it, I go, 'Michael, who do you think you are saying you don't like my stuff? The fuck you know about it?' Or, check this out, 'Hey Michael, anybody ever tell you—'"

Brian stopped me. "I take your point. But no, not like that. You go in and say, 'I understand that you're dissatisfied with my work at Comedy Central.' Be very humble. Deferential."

"Hold on, I'm writing this down…Okay, then what?"

"Nothing. That's it."

"That's it?"

"Yeah. You say that and wait to hear what he says. Sounds like Michael's not the shy, retiring type. He'll jump right in, tell you what he's concerned about. Or maybe not. But even if he gets pissed and starts yelling—which he probably won't—at least you'll know. If it looks bleak, you start looking for another job."

"I don't know…"

"Well, you asked, that's what I think you should do."

"He may not even see me."

"Art, if he won't meet with you, then you've got your answer." I thought about that for a few seconds. It seemed to make sense.

"Thanks for the advice," I said. "Let me think about it. I'll let you know what happens."

I walked into the family room. Carrie was curled up on the couch, reading a magazine. I asked her what she thought of Brian's advice.

"I like it," she said. "Call his office tomorrow and see if you can get in soon. Not knowing is driving you crazy."

When I got to the office the next morning, I was tired. I'd tossed and turned all night trying to decide what to do. If I decided to go ahead with Brian's advice, there were some looming questions. First, would Michael even agree to see me? Second, I only had one set of balls, not a larger pair stored somewhere for the tougher moments in life as Brian suggested; were my balls big enough to do this? And finally, should I tell Bob that I intended to meet with Michael so he wouldn't hear about it from someone else and think I was an insubordinate asshole?

I stared at the phone. When I picked it up and started to dial Michael's number, it occurred to me that telling Bob in advance was, if nothing else, an excellent way to procrastinate. And, maybe even better, Bob could say he'd prefer I not meet with Michael, a reasonable enough response, given Michael's position as chairman of the board. I put down the phone and headed for Bob's office.

Bob's assistant hadn't arrived yet, but Bob's office door was open. I knocked on the doorframe, and Bob looked up from his newspaper and invited me in.

"Bob, if it's all right with you, I'd like to meet with Michael and ask him why he wanted me out, you know, right before Christmas."

Bob shrugged. "I can see that. Good luck getting an appointment with him."

"Yeah, I know, but I'd still like to give it a shot."

"Fine by me. Anything else?"

"No, that's it. Thanks, Bob." Bob went back to his paper. I was surprised by his casual response, but that wasn't unusual. Some days he was calm, rational, supportive. Other days he changed, for no apparent reason. I had trouble reading his moods and anticipating his reactions, which made my life that much crazier.

When I got back to my office, I picked up the phone and dialed Michael's number.

After just one ring, Merav picked up.

"Hi, Merav, it's Art Bell."

"Hello, Art. How are things at Comedy Central?"

"Hilarious as usual." Merav laughed, but I guessed she sensed the irony. It occurred to me she knew more about what was going on at Comedy Central than I did. She probably knew why Michael wanted to fire me. Rather than continue the pleasantries, I asked Merav as confidently as I could (so as not to betray my trepidation) for a meeting with Michael. Without the slightest hesitation, she said he could see me the next day at two o'clock.

I put the phone down and sat back in my seat. Bob had just told me minutes ago that getting a meeting with Michael would be difficult. I thought I'd have to wait days if not weeks. I looked at my watch and calculated that I'd be in Michael's office in less than twenty-two hours. This was coming down faster than I'd expected.

I noticed I hadn't taken off my jacket, so I got up and grabbed the hanger on the back of my door, hung it up, and sat down again. That's when I realized that I was wearing my best suit and my favorite tie.

Oh, shit. What would I wear tomorrow?

That night when I arrived home from work, I walked in, dropped my briefcase on the floor, and said, "Guess what? I'm meeting with Michael tomorrow."

Carrie was at the stove stirring something. "That's great. Right? Isn't that what you wanted?"

I nodded. "I'm going up to change. How 'bout some wine with dinner?"

"White or red?"

"Both."

CHAPTER 31

Betrayed

The day of the meeting, I pretended to work but was too distracted to do much. I normally made a point of never skipping lunch, but I wasn't hungry, so I just took a walk around the block. At 1:15 I started walking down Broadway. Sometimes Broadway is so crowded with tourists that walking is difficult, but that day was bitterly cold, and the crowd was manageable. I needed to walk. I liked walking to important meetings, even if it was a long way. It distracted me from whatever was coming, but it also let me sort things out a little, think about what I would say, and get myself psyched. Both hands were in my pockets to keep them warm. I'd left my briefcase at the office. No reason to have even a notepad at this meeting. As I walked, I adjusted my posture, stood up straight, put my shoulders back. I felt strong, maybe even a little noble, marching to Michael's office. I felt good.

I arrived at the HBO building with plenty of time to spare. I walked into the guest reception area, signed in, and affixed my visitor pass to my jacket. Since I'd worked in this building for six years and used to walk in by just flashing my HBO ID at the guard, it felt funny to have to sign in as a visitor. I headed for the elevators at the rear of the lobby. I still knew just about everyone at HBO, and people said, "Hi, how ya doing, good to see you," as I walked by.

Walking into the HBO building was like coming home.

The rear elevators went straight to the executive floor. When I got off the elevator, I turned left and walked through the double doors. The décor was lush, the paintings original, and the beige carpet so thick that all sound was muted almost to silence. A young woman was seated at a reception desk that served as a forbidding gateway to the executive floor. Behind the receptionist was a waiting area with two large couches and a coffee table. It looked like the lobby of a small luxury hotel. I was about to enter the rarefied domain of the half-dozen top executives who ran HBO. Their offices were down the corridor to the right. Michael's office suite was to the left, hidden around the corner.

I introduced myself in an appropriately hushed tone to the receptionist. She gave me a welcoming smile, asked me to have a seat, and assured me that she would tell Merav that I had arrived. She picked up the phone and started to dial Merav.

"Art, is that you?" It was Merav, calling to me from outside Michael's office.

"Hi Merav. Yes, it's me."

I heard her say, "Michael, Art's here." And then, "Come on in, Art. Michael will be right with you." I thanked the receptionist and walked down the hall to Michael's office suite. Merav gestured for me to go in.

When I walked in, Michael was just getting up from behind his desk. I'd been in this office a dozen times over the years, but it still overwhelmed me. I looked around to see what, if anything, had changed. The desk was still a big slab of glass. The door to the private bathroom was still in the left rear corner. There was a "living room" area with two white leather couches that faced each other, a coffee table, three side chairs, and a floor lamp. Behind that and to the left was a round conference table accompanied by six chairs. As far as I could tell, nothing much had changed.

"Arrrrt," Michael said, drawing out my name. He walked slowly around his desk, casually hitching up his pants. He wore a white shirt tailored tightly against his arms and torso. He shook my hand and aimed me toward one of the chairs in the living room. I was glad we weren't on a couch. Those couches were soft; they swallowed you whole. For this meeting I wanted to be seen. I sat down in a chair and Michael sat down across from me, but the chairs were pretty close to each other. He was wearing cologne. "What can I do for you?" He wasn't smiling, but he certainly didn't seem hostile.

"Thanks for seeing me, Michael." I cleared my throat and checked to see that I was sitting up straight. "The reason I'm here is, well, I understand you're not happy with my work and you want me fired." Michael frowned and shifted in his seat. He seemed slightly agitated.

"Who told you that?" he said. I felt like he was accusing me of something, of knowing something I shouldn't, and the question and his tone caught me completely off guard. I didn't answer right away. Michael leaned forward in his chair.

"Did Bob tell you that?"

I nodded.

"Bob told you I was unhappy with your work and I wanted you, what, fired? Really?" This was suddenly a very confused conversation. "I can't believe it," he said. "I never said anything about your work, or that I want you fired. It's Bob who should be fired."

I almost couldn't believe what Michael was saying. Not only was he telling me that Bob had lied to me, but he was saying that Bob should be fired.

"Don't you think he should be fired, Art?"

"I didn't come here to sell out my boss. I came—"

"No, you wouldn't do that. I know you wouldn't come here for that. But, Art..." He paused, and his voice got a notch quieter. "Don't you think Bob should be fired?"

Michael wanted me to answer. I was thinking fast, trying to figure out not only what to say, but why Michael was so intent on my opinion. I sat, frozen, with Michael's eyes locked on mine. If I moved my eyes or my head, would that telegraph an answer?

Yes would be disloyal and devastating to my boss, but that was the answer Michael was looking for. He'd said, "Don't you think," implying he knows that's what I think. I thought briefly of trying to worm my way out of this with a noncommittal response, like, "It's not for me to say," or, "I'm just relieved to hear that you're not disappointed in me." But Michael wanted me to say yes. He wanted me to affirm his decision to fire Bob. He was making it a rhetorical question.

Michael stood up, walked back to his desk, and poured himself a glass of water from a pitcher. "Don't you think I know what's going on up there? Don't you think I've heard from others at Comedy Central? For months now?" My discomfort was probably radiating from me, because then he said, "Don't worry. I'm going to fix this. It's already in the works."

Michael took a drink of water, put the glass down, and walked over to me with his hand extended. "Thanks for coming in, Art." The meeting was over.

On my way out, I thanked Merav, and she told me to take care. She'd probably heard the whole thing; the door had been left open. She probably knew how emotionally fraught the meeting was for me. But then, Merav had probably seen and heard a lot sitting outside that office, seen a lot of people walk out of there looking more worried, more confused, and more rattled than when they'd walked in. She was like the admitting nurse at the emergency room who's seen just about everything and knows tomorrow will be more of the same. She was seemingly unfazed by screaming, crying, or the sight of blood. It was all just part of her job.

I'd originally planned on taking a cab back to the office, but when I hit the street, I started walking. I needed to digest. I went over every word of our conversation. Michael answered my question: he wasn't out to fire me. Could I trust that? He'd have no reason to lie.

He said he knew what was going on at Comedy Central, that others had told him. Who? My guess was Becca Slater, our CFO. She'd had it in for Bob from the day he took over. I remember her walking into my office on the day Bob started. She'd closed the door and said, "We gotta get this guy Bob out of here. He has no idea what he's doing." I told her he'd just started, and we should give him a chance, but I knew Becca wanted to be president of Comedy Central. She was probably checking in to see if I was an ally or potential foe. It made sense that she'd been whispering in Michael's ear all along, telling him that the company was a mess.

Finally, Michael told me something I didn't even suspect: Bob had lied to me. He'd called me a week before Christmas and scared me into thinking I'd be fired if I didn't do something spectacular. I didn't know for sure, but it seemed possible that Michael had given Bob that challenge, and Bob had just passed it on to me.

When I got to my office, there was a message on my desk from Bob asking me to please stop by when I had a minute. I took off my overcoat and hung it up, then took the long walk to Bob's office. His assistant looked up. "You can go in. Bob, Art's coming in."

Bob was writing something, but he put it aside. "How'd your meeting with Michael go?"

"Good, I think." I looked at Bob, and he looked at me. I was quiet. I didn't offer up any details of the meeting, and he didn't ask. In any other circumstance, Bob would have me sit down and give him a blow-by-blow account, and together we'd look for clues, scraps of information, anything that might tell us what Michael was really thinking. And we'd maybe plan our next board meeting using those insights; we'd sleep better having that little extra knowledge that might keep this all going smoothly under Michael's watchful eye. But no, Bob didn't ask what happened because he knew what had happened. And I volunteered nothing. In that moment, questions went unasked and unanswered; whole paragraphs went unspoken. There was a stillness between us. I finally broke it by repeating myself. "Yeah, Bob, I think it went really well."

"I'm glad," he said. Then he went back to what he was doing, and I walked out.

CHAPTER 32

Conference Call

A few weeks after my meeting with Michael, Bob called a meeting to brainstorm new ideas for the channel. We'd booked a conference room in the Essex Hotel, just around the corner from our office. As I walked into the conference room, I said hello to everyone, dumped my coat and briefcase on a chair, and walked to the window to check out the view of Central Park. I watched the tourists, bundled up against the cold, climb into hansom cabs and cover themselves with the wool blankets provided for the ride around the park. The horses looked tired and disengaged, and that made me feel sad. I went back to the conference table and took a seat opposite the windows, grateful for the natural light and the view.

I scanned the room. There was Bob, Becca, Vinnie, and three other Programming executives. Conspicuously absent was a head of Programming. Several months had passed since Bob fired Mitch Semel, our former head programmer. Whether it was because he couldn't find good candidates or because he felt he could run Programming himself, Bob seemed in no hurry to hire a replacement. Unfortunately, Comedy Central's programming seemed adrift. The lack of leadership contributed to a lack of inspiration. That's what led to Bob calling this meeting and inviting a special guest: noted TV sitcom writer/producer Bill Persky.

Bill Persky was the creator of *That Girl* starring Marlo Thomas. He'd also had a hand in a lot of classic television comedy, like *The Dick Van Dyke Show* and *McHale's Navy*. Bob introduced Bill, and we began by telling him about our current programming and what new shows were in development. He complimented us and said we'd "made a helluva channel." He asked a question now and then ("When is that show scheduled?" or "How many episodes are you producing?"), but mostly he listened.

An hour into the meeting the telephone in the middle of the conference table rang so loudly I jumped. Bob grabbed the receiver. He mouthed "Marie" to the rest of us, indicating his assistant was on the line, and spoke briefly. After hanging up, Bob told us matter-of-factly that Tom Freston (cochairman of the Comedy Central board of directors) was looking for him. Apparently, he wanted Bob in his office right away, although he hadn't said why. Bob put on his overcoat and told us to continue the meeting without him. He'd get back as soon as he could. Bob chuckled as he reached the door. "If I don't come back, consider that a bad sign." He opened the conference door and walked out.

When the door closed, Becca shot me a look that meant "What's this about?" I shrugged as if I had no idea. Of course, ever since my meeting with Michael, I'd been bracing myself for the inevitable reckoning. This might be it.

An hour later we took a break. I was heading to the men's room when Vinnie caught up to me. "Where the fuck is Bob?" he asked. He sounded worried. "It's been over an hour and still no sign of him."

"I'm thinking alien abduction," I said, but the joke fell flat.

"Is Bob getting fired?"

"I don't know, Vinnie. Freston didn't check in with me. It could be that. Could be something else."

"Like?"

"Like maybe Bob's getting an ultimatum. Or Freston's suggesting somebody as the new head of Programming."

"Yeah, how crazy is it that Bob never replaced Mitch?" Vinnie shook his head. "Bob's the CEO. He's a Finance guy, not a programmer."

Becca walked up and joined us. "What are you guys talking about?"

"Nothing...," Vinnie said.

"Oh," Becca said. "I thought maybe you were talking about Bob. You wanna know what I think?" Becca's eyes were shining, wide with excitement, and she was smiling. "I think he's getting canned." She made no effort to hide her delight. It reminded me that right after Bob became our boss, she had come into my office, pronounced Bob "clearly incompetent," and asked for my help in getting him fired. I politely declined, but from then on I knew Becca wanted him out. Becca looked at me. "One of *us* should be running this channel, Art," Becca said, meaning *she* should be running the channel, "and you know it." Vinnie and I just stared at her as she turned and disappeared into the bathroom.

I returned to the conference room and grabbed a cup of coffee. Ten minutes later there was a tentative knock and Marie, Bob's assistant, opened the conference room door just wide enough to get her head through. Becca waved her in. "Sorry to interrupt," Marie said. "I'm just here for Bob's briefcase." Becca pulled it out from under the table near Bob's chair. Marie took it, thanked us, and started to leave.

"Wait a second, Marie," Becca said, and Marie stopped. "Bob's not coming back?" Marie slowly looked around the room before shaking her head in a way that made me think of a doctor in a soap opera saying someone just died on the operating table. Then, without a word, she walked out, closing the door as quietly as she could.

For a few seconds nobody said anything. I looked at Becca and she looked at me. Finally, Bill Persky spoke up. "What's going on?"

Everyone turned to Persky. "This is kind of awkward, Bill," I said, "but it looks like our boss just got fired."

·   ·   ·

We stayed at the hotel for a while, slightly traumatized but not surprised by Bob's abrupt dismissal. And, naturally, the big question was who was going to be the new president. For a lot of reasons, I hoped it wasn't Becca.

I got back to the office feeling disoriented. For some reason, I wanted to know that Bob was "all right," although I knew he was, on some level, devastated. Bob called me late in the afternoon, and that gave me the opportunity to tell him that I felt bad for him. I did my best to be supportive, noting how much Bob had accomplished as the first president of Comedy Central, wishing him luck with his next job, whatever that was, and promising to stay in touch. When we finished, I thought about how fraught our relationship was, especially after the "spectacular" episode. But as I thought back on it, I realized he had probably been afraid of being fired and hadn't known what to do.

CHAPTER 33

Sunshine in Siberia

On the same day that Bob Kreek left Comedy Central, the board announced that the new president and CEO, effective immediately, would be an MTV Networks executive named Doug Herzog. I had heard of Doug but knew little about him. Tom Freston, chairman of MTV Networks, phoned me. "Art, how are you doing?" He didn't wait for an answer. "Bob had to go. We're lucky we could put Doug in there. He's great—you're gonna like him, I know it. Don't worry."

I worried.

That night, when I told Carrie, she looked worried. "What do you think will happen?" she asked.

"I don't know. Freston said don't worry, but I don't know the new guy, Herzog, and he doesn't know me. Sometimes these guys come in and clean house, bring in their hand-picked staff right away."

"You think this new guy will do that?"

"We'll see. It doesn't help that I'm not an MTV alum. But the channel's been doing pretty well. Ratings are up, we're getting lots of press, we're almost making money. It's not like Herzog's taking over some kind of losing enterprise."

That was how I saw the situation. For all I knew, Doug Herzog did consider it a losing enterprise, a channel that needed to be saved. But I'd know soon enough. Doug was starting the next day.

•   •   •

Doug brought a bunch of people with him from MTV, and one of them stole my job as head of Marketing. I was sent to the basement (actually, just an office one floor down from where I had been, but it felt like the basement) along with Vinnie, who'd been kicked out of Programming. The head of Human Resources informed us that we would be in charge of New Business Development. I'd been in New Business Development at HBO, and we took care of anything that wasn't in HBO's current businesses, such as exploring new channel ideas, investment opportunities, and joint ventures with other companies. New Business Development hardly existed at Comedy Central, so I didn't consider it a plum reassignment and neither did Vinnie.

I reported to the new president, but I'd been banished to the Siberia of the org chart. My box on the org chart still had my name on it, but it was left dangling, awaiting the inevitable shudder that would send it plunging into the unemployment abyss. Even so, I felt I wasn't ready to leave Comedy Central.

On our first day as New Business Development execs, Vinnie and I sat in my new (much smaller) office, me at my desk and

Vinnie, his thick blond hair framing sad eyes, in the chair across from me. In the seven years we'd worked together, I'd never seen Vinnie like this. He typically had the wide-eyed enthusiasm of a sixteen-year-old kid who'd just had sex for the first time. And he looked like a sixteen-year-old kid: long dark blond hair, wide brown eyes always bursting with the excitement of being alive. His face was plump and smooth, and his voice was pitched high. Vinnie and me, we once owned this place. Now we were the uncool kids in the corner of the playground, chum to bullies, hoping to make it through recess without getting harassed by some random asshole.

I loved Vinnie. He was one of our first employees at The Comedy Channel, and when we'd met, he'd said to me, "I'm the luckiest guy on earth. My whole life I've dreamed of a job like this, where being funny was in the job description. I was born to work at The Comedy Channel." And he was. Despite starting in the bowels of the Ad Sales department, everyone quickly recognized Vinnie for the talent he was. I once asked him how he knew so much about television. "I have every *TV Guide* since the December 14, 1965, issue in my closet," he said. "I like to read them late at night when I can't sleep."

We sat without saying a word for a while, and I took some comfort from having Vinnie there. It felt like we were a couple of castaways just washed up on a desert island with nothing to do and nowhere to go, baking in the sun and pondering our fate with only the faintest hope of a rescue.

"They're gonna fire us. Right? Don't you think they're gonna fire us?" Vinnie mumbled.

"Nah," I lied. "If they were gonna fire us, they would have just done it. Why keep us around at all?" Vinnie didn't look convinced. "More likely they're giving us the Corporate Kiss-Off."

"Never heard of it. I'm not sure I wanna know what it is."

"Yeah, the CKO," I said. "Developed in Japan in the '60s before becoming popular in American business."

Vinnie laughed. "I know you're making this up."

"I swear it's real," I said, keeping a straight face. "In Japan the office workers were guaranteed a job for life, which means when somebody fucked up at work, they couldn't be fired. So the company would banish the hapless worker to a windowless basement office with nothing to do. Just the guy, his phone, and a coffee maker."

"You mean a tea maker."

"Okay, yeah, a tea maker. He keeps coming to work since he's like, 'I have my pride. I will *not leave my company*.' After a couple weeks, they start to dim the lights a little bit each day. It's a slow process, but after a couple months his office is almost pitch black. The poor guy sits in the dark for a few days, terrified. He keeps trying the light switch, but...nothing. He reads the newspaper by the light of his luminous watch dial. Finally he can't take it anymore and quits."

"Bullshit."

"True! I read about it in business school. Is that diabolically great or what?"

Vinnie got quiet again for a few seconds. "Well, as long as we got windows and lights, we should probably find something to do."

And then, something to do found us. The worldwide web was just getting a foothold, and Comedy Central needed a website. The new president called Vinnie and me into his office and handed us the project. "It's new business, so it comes under you guys." He looked over at me. "You cool with that, man?" That's how Doug talked. Everyone from MTV talked like they were transacting a drug deal. I nodded and said, "Yeah, I'm cool." So Vinnie and I rushed back to our basement offices, called a computer guy who knew how to build websites, and prepared to march into the brave new world of online comedy.

Vinnie and I began by looking at other websites to get some ideas. "Wow, look at all the stupid websites out there," Vinnie said as we bounced around the web. "We can't have a stupid website." I agreed. We considered that for a few seconds, then began tossing out ideas for what could go on the website: program schedule, a "what's on right now" feature, information on each of our shows, interviews with comedians, viewer feedback, contests.

Vinnie put his hand up and said, "Stop. How fucking boring is this? We're a comedy network. Our website should be funny." We got to work.

We weren't comedy writers, but after years of hanging around comics we were ready to give it a shot. We sat in our offices laughing like schoolgirls, making up funny stuff, mostly about the news, and putting it on our website. But we soon realized our work wasn't all that funny. We needed professional help. As if by magic, somebody showed up.

Dr. Dave Kolin had a business doing comedy bits, funny voices, and audio comedy of all kinds for radio stations. He'd gone into radio after suffering through years of dental school. On the day he graduated with a degree in orthodontics, he took a job with a New York radio station and went on the air as Dr. Dave. Now he had a radio syndication business that was so successful that Dick Clark had bought it. Somewhere in the eighties he had a couple of successful comedy shows on HBO and MTV, but that was then. Now, Dave was dying to get back on television, and he was constantly pitching us crazy show ideas, none of which made it on the air.

One day Dave came in to pitch us on putting some of Comedy Central's stand-up comedy on the radio. "How much money do we make?" I asked, slapping on my New Business Development hat.

"You pay us," Dave replied. Here was my New Business Development experience in a nutshell.

"What? I'm not paying you. You pay us."

"Okay, never mind that, we'll figure something out."

"Hey, Dave," Vinnie said, "you wanna see some web stuff we're working on?" The next thing we knew, Dave started coming up with great material to put on the site. So we hired him.

One of our early bits was called "Web Sites We'd Like to See," where we'd do parody websites based on current news events. Around that time, mad cow disease was in the news, and everyone in the world was afraid that they'd eat mad cow–infected beef and their brains would shrivel and die. It was an "end-of-civilization" disease, because you couldn't identify tainted meat. But the cows that got it staggered and stumbled a lot, which made them easy to spot and yank out of the slaughter line before they hit the food supply. So we put up a web page called "How to Tell If Your Cow Has Mad Cow Disease." It showed a picture of a cow looking into the camera. Underneath were two buttons, one that said "Healthy Cow" and the other "Diseased Cow." When the healthy-cow button was clicked, the cow said, "MOOO." But when the diseased-cow button was clicked, the cow's eyes started spinning and the cow went into a long "MOOO" that sounded like the cow was going off the deep end. The "MOOO" morphed into a crazed cackle, a combination of Daffy Duck at his most manic and a cow screaming for its life. Dave did the sound effects and they were hilarious. Our Mad Cow page first gained notoriety among the Wall Street guys (they were always looking for funny stuff to pass to their friends and coworkers). Before long it had amassed a huge number of viewers. It was our first online comedy hit.

One day, when we were trying to come up with ideas for "Web Sites We'd Like to See," Vinnie asked, "Couldn't we make a book out of these?" None of us had any idea how to go about this, but Dave had a friend whose daughter worked at Simon and Schuster. She steered us to the right department—the one that did funny novelty books, the kind bookstores have at the cash register that everyone looks through when they check out. I figured we had no chance, but the lady we spoke to said she loved Comedy Central. If we would put the book out as a Comedy Central book, they'd consider it. A couple of meetings later, we had a deal.

So Vinnie, Dave, and I, along with our trusty web designer Chris, created hundreds of satirical websites, some funny, some less so. We were definitely critical of each other's ideas.

"Okay, I got one," I said one morning. "The Mayonnaise Council website. It's just a big picture of a mayonnaise bottle, and there's only one link on it: tuna."

"That's not funny," said Vinnie.

Dave laughed, but said, "Not funny."

"Yeah? Well, I thought of it and I think it's a riot."

"It'll ruin the whole book!" Vinnie whined.

Dave came to my rescue. "It's stupid and really not funny, but what the hell, let's put it in." And we did.

After working frantically for six weeks to meet the publisher's deadline, we handed in our draft. The editor loved it. Several weeks later, we were published. *Comedy Central Presents Web Sightings: A Collection of Web Sites We'd Like to See*, by Art Bell, Vinnie Favale, and David "Dr. Dave" Kolin was Comedy Central's first book.

Coliseum Books, one of the great independent New York City bookstores, was downstairs. Every day at lunch time, Vinnie and I would stop in and go to information.

"Do you have a book called *Web Sites We'd Like to See*?" we'd ask. They didn't. But we kept asking. After a while the guy at information would see us coming and shake his head no. Then one day, he said, "Aisle seventeen. It's in the comedy section." We pushed through the lunchtime crowd like a couple of kids trying to get a great view of the passing parade. I saw it first and pulled a copy from the shelf.

"Yes!" I screamed. People looked over. Vinnie and I were high fiving and laughing. "We did it!" We grabbed a handful of the books and hurried over to the register.

After the publication, Doug, the president of Comedy Central, walked into my office with his usual greeting. "Art, what's happening?" He held up a copy of the book. "This is great, man. No, really, this is really great. Really." I was flattered. For a few minutes after he walked out of my office, I thought, I'm not going to get fired. We're kicking ass here in New Business Development.

CHAPTER 34

The Firing

Two days later, Doug Herzog asked me to come to his office.

"Hey, man, what's happening? You want some water or anything?"

"No, I'm good." Mostly I was on alert. It was unusual for Doug to ask to see me.

"Okay, here it is. I'm having you and your New Business department report to Becca."

"Doug, you gotta be kidding. Becca? But she runs Finance! She doesn't know what we do or how we do it. That's a really bad idea."

"Art, she thinks the world of you, man. She says you're great, and I want her to get some experience managing a team that's a little more creative than Finance."

"It'll be a disaster. Don't make me report to her. Please. She'll..." I hesitated.

"What?"

"What if it doesn't work out?"

"She loves you, man. She'll learn a lot from you. I got your back. Don't worry."

I worried.

I went back to my desk and wished Vinnie were still here. I needed to talk to him.

A few weeks earlier he'd come into my office. "Mitch just called. He offered me a job at CBS." Mitch Semel, former Comedy Central programmer, had landed a job at CBS as head of East Coast Production.

"You gonna take it?" I asked, just to keep the conversation going.

"Are you kidding? You think I should hang around here until I get fired?"

"No." I felt like the death-row convict whose best friend had just been exonerated. "Take the job, of course you should take it. I'm happy for you. I'm proud of you, too. You and Mitch are gonna have a great time together."

"I know. We are." Vinnie looked at me. "I can't believe it's ending for us like this."

"Me neither. I ought to start looking for another job. I just can't bring myself to say it's over."

Vinnie left a week later. No party, no fanfare, not even much of a thank-you from the company, even though he'd worked so hard to help build it. So I thanked him.

I got to the office the next day and felt completely alone. With Vinnie gone, I had no one to commiserate with, to laugh with, to work with. I sat at my desk and spun around in my office chair while I assessed the situation. I was forty years old, and I'd been working for thirty of them, starting with mowing lawns and moving on to babysitting, crazy summer jobs, consulting, and, for the last twelve years, television. Never during that time had I felt as useless as I felt at that moment.

I stopped spinning in my chair.

Then I wondered what was next for me.

·   ·   ·

Two months later, on a cold Thursday evening, Comedy Central's company Christmas party was in full swing at a downtown restaurant. Nobody goes to their office Christmas party without some kind of agenda: flirt with that incredibly cute designer in Graphics, or get drunk enough to tell someone what you really think. Mine was to confirm a hunch that my Comedy Central days were numbered. My new boss, Becca, had been avoiding me for the past few days, which was unusual for her.

I looked around and spotted Becca standing across the room, holding a drink, leaning on the bar and chatting amiably with a guy from Accounting. Becca was about my height with straight blond hair. She wore her usual investment-banker getup that involved a white blouse, a sweater, and a scarf at the neck. She reserved her biggest smile for when she knew something you didn't. After a few minutes the guy she was talking to wandered away.

I walked up to her and said, loudly enough to be heard over the music, "Becca? Are you going to fire me tomorrow?"

She looked at me wide eyed and open mouthed and started to say something but froze. I stood stock still, waiting for an answer. She stirred her drink with the brown plastic swizzle stick and took a sip, then shot another glance at me over the glass but said nothing. Someone called her name and she held my gaze for a second then dissolved into the crowd, leaving a blank space where she stood. I stared at the blank space, expecting to see a little puff of cartoon smoke because she'd left so fast.

Nobody had told me she was about to fire me. I felt it in the way she'd avoided me, deflected my questions, put off a couple of meetings, sped up when she walked by me in the hall. Discomfort radiated from her like sparks. She crackled with unease. Yeah, I felt it coming.

The next morning, with the roar of the Christmas party still ringing in my ears, with the afterburn of four gin gimlets still scalding my esophagus, my phone rang. It was Becca's secretary. Could I please come to Becca's office? Immediately? I hung up the phone and looked around my office, knowing that this was it but wanting to believe it wasn't. I pushed my chair back, got up, put on my jacket and straightened my tie, and started down the hall toward her office. When I got there, the secretary turned toward Becca's open door and said, "Becca, Art's here. Are you ready for him?"

Are you ready for him. Ready. For him. It bounced around in my head; the more I thought about it, the more ridiculous it sounded. I walked in.

"Are you ready for me, Becca?"

"Hi, Art." She got up and walked around her desk. "Please sit." I sat on her couch and looked around her office, noticing, not for the first time, that it was the second-biggest office in the place. A couch, an overstuffed black leather chair, a meeting area with a dark wooden table and chairs, a big glass desk with a tall desk chair swiveling behind it. Her power office closed in on me as I sat down and sunk into the couch. She sat on one of the chairs across the coffee table and crossed her legs. I noticed she left her coffee on her desk. Looked like she planned to finish with me fast enough to get back to her coffee before it cooled down.

Becca looked at me through small, brown horn-rimmed glasses, which she seldom wore. They made her look like a school principal. When I was in third grade, my school principal was Miss Parmentier, and she was gigantic, thin, and had small horn-rimmed glasses. I remember sitting in her office, sent there by my teacher for being a wise guy in class, and Miss Parmentier taking me apart so fiercely that I started crying. I resolved not to cry now.

"Art. I was so excited when Doug told me that you would report to me. I thought we could really accomplish a lot together, that we'd be a great team." She paused. "I really thought we'd be a great team. But you clearly didn't like this arrangement, and you were insubordinate on several occasions. I can't have that."

"I wasn't insubordinate, Becca. Disagreeing with you isn't insubordination. It's having a difference of opinion. I always tried to be respectful when we disagreed. I'm sorry you feel differently."

"Art. You've been rude to me. You've been dismissive of my ideas, and you obviously hated working for me. Why, I don't know. I certainly tried my best to be a great manager to you. I went to bat for you several times. Maybe I shouldn't have, but I did." She looked at me like she was waiting for me to say something. I just nodded, because I didn't know what else to do. "I discussed this with Doug, and we thought it best that you leave Comedy Central." She paused. "So you're being terminated, effective immediately."

I blinked, not because I wasn't expecting it, but because it sounded so odd. I'm being terminated? Becca's face never softened. Shouldn't she have some regret in firing me, shouldn't she feel a little bit bad? I didn't move, just stared at her. She said, "Do you understand what I'm saying to you?"

"Yes, I understand."

"When you leave my office, go see Ann." Ann was the head of Human Resources. "She'll explain the procedure." Procedure. Terminate. This all sounded so clinical, like surgery. I stood up quickly, turned away from her. Then I reflexively started to say "Thank you," as I typically did after a meeting, but I caught myself and walked out without saying a word.

CHAPTER 35

Last Call

I made my way to the Human Resources department. People I passed on the way looked at me, letting their gazes linger on my face as they said hello, turning slightly as I went by, trying to figure out if something was wrong—or maybe that was my acute discomfort turning into paranoia. Larry Divney, our head of Ad Sales, saw me and asked if something had happened. When I told him, he said, "Yeah, I can see that." He shook my hand and offered to help me out if he could.

I felt strange, as if I'd been transferred into someone else's body, or like I'd just woken up in a hospital bed with people asking me questions about an accident I couldn't remember, imploring me to piece together events, to tell them what went so wrong.

I walked into the HR office and said I was there to see Ann Reagan, the head of HR. Ann wasn't in the office due to some personal emergency, so I was briefed on the termination particulars by her second in command, Melanie Fischer. I liked Melanie. She was smart and well intentioned and had a warm smile; she clearly enjoyed the human side of human resources. However, she'd been on the job for less than a year, half of that as Ann's assistant. When I walked in, she said hello, stood up, and shook my hand. She looked at me with eyes so full of sympathy and compassion that for a moment I thought she might tell me the whole thing had been a mistake, that Becca was fired instead, and she was truly sorry for the mix-up.

"Art, I'm here to explain how your termination from Comedy Central will proceed. If at any time during the process you have any questions or concerns, please ask me. I will answer any questions and address any concerns. If, for whatever reason, I'm unable to adequately answer your questions, I will make every effort to find answers and get back to you promptly."

I turned around to see if she was reading off cue cards, or if she'd tacked her remarks on the wall behind me.

"Thanks, Melanie. This your first termination?"

"Oh, no," she said with confidence and a good deal of pride. "I mean, I've helped Ann with lots of terminations in the last few months since Doug Herzog took over." She paused and her voice became tentative. "Actually, this is the first time I've handled one on my own. And I've never even helped Ann on a termination of a senior executive."

"So I'm the most senior person you've ever processed out?"

She nodded. "In a way you're my most important termination yet."

"Mine, too," I said. Melanie looked away, as if she realized the conversation was getting away from her. I said, "Don't worry, I'm not going to be an asshole about this. At least not to you."

She laughed. "Sorry, this isn't easy for me, either."

I pointed to the red file folder in front of her. "What's in there, something I need to sign, or review, or what?"

She looked down at it, as if she were seeing it for the first time, and said, "Oh. Yes. This is for you."

Melanie fully recovered her professional posture, opened the folder in front of us, and reviewed the situation with me. The one small mercy was that I wasn't being escorted out of the building by security guards. They sometimes did that when they fired someone. I was spared the indignity of being dumped on the sidewalk outside my office building holding a small cardboard box full of the personal stuff (photos, a desk clock, some favorite pens) I'd collected over the last eight years. Either they didn't view me as much of a security risk, or this was just their way of saying thanks.

I also learned I could use my office for the rest of the week and they'd help pack my stuff and get it to my house.

I waited for more from Melanie. While senior executives were usually provided outplacement counseling for a number of weeks or months at the company's expense, Melanie told me the company wouldn't provide outplacement services to me. The rest of the news was equally bad. But I would need to take that up with lawyers. Melanie was just the messenger.

Up to this point, my morning had taken on a dream-like, surreal quality, but the reality of it was starting to take over. I realized that my life had changed, that I was unemployed, and that until I found another job and settled in, I would be living with a lot of uncertainty. I got scared and a little angry. That was the dark moment when I first considered the possibility, however remote, that I might never get another job. Sometimes you go right to the heart of the abyss when even moderately bad things happen. You imagine a horrible future, failure upon failure, breakdown of everything. At that moment I went to the heart of the abyss. I looked around for a few seconds, then told myself, Don't be crazy.

Just as we were finishing up, Melanie's phone rang. "Yes, he's still here...Okay, I'll tell him. Thanks," she said and hung up. "That was Doug Herzog's office. Doug wants to see you when you're done here." I should have expected that Doug would ask to see me before I left. Maybe he'd say he regretted that Becca and I hadn't found a way to work together. Or maybe he'd say that if it were up to him I wouldn't be fired, but since Becca was my boss and in possession of all the facts, it was her call. Or maybe he'd just say goodbye and leave it at that.

Holding the red folder Melanie had given me, I took the elevator up one floor to Doug's office. When the elevator doors opened on Doug's floor, the folder slipped out of my hand and papers spilled everywhere. I was the only one in the elevator, so I scrambled to collect everything before the doors closed and I was whisked away on an elevator ride to nowhere. A couple of people who were waiting for the elevator realized what was happening and held the elevator door until I got everything back in the folder.

I got to Doug's office and his assistant waved me in. Doug was sitting behind his desk. He stood up and told me to take a seat on the couch. He took the chair across from me. There was a glass coffee table between us with nothing on it. I put the red folder on my lap and crossed my arms across my chest.

"What's happening?"

I wanted to say, "Oh, I thought you knew? Becca fired me a half hour ago. What's happening with you?" Instead I just waited for him to get on with whatever he intended to say.

"I know this is tough for you, Art, but I had to let you go." Ah, now I see. Becca pulled the trigger, but Doug handed her the gun. "Your fingerprints are all over this place. Everyone knows that. But if I'm going to run Comedy Central my way, I need to make a fresh start." He paused for my response. Did he expect me to tell him I completely understood and that I would have done the same thing had the situation been reversed? If Doug was explaining himself in order to feel better about firing me, I sure as hell wasn't going to help.

As he spoke, I marveled at the incongruity of his demeanor and the circumstances. While Becca had been imperious, abrupt, even angry, and Melanie had overflowed with compassion and warmth, Doug behaved unremarkably, as if he'd called me to his office to ask my opinion on last night's ratings or the latest programming schedule.

He continued. "I'm not worried about you. You're good, you'll get another job." I sat there without saying a word. A few seconds went by before he realized I wasn't going to talk to him. He stood up and extended his hand. I shook it, reflexively, regrettably. As I turned to leave, Doug said, "And Art, if there's something I can do to help…"

"Like what?" I asked. I knew he had no intention of helping and that he wasn't genuinely offering help. He'd said it because it was something people say to make themselves feel better in awkward situations. I stood looking at Doug, waiting for him to say something, daring him to say something, wondering if he felt uncomfortable. But he stayed quiet.

"Well, if you think of something...," he said.

I walked out.

I went back to my office and tossed the red folder on my desk. I glanced at the clock: 11:15. Carrie still didn't know what was going on. It was time I called home to tell her I'd been fired.

"Oh, no! Oh, Art, I'm so sorry. Are you okay?"

"No, not really. Should I be?"

"No, of course not. Those bastards. Who fired you? Becca? You always said she wanted to get rid of you."

"Yeah, Becca told me, but Doug was behind it, too."

"Come home," Carrie said. "I want you to come home. I don't think you should stay at work a minute more than you have to. Can you leave right now?"

"I don't know. I guess. I went to HR, and they gave me a bunch of paperwork to look over. They said I could use my office for the rest of the week. Maybe I should stay and pack up."

"Forget that. Do it tomorrow. Just come home."

I wanted to go home, but it wasn't even noon. I realized that leaving the building in the middle of the day would make it true: I'd been fired after eight years at Comedy Central. I wasn't sure I was ready. As of the moment I was fired, I'd been with Comedy Central longer than anyone else in the world, because I'd started it. I told Carrie, "I'll call you when I'm on the train. See you soon."

I hung up the phone, stood up, and walked around my desk to the window. Broadway was buzzing fourteen stories below me. Cars jockeyed for position, trying to make the light before it went from yellow to red; pedestrians scurried around, somehow not bumping into each other; people crossed against the light, hoping the cars would stop for them, jumping out of the way when they had to. Everyone went about their business as if nothing had changed.

The phone rang and I thought, Okay, one last call. I picked up the phone and said hello. "Hello, Art. It's Merav in Michael Fuchs's office. Please hold for Michael." Michael? He wasn't even Chairman of HBO anymore. He'd left almost a year earlier to become Chairman of the Warner Music Group. I hadn't seen him or spoken to him in a long time. Had Michael ever called me? I couldn't remember.

Michael picked up. "Arrrrrt," he said, drawing out my name the way he used to. "I just heard. I'm really sorry." Of course Michael would have heard by now. Of course.

"It's nice of you to call, Michael," I said. "Yeah, Becca told me about an hour ago."

"Becca Slater? She still there?"

"So far. I guess Doug's getting rid of a bunch of us ex-HBOers but not everyone."

"I figured Doug would do something like that. Freston and the MTV guys are in charge now."

"They are. That wouldn't have happened if you were still here."

Michael paused for a few seconds, and I thought the phone call was over. I was about to thank him again when he said, "Art, if I was still there, you'd have a job for life. You're the founder. Without you there wouldn't *be* a Comedy Central."

"Thank you for saying that, Michael."

"Well, it's true," he said. "Take care, Art. Good luck." Then he was gone.

I took one last look around my office, then pulled my coat off the hanger behind the door. The hanger clattered to the floor. I didn't bother to pick it up.

Epilogue

I used to assume anyone who got fired sucked at their job, or had a bad attitude, or had made some colossal mistake with profound consequences. But the day I got fired, *because* I got fired, I realized I was wrong. People like me, people who perform their work seriously, passionately, and effectively, get fired, too.

During the next few months I met with dozens of media executives, ostensibly to get advice on finding my next job. But more than that, I hoped these conversations might help me make sense of my Comedy Central journey, a wonderful, eye-opening odyssey that ended with me sitting bruised and bewildered on the side of the road. One of my first meetings was with the chairman of a large media company, who told me, "If you don't get fired now and then, you probably aren't having an impact." While that was not exactly heartwarming, I realized I would never be someone who kept my head down in an effort to avoid getting fired. I needed to have an impact.

When I left Comedy Central at the end of 1996, I was forty-one years old and had a wife and two kids. The prospect of being out of work terrified me. My wife was supportive, certain that I'd land my next job quickly, but she was wrong. Finding work proved more difficult than either of us expected.

But people were kind. Comedy Central's head of Advertising Sales, Larry Divney, came to my rescue by getting me a consulting engagement at A&E. Consulting assignments at other entertainment companies followed. Over the next two years, my consulting work was varied and interesting: I helped launch a children's television network; I developed strategic objectives for a broadcast television channel; I guided a group of young entrepreneurs on a start-up college television network. But I still wanted a full-time job.

In addition to consulting, I joined the millions of people who started a business at the dawn of the internet. Six months after leaving Comedy Central, my friend Dave Kolin (my coauthor on *Web Sites We'd Like to See*) suggested we create comedy bits for websites, the way we had for Comedy Central. The idea was to deliver web content to local radio and television stations for a fee. We put together a package of web comedy (funny games, topical news bits, some animation), sold it to a New York radio station and to a Los Angeles television station, and signed them up for regular updates. Suddenly we were in the web-comedy business, supplying comedy to radio and television companies. The business initially showed promise, but the stations quickly got the hang of how to build their own websites. We shut down after a year. I resumed my consulting, but after two years I wanted to get back to being a part of a team, to building something. I wanted to re-create the excitement I'd felt at Comedy Central.

Finally my efforts paid off: I got three job offers in one week and accepted a senior executive position at Court TV.

Despite the hype around the O. J. Simpson murder trial, Court TV was floundering. The owners (Time Warner and Liberty Media) hired an industry veteran, Henry Schleiff, to turn things around, and a week later, Schleiff hired me. Together, we transformed the channel by adding a prime-time schedule of crime documentaries and crime shows, like *Homicide* and *Cops*. It became a channel about all aspects of the criminal justice system, from beat cops to lawyers and judges, to criminals and crime solvers. And in the same way that comedians found a home at Comedy Central, famous lawyers, detectives, and forensic investigators came to Court TV wanting to get involved and to share their stories.

People asked, "How did you go from Comedy Central to Court TV?" It was certainly a different world, but like comedy, it was a world unto itself, with heroes and villains and superstars hoping to make a name for themselves on television.

When I first left Comedy Central, I assumed I would always think of it as the pinnacle of my television career, my greatest hit. It felt personal, because I'd started it and struggled so hard to make it succeed. But Court TV was a different kind of career experience, and I think it's because I went to Court TV as a seasoned executive. I spent eight years there, the last half as president of the company, and then left in 2006 when the channel was sold to Turner Broadcasting.

Meanwhile, Comedy Central was on its way to becoming one of the most powerful creative comedy institutions in entertainment ever, rivaled only by Lorne Michaels's *Saturday Night Live*. Just before I left, Comedy Central decided to launch two shows that were each, in its own way, transformative. The first was *The Daily Show*, ultimately hosted by Jon Stewart. Comedy Central's commitment to covering news events comedically, which had started with Al Franken and *InDecision '92*, was honed by Jon Stewart and *The Daily Show*. *The Daily Show* became the primary news source for a generation of young viewers. Stephen Colbert, a correspondent on *The Daily Show*, was spun off into his own show, *The Colbert Report*, which ran for nine years before Colbert was hired by CBS to replace David Letterman.

The second show was *South Park*. The pilot was an unsolicited short animated film masquerading as a Christmas greeting, featuring a bunch of cartoon kids massacring Christmas in the most offensive and profane way imaginable. This pilot made the rounds of television channels, and by the time the tape got to Comedy Central, everyone at the company was dying to see it. Doug Herzog instantly recognized that the show could help take Comedy Central to the next level, and he fought hard to land the show for the channel. The head of Advertising Sales almost had a heart attack when he saw it—advertisers generally run from the offensive and profane. But he said he'd do his best to sell it despite the profanity. A few years later, the show was on the cover of *Time* magazine, and the creators, Trey Parker and Matt Stone, went on to produce hundreds of episodes for Comedy Central.

Over the years Comedy Central made the careers of countless comedy writers and performers who otherwise might not have had a platform. Comedy Central created and showcased thousands of hours of innovative television comedy. And most importantly to me, Comedy Central became what I intended: the center of the comedy universe.

And that was the idea.

THE END

Acknowledgments

This book mentions only a few of the people I worked with at The Comedy Channel and Comedy Central. I'd like to acknowledge all of them, as well as the hundreds of smart, talented, and creative people who built the channel, and the hundreds more who made sure that there was a Comedy Central for me to write about thirty years later.

There were many people who taught me, inspired me, and guided me as I wrote this memoir. Danny Abelson, Gerry Albarelli, Larry Bell, Kathy Curto, Lynn Edelson, Reyna Gentin, Lisa Donati Meyer, Allen Kay, Steve Lewis, and Michael Weithorn all read various chapters and offered their advice and wisdom. My wonderful editor, Jane Rosenman, made everything about the book better. Keith Riegert, publisher at Ulysses Press, took a chance on me and warmed me with his enthusiasm. Comedy Central alumni Ken Olshansky, Vinnie Favale, Mitch Semel, and Ben Zurier jogged my memory on names, dates, places, and events. More importantly they reminded me how much we laughed through good times and tough times, and how much we enjoyed working together.

My children, Thea and Julia, listened to and laughed at my stories about the comedy business. When I started repeating myself I knew it was time to write the book. They also served as the official spokespeople for their generation. "Dad, you can't say that…it's 2019!" Any culturally insensitive, anti-feminist, or otherwise inappropriate parts of the book are in no way their fault—they tried to warn me.

Finally, I couldn't have done any of this without Carrie, my wife. She encouraged me to write by signing me up for a memoir class. She was the first person to read everything I wrote and the last person to edit the manuscript. She literally and figuratively held my hand throughout my career and through the writing of this book.

About the Author

Art Bell is a former media executive best known for creating, building, and managing successful cable television channels. While working at HBO he pitched the idea of a 24-hour comedy network which he helped develop and launch. Art went on to hold senior executive positions in both programming and marketing at Comedy Central. During that time he also coauthored a humor book entitled *Web Sightings: A Collection of Websites We'd Like to See*. After leaving Comedy Central, Art became president of Court TV, where he was a guiding force behind one of the most successful brand evolutions in cable television.

This is his first memoir. In addition to writing, he plays piano and jazz drums.

Art Bell currently resides in Greenwich, Connecticut, and Deer Valley, Utah, with his wife.

Find out more about Art Bell at artbellwriter.com.